Module E

IMPROVING SAFETY, MANAGING CONFLICT & REDUCING BULLYING

Module 5 of 6 in *Foundations: A Proactive and Positive Behavior Support System* (3rd ed.)

Randy Sprick
Jessica Sprick
Paula Rich

Module E

To view videos and download print resources licensed exclusively to Sunnyside Intermediate, go to: www.pnwpvideos.com

School Code: E3J6F4E2

Use Google Chrome, Internet Explorer, or Microsoft Edge browser.

© 2014 ANCORA PUBLISHING

Except as expressly permitted below and under the United States Copyright Act of 1976, no materials in this book may be used, reproduced, or distributed in any form or by any means, electronic or mechanical, without the prior written permission of the publisher.

The purchaser is granted permission to use, reproduce, and distribute the materials provided on the CD or streaming video site solely for use in a single school. The purchaser does not have permission to assign, use, or reproduce and distribute the materials to another school.

The *Foundations* videos are licensed for use in a single school.

Published in the United States by
Ancora Publishing
21 West 6th Ave.
Eugene, Oregon 97401
ancorapublishing.com
ISBN: 978-1-59909-073-3

Part of *Foundations: A Proactive and Positive Behavior Support System* (3rd ed.)
ISBN: 978-1-59909-068-9

Cover by Aaron Graham
Book design and layout by Natalie Conaway

Eugene, Oregon | ancorapublishing.com

Any resources and website addresses are provided for reader convenience and were current at the time of publication. Report any broken links to info@ancorapublishing.com.

CONTENTS

About the Authors v
Safe & Civil Schools vii
Acknowledgments xi
How to Use Foundations xiii

Overview of Modules 1

Presentation 1: Keeping Students Safe From Physical and Emotional Harm . . . 5
    Introduction to Module E 6

Presentation 2: Attributes of Safe and Unsafe Schools 11
    Introduction 12
    Task 1: Understand the Attributes of Safe and Unsafe Schools. 13
    Task 2: Assess Emergency Preparedness 23
    Task 3: Teach Lessons to Increase Connectedness and Safety 33

Presentation 3: Teaching Conflict Resolution 53
    Introduction 54
    Task 1: Determine Whether STP Meets the Needs of Your Students 57
    Task 2: Develop an STP Program in Your School 76
    Task 3: Educate Parents About STP 84

Presentation 4: Analyzing Bullying Behavior, Policies, and School Needs 89
    Introduction to Presentations 4 and 5 90
    Task 1: Understand Bullying Issues 93
    Task 2: Collect Data on Bullying in Your School 103
    Task 3: Define and Refine Your Bullying Policy 118
    Task 4: Analyze Bullying Data and Determine Priorities 133

CONTENTS

Presentation 5: Schoolwide Bullying Prevention and Intervention 141

    Task 1: Train Staff to Respond To and Prevent Bullying. 142
    Task 2: Help Students Prevent Bullying 155
    Task 3: Partner With Families to Prevent Bullying 189
    Task 4: Actively Engage Students to Prevent Bullying. 207

Bibliography 219
Appendix A: Foundations Implementation Rubric and Summary 231
Appendix B: Module E Implementation Checklist 241
Appendix C: Guide to Module E Reproducible Forms and Samples 249

ABOUT THE AUTHORS

Randy Sprick, Ph.D.

Randy Sprick, Ph.D., has worked as a paraprofessional, teacher, and teacher trainer at the elementary and secondary levels. Author of a number of widely read books on behavior and classroom management, Dr. Sprick is director of Safe & Civil Schools, a consulting company that provides inservice programs throughout the country. He and his trainers work with numerous large and small school districts on longitudinal projects to improve student behavior and motivation. Efficacy of that work is documented in peer-reviewed research, and Safe & Civil Schools materials are listed on the National Registry of Evidence-Based Programs and Practices (NREPP). Dr. Sprick was the recipient of the 2007 Council for Exceptional Children (CEC) Wallin Lifetime Achievement Award.

Jessica Sprick, M.S.

Jessica Sprick, M.S., is a consultant and presenter for Safe & Civil Schools and writer for Ancora Publishing. Ms. Sprick has been a special education teacher for students with behavioral needs and Dean of Students. She is a coauthor of *Functional Behavior Assessment of Absenteeism & Truancy, Absenteeism and Truancy: Interventions & Universal Procedures, Functional Behavior Assessment of Bullying,* and *Bullying: Interventions & Universal Procedures* with William Jenson, Randy Sprick, and others. Ms. Sprick's practical experience in schools with positive behavior support techniques drives her passion to help school personnel develop and implement effective management plans.

ABOUT THE AUTHORS

Paula Rich, B.Mus.Ed., M.Mus.

Paula Rich, B.Mus.Ed., M.Mus., has been a substitute teacher in public schools, was a freelance musician, and taught private music lessons for many years in the Boston, Massachusetts, area. More recently, she contributed original stories and poems to the *Read Well* curriculum for second-grade readers and edited several of Randy Sprick's staff development and behavior management books and papers. She was instrumental in developing Connections, an online check-and-connect program available through Ancora Publishing.

SAFE & CIVIL SCHOOLS

THE SAFE & CIVIL SCHOOLS SERIES is a comprehensive, integrated set of resources designed to help educators improve student behavior and school climate at every level—districtwide, schoolwide, within the classroom, and at the individual intervention level. The findings of decades of research literature have been refined into step-by-step actions that teachers and staff can take to help all students behave responsibly and respectfully.

The hallmark of the Safe & Civil Schools model is its emphasis on proactive, positive, and instructional behavior management—addressing behavior before it necessitates correction, collecting data before embarking on interventions, implementing simple corrections before moving to progressively more intensive and time-intrusive ones, and setting a climate of respect for all. As a practical matter, tending to schoolwide and classwide policies, procedures, and interventions is far easier than resorting to more costly, time-intrusive, and individualized approaches.

Foundations and PBIS

Positive Behavioral Interventions and Supports (PBIS) is not a program. According to the U.S. Department of Education, PBIS is simply a framework to help provide "assistance to schools, districts, and states to establish a preventative, positive, multi-tiered continuum of evidence-based behavioral interventions that support the behavioral competence of students" (A. Posny, personal communication, September 7, 2010). That framework perfectly describes *Foundations*. *Foundations* provides instructions for implementing such an approach—with detailed processes and hundreds of examples of specific applications from successful schools. Furthermore, *Foundations* provides step-by-step guidance for involving and unifying an entire district staff to develop behavior support procedures that will prevent misbehavior and increase student connectedness and motivation. *Foundations* moves well beyond a simple matrix into how to guide and inspire staff to take ownership of managing and motivating all students, all the time, every day.

SAFE & CIVIL SCHOOLS

Resources in the series do not take a punitive approach to discipline. Instead, Safe & Civil Schools addresses the sources of teachers' greatest power to motivate: through structuring for student success, teaching expectations, observing and monitoring student behavior, and, above all, interacting positively. Because experience directly affects behavior, it makes little sense to pursue only the undesired behavior (by relying on reprimands, for example) and not the conditions (in behavioral theory, the antecedent) that precipitate experience and subsequent behavior.

The Safe & Civil Schools Positive Behavioral Interventions and Supports (PBIS) Model is listed in the National Registry of Evidence-based Programs and Practices (NREPP) after review by the Substance Abuse and Mental Health Services Administration (SAMHSA).

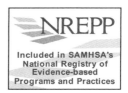

Inclusion in NREPP means that independent reviewers found that the philosophy and procedures behind *Foundations*, *CHAMPS*, *Discipline in the Secondary Classroom*, *Interventions*, and other Safe & Civil Schools books and videos have been thoroughly researched, that the research is of high quality, and that the outcomes achieved include:

- Higher levels of academic achievement
- Reductions in school suspensions
- Fewer classroom disruptions
- Increases in teacher professional self-efficacy
- Improvement in school discipline procedures

For more information, visit www.nrepp.samhsa.gov.

The most recent evidence of the efficacy of the Safe & Civil Schools PBIS Model appeared in the October 2013 issue of *School Psychology Review*. "A Randomized Evaluation of the *Safe and Civil Schools* Model for Positive Behavioral Interventions and Supports at Elementary Schools in a Large Urban School District," by Bryce Ward and Russell Gersten, shows how the Safe & Civil Schools PBIS Model improves student behavior and school climate. Thirty-two elementary schools in a large urban school district were randomly assigned to an initial training cohort or a wait-list control group. Results show reduced suspension rates, decreases in problem behavior, and evidence of positive academic gains for the schools in the training cohort.

SAFE & CIVIL SCHOOLS

Observed improvements persisted through the second year of trainings, and once the wait-list control schools commenced Safe & Civil Schools training, they experienced similar improvements in school policies and student behavior.

 Download and read the full article at: www.nasponline.org/publications/periodicals/spr/volume-42/volume-42-issue-3

Safe & Civil Schools acknowledges the real power educators have—not in controlling students but in shaping their behavior through affecting every aspect of their experience while they are in school: the physical layout, the way time is structured, arrivals and departures, teaching expected behavior, meaningful relationships with adults, and more. These changes in what adults do can create dramatic and lifelong changes in the behavior and motivation of students.

ACKNOWLEDGMENTS

As lead author, I owe a huge debt to many people who have guided the development and revision of *Foundations* over the past three decades. Betsy Norton, Mickey Garrison, and Marilyn Sprick were instrumental in the development and implementation of *Foundations* long before the publication of the first edition in 1992. Dr. Jan Reinhardtsen received the very first federal grant on the topic of positive behavior support and, with Mickey, implemented the first edition of *Foundations* as the basis for Project CREST in the early and mid-1990s. Jan also came up with Safe & Civil Schools, which became the name of our staff development services. Dr. Laura McCullough implemented a brilliant state-level Model School project in Kentucky, followed by the Kentucky Instructional Discipline System (KIDS) project that taught me so much about the importance of training and coaching to assist schools with implementation of both schoolwide and classroom behavior support.

I want to thank my coauthors of the different modules within this edition. Susan Isaacs, Mike Booher, and Jessica Sprick are outstanding trainers of *Foundations*, and their respective expertise has added depth to the content that makes this edition more practical, rich, and fun than previous editions. Paula Rich has provided both organizational skill and writing expertise to weave together a vast amount of content with many school- and district-level examples to create a highly accessible and user-friendly resource.

Thanks to the awesome staff of Ancora Publishing: Aaron Graham and Natalie Conaway with design, Sara Ferris and K Daniels with editing, Matt Sprick for directing both video and print development, Sam Gehrke for video editing, Robert Consentino and Jake Clifton for camera and sound, and the rest of the Ancora Publishing and Safe & Civil Schools staff—Jackie Hefner, Karen Schell, Sarah Romero, Kimberly Irving, Brandt Schram, Caroline DeVorss, and Marilyn Sprick—for their great work.

Implementation of *Foundations*, *CHAMPS*, and *Interventions* would not have thrived without the skill and dedication of great staff developers and trainers: Tricia Berg, Mike Booher, Phyllis Gamas, Laura Hamilton, Andrea Hanford, Jane Harris, Susan Isaacs, Debbie Jackson, Kim Marcum, Bob McLaughlin, Donna Meers, Carolyn Novelly, Robbie Rowan, Susan Schilt, Tricia Skyles, Pat Somers, Karl Schleich, Jessica Sprick, and Elizabeth Winford as Director of Professional Development.

ACKNOWLEDGMENTS

Fresno Unified School District and Long Beach Unified School District in California allowed us to visit with the Ancora Publishing video crew to capture the excitement, professionalism, and commitment of school and district personnel. These districts have taught us so much about the importance of common language and district support in creating a sustainable implementation.

Lastly, I want to the thank the schools and districts that have implemented *Foundations* over the years and graciously shared their lessons, posters, staff development activities, forms, and policies that you will find as examples throughout the print and video presentations. These real-world examples will help your implementation process by illustrating how other schools and districts have successfully implemented and sustained *Foundations*.

—R.S.

HOW TO USE FOUNDATIONS

This third edition of *Foundations* is constructed as six modules to accommodate schools that are just beginning their implementation of multi-tiered systems of behavior support (MTSS) as well as schools that already have some, but not all, pieces of behavior support firmly in place. For example, a school may have done great work on improving behavior in the common areas of the school but very little work on intentionally constructing a positive, inviting climate or addressing conflict and bullying in a comprehensive way. This school could go directly to Module C: *Conscious Construction of an Inviting Climate*, and after implementing those strategies, move to Module E: *Improving Safety, Managing Conflict, and Reducing Bullying*.

Each module incorporates multiple resources to assist you: video presentations, the book you are reading now, and forms and samples that you can reproduce. The videos, provided as either streaming video or on DVDs, can guide a building-based leadership team through implementing *Foundations*. The same content is available in print format; we provide eight copies of this book for each module, one for each member of the leadership team. Teams can decide which content delivery form works best for them—video or print.

Each module features reproducible forms, examples of policies and procedures from real schools that have implemented *Foundations*, and other implementation resources. PowerPoint presentations that correspond directly to the video and print content are also provided. Your leadership team can use these presentations to deliver the most relevant *Foundations* information to the entire staff.

Beginning Behavior Support

For schools and districts that are just beginning with behavior support or are unsure where to begin, we suggest starting with Module A: *Foundations of Behavior Support—A Continuous Improvement Process*. This module is the foundation of *Foundations*. It describes the importance of a well-designed leadership team, a formalized continuous improvement cycle, how to use multiple data sources to drive that cycle, and how to involve and unify the staff in implementation. Without laying this groundwork, any specific work on procedures, such as improving the cafeteria, is unlikely to be effective or sustainable.

HOW TO USE FOUNDATIONS

Once your team is collecting and analyzing data, you will probably move through Modules B–F (described below) in order. You'll work on the common areas of the school, then positive climate, and so on. Once a module has been implemented, you are not done with that module. For example, after implementing the procedures in Module B for a couple of common areas and a couple of schoolwide policies, such as dress code, you may move on to Module C to work on improving school climate. However, you will concurrently continue to implement Module B procedures for additional common areas and schoolwide policies. Working through all six modules will take about two to five years of development and implementation.

MTSS in Progress

Schools and districts that have been effectively implementing other approaches to PBIS should follow these guidelines when implementing *Foundations*.

You may be able to use the modules in a nonlinear fashion if your school has a highly functional team, uses multiple data sources to involve the entire staff in continuous improvement of behavior support, and has worked to improve several common areas or schoolwide policies. To self-assess where to begin, a resource called the Foundations Implementation Rubric and Summary is included in Appendix A of the book and with the reproducible print resources for each module. The rubric can help your leadership team assess which modules have information useful to your school at this time and help you make judgments about where to begin. Print the rubric, work through it as a team, and summarize your findings, and you will see patterns emerge. (Instructions are included with the rubric.)

For example, if all the conditions described at the beginning of this paragraph are in place, you will probably find that you are already implementing many of the procedures delineated in Modules A and B. One school may have an urgent need to go directly to Module E because the school has no programs or policies to address conflict and bullying, whereas another school may go directly to Module D because staff are very inconsistent about when and how to use disciplinary referral to the office. Another school may go directly to Module F because their schoolwide structures are relatively well established, but they have yet to address classroom management or the integration of universal, targeted, and intensive interventions.

HOW TO USE FOUNDATIONS

Appendix B of each module presents an Implementation Checklist for that module. The Implementation Checklist details the summarized items on the rubric. You will use this tool as you near completion on any module to ensure that you have fully implemented it, and it's also useful for reviewing the implementation every three years or so. The checklist can identify strengths to celebrate and catch gaps in your implementation that you may be able to fill before a major problem emerges.

Videos and Print Resources

The method you use to view the videos and access the print resources depends on the version of *Foundations* your school or district purchased. Print resources include reproducible forms, samples, PowerPoint presentations, and other implementation tools (see Appendix C).

Foundations DVD option. Videos are provided on a set of DVDs. The CD in the DVD case contains the print resources.

Foundations streaming video option. Find your School Code on the title page of this book. Go to the website streaming.ancorapublishing.online and enter your School Code and your school email address. Be sure to enter this email address each time you log in.

Note: The only web browsers supported are Chrome, Internet Explorer, and Edge. Use of other browsers may cause problems with viewing the videos.

After you log in, click on Foundations to see the menu of modules. Click on a module to see the menu of tasks. Click on a task to open the video. Click on the Play icon below the video screen to play the video (if needed, scroll down to see the icon). Change the video resolution by clicking the HD icon in the lower right corner of the video screen.

To access print resources, click the Download Print Resources link that appears to the left of the menu of tasks for each module. A menu of print resources opens in a new browser window. Click on the links to view or download files. Note that you must download files to your computer to modify them or use the fillable PDF features described in the Using the Files document.

HOW TO USE FOUNDATIONS

Another school may go directly to Module F because their schoolwide structures are relatively well established, but they have yet to address classroom management or the integration of universal, targeted, and intensive interventions.

Appendix B of each module presents an Implementation Checklist for that module. The Implementation Checklist details the summarized items on the rubric. You will use this tool as you near completion on any module to ensure that you have fully implemented it, and it's also useful for reviewing the implementation every three years or so. The checklist can identify strengths to celebrate and catch gaps in your implementation that you may be able to fill before a major problem emerges.

OVERVIEW OF MODULES

The modules in *Foundations* are designed to be used sequentially by a school or district that is just getting started with behavior support. However, if a school or district is already implementing a team-based, data-driven approach to continuous improvement of climate, safety, discipline, and motivation, the modules can be used in any order.

This module—**Module E: *Improving Safety, Managing Conflict, and Reducing Bullying***—guides the Foundations Team in assessing school strengths and weaknesses related to safety, conflict, and bullying. The module begins by examining the attributes of safe and unsafe schools and offers suggestions for moving your school toward the evidence-based attributes that contribute to safety. One potential risk to safety is poor conflict management, so this module includes a simple conflict resolution strategy that students can use to manage conflict in peaceful and mutually beneficial ways. Bullying is another serious risk to safety. Module E provides a step-by-step process for analyzing strengths and gaps in your school's bullying policies and procedures as well as suggestions and examples for turning gaps into strengths. This module includes lessons for students on safety, conflict, and bullying prevention and intervention.

- Presentation 1: Keeping Students Safe From Physical and Emotional Harm
- Presentation 2: Attributes of Safe and Unsafe Schools
- Presentation 3: Teaching Conflict Resolution
- Presentation 4: Analyzing Bullying Behavior, Policies, and School Needs
- Presentation 5: Schoolwide Bullying Prevention and Intervention
- Appendix A: Foundations Implementation Rubric and Summary
- Appendix B: Module E Implementation Checklist
- Appendix C: Guide to Module E Reproducible Forms and Samples

Other modules in *Foundations: A Proactive and Positive Behavior Support System* are:

Module A: *Foundations of Behavior Support—A Continuous Improvement Process* covers the essential processes for involving the entire staff in developing, implementing, and sustaining positive behavior support. It includes detailed information about establishing a building-based leadership team (Foundations Team) to represent the entire staff. This module advises the team on how to collect and analyze data, identify and rank a manageable number of priorities for improvement, and guide the staff in revising, adopting, and implementing new policies and procedures for each priority. This process creates a cycle of continuous improvement that empowers and unifies the entire staff.

- Presentation 1: Foundations: A Multi-Tiered System of Behavior Support
- Presentation 2: Team Processes
- Presentation 3: The Improvement Cycle
- Presentation 4: Data-Driven Processes
- Presentation 5: Developing Staff Engagement and Unity
- Appendix A: Foundations Implementation Rubric and Summary
- Appendix B: Module A Implementation Checklist
- Appendix C: Guide to Module A Reproducible Forms and Samples

Module B: *Managing Behavior in Common Areas and With Schoolwide Policies* delineates processes for ensuring that common areas (arrival, cafeteria, hallways, and so on) and schoolwide policies (dress code, electronics use, public displays of affection, and so on) are structured for success and that expectations for behavior are directly taught with clarity and repetition to students. In addition, this module includes detailed information for all staff about how to provide positive and systematic supervision and how to correct misbehavior calmly, consistently, and respectfully.

- Presentation 1: Laying the Groundwork for Consistency in All School Settings
- Presentation 2: Structuring Common Areas and Schoolwide Policies for Success
- Presentation 3: Teaching Expectations to Students
- Presentation 4: Effective Supervision, Part 1—Protect, Expect, and Connect
- Presentation 5: Effective Supervision, Part 2—Correct and Reflect
- Presentation 6: Supervising Common Areas and Schoolwide Policies—for All Staff
- Presentation 7: Adopting, Implementing, and Monitoring Improvements to Common Areas and Schoolwide Policies
- Appendix A: Foundations Implementation Rubric and Summary
- Appendix B: Module B Implementation Checklist
- Appendix C: Guide to Module B Reproducible Forms and Samples

Module C: *Conscious Construction of an Inviting School Climate* guides the entire staff in creating and sustaining a school environment that makes all students feel welcomed and valued. This process includes developing Guidelines for Success, a set of behaviors and traits that provides a common language and common values among staff, students, and parents. This module explains how and why to maintain at least 3:1 ratios of positive interactions and covers the importance of regular attendance and strategies for improving attendance. Strategies for meeting the basic human needs of all students are also discussed. Finally, the module outlines how to welcome and orient staff, students, and families who are new to the school in a way that connects them to the school community.

- Presentation 1: Constructing and Maintaining a Positive Climate
- Presentation 2: Guidelines for Success
- Presentation 3: Ratios of Positive Interactions
- Presentation 4: Improving Attendance
- Presentation 5: School Connectedness—Meeting Basic Human Needs
- Presentation 6: Programs and Strategies for Meeting Needs
- Presentation 7: Making a Good First Impression—Welcoming New Staff, Students, and Families
- Appendix A: Foundations Implementation Rubric and Summary
- Appendix B: Module C Implementation Checklist
- Appendix C: Guide to Module C Reproducible Forms and Samples

Module D: *Responding to Misbehavior—An Instructional Approach* focuses on the vital importance of an instructional approach to correction in reducing future occurrences of the misbehavior. It provides information on training and inspiring all staff to correct all misbehavior by giving students information about how to behave successfully and by using the mildest consequences that reasonably fit the infractions. Module D describes how to get consensus among staff about when (and when not) to use office discipline referral. It provides menus of corrective techniques for mild and moderate misbehavior, from gentle verbal correction to time owed after class to restorative justice. All staff learn strategies for de-escalating emotional situations, and administrators are introduced to a comprehensive game plan for dealing with office referrals and implementing alternatives to out-of-school suspension. This module includes sample lessons for students on how to interact with people in authority.

- Presentation 1: The Relationship Between Proactive Procedures, Corrective Procedures, and Individual Student Behavior Improvement Plans
- Presentation 2: Developing Three Levels of Misbehavior
- Presentation 3: Staff Responsibilities for Responding to Misbehavior
- Presentation 4: Administrator Responsibilities for Responding to Misbehavior
- Presentation 5: Preventing the Misbehavior That Leads to Referrals and Suspensions
- Appendix A: Foundations Implementation Rubric and Summary
- Appendix B: Module D Implementation Checklist
- Appendix C: Guide to Module D Reproducible Forms and Samples

Module F: *Establishing and Sustaining a Continuum of Behavior Support* outlines how the Foundations Team can analyze and guide an integration of universal prevention, targeted support, and intensive support for students. This process includes adopting and supporting a schoolwide or district approach to classroom management that creates a common language and ensures that teachers, administrators, and support staff are on the same page about classroom organization and management. For students who need individual support, this module provides staff training in early-stage interventions and a variety of problem-solving structures that match the intensity of student need to the intensity of school- and district-based resources. Finally, Module F provides guidance in sustaining *Foundations* at the building and district level so that effective procedures are maintained and improvement continues, even when school administration changes.

- Presentation 1: The Vision of a Continuum of Behavior Support
- Presentation 2: Supporting Classroom Behavior—The Three-Legged Stool
- Presentation 3: Articulating Staff Beliefs and Solidifying Universal Procedures
- Presentation 4: Early-Stage Interventions for General Education Classrooms
- Presentation 5: Matching the Intensity of Your Resources to the Intensity of Student Needs
- Presentation 6: Problem-Solving Processes and Intervention Design
- Presentation 7: Sustainability and District Support
- Appendix A: Foundations Implementation Rubric and Summary
- Appendix B: Module F Implementation Checklist
- Appendix C: Guide to Module F Reproducible Forms and Samples

Keeping Students Safe From Physical and Emotional Harm

CONTENTS

Introduction to Module E
For the Foundations Team

INTRODUCTION TO MODULE E

Module E is about integrating efforts to encourage school safety, reduce bullying, and provide students with strategies for managing and resolving conflict. Parents want and expect many things from schools, but the absolute expectation is that schools will make every effort to keep children free from physical and emotional harm.

Figure 1a   *Foundations continuum of behavior support*

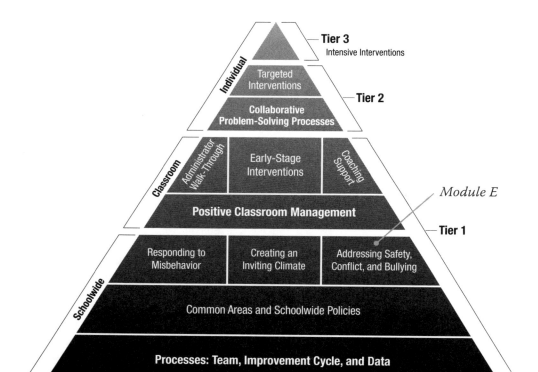

Despite what you might think because of the school shootings that get so much media coverage, schools do a good job keeping students safe from homicide. According to the Centers for Disease Control and Prevention (CDC; 2012), the percentage of all youth homicides occurring at school has been less than 2% since the CDC started collecting those data in 1992, even though, by our rough calculation, students spend about 25% of their waking hours in school. So schools are keeping children safe from homicide at a significantly better rate than nonschool settings. School personnel can be proud of that fact.

Before you begin congratulating yourself, however, read some other information from the CDC (2012) that relates to violence in school: In a 2011 nationally representative sample of youth in grades 9 through 12, 12% of respondents reported being in a physical fight on school property in the 12 months preceding the survey, and 5.9% did not go to school on 1 or more days in the 30 days preceding the survey because they felt unsafe at school or on the way to or from school. Weapons—guns, knives, or clubs—were carried by 5.4% of students on 1 or more days in the 30 days preceding the survey, and 7.4% of high school students reported being threatened or injured with a weapon on school property 1 or more times in the 12 months preceding the survey. So there are significant concerns about violence to consider.

Safety is not just an issue of violence, however. The playground, a staple at almost every elementary school in the country, can be an unsafe setting. At one elementary school we worked with, for example, the playground was initially not a high priority in their improvement process. But one of our trainers observed the playground and expressed concern about the chaotic activity—so much so that he asked the school nurse about the injury rate. The school nurse reported 242 injuries as of Month 6 of the school year. That's a lot of injuries for a school of fewer than 500 students.

Physical harm is not the only safety issue schools need to worry about. The emotional harm that bullying can inflict is also a concern. In the CDC study (2012), 20.1% of high school students reported being bullied on school property in the 12 months preceding the survey. Regardless of socioeconomic status, racial makeup, and location, all schools can potentially be affected by bullying.

If you have administered surveys to gather anonymous information from staff, students, and parents about their perceptions of the school, you may have already learned that staff and parent perceptions of safety and bullying can be quite different from student perceptions. We frequently find this disparity in schools. Here are some real data from one school we worked with in response to the survey item: Does this school have a problem with students bullying other students? Only 11% of staff agreed that bullying was a moderate or severe problem in the school, but 43.3% of students agreed that bullying was a moderate or severe problem.

An example of how bullying can fly under staff radar comes from one of our *Foundations* trainers. She was conducting a site visit at an elementary school in a fairly affluent community. At first glance, she thought the playground was very orderly and respectful. But as she walked around the playground to better hear as well as see how the children were interacting, she moved near three young girls on the swings. The girls were smiling and looked as though they were behaving very appropriately, but when the trainer was close enough to hear them speak, she heard one girl say to another, "You need to get those nasty Kmart shoes off of our school's swings." If this type of interaction is representative of the school's students, the school clearly needs to address respectful student interactions and bullying issues.

In this module, we discuss what your staff members need to know and what they can do to enhance safety, help students manage conflict, and reduce bullying in your school. Remember this guiding principle that we've applied to other areas of *Foundations*: If everyone does a little, no one has to do a lot. And by extension: If anyone is *unwilling* to do a little, the rest of the staff is unlikely to be able to fill in the gaps that result.

We also discuss what students need to know and do. We include many sample lessons that can be used as is or modified to fit your needs. (Lessons can be printed from the reproducible materials and also appear at the end of their corresponding presentations in this book.) The lessons present what we think is essential information that students need to know about their role in keeping the school safe, handling conflict, and preventing and dealing with bullying.

You may already have a comprehensive curriculum that addresses one or more of the topics in this module. If so, we recommend that the Foundations Team compare the *Foundations* information with your current approach and consider whether any of the suggested actions and resources would benefit your school.

This module contains five presentations.

- Presentation 2, "Attributes of Safe and Unsafe Schools," can serve as a reality check on your current safety efforts related to natural disasters, man-made emergencies such as intruders, and behavioral emergencies such as out-of-control students and fights. Seven sample lessons address integrating school safety with a positive and welcoming climate.

- Presentation 3 describes a simple conflict resolution strategy for students and staff. They learn the difference between disagreements and conflicts that can escalate, and they learn to Stop, Think, and Plan (STP) when conflict arises. A common language—the key to resolving conflict peacefully—is created among students and staff. This presentation includes seven sample lessons on managing conflict in peaceful ways.

- Presentations 4 and 5 cover the complex issues surrounding bullying. Presentation 4 suggests ways to establish a foundation for reducing bullying, such as collecting initial data that will help you set priorities for improvement and implementing methods for ongoing data collection and reporting. We provide tips for analyzing your existing bullying-related policies and revising them, if necessary. We also suggest ways to set priorities for the universal prevention of bullying in your school.

- In Presentation 5 we discuss concrete strategies for preventing and intervening with bullying, including training staff and students and providing information to parents about how they can support the school's antibullying efforts. We also cover information on schoolwide prevention methods, such as improving student engagement and connection with the school, and provide 11 sample lessons that relate to bullying issues.

Action Steps & Evidence of Implementation

Action Steps	Evidence of Implementation
1. Review Module E, either as a team or in smaller groups of two or three team members (one group reviews Presentation 2, one reviews Presentation 3, and one reviews Presentations 4 and 5).	Foundations Process: Meeting Minutes, Presentations/ Communications With Staff
2. As a team, decide whether current school policies and procedures are accomplishing some or all of the *Foundations* recommendations. If so, are there any minor gaps not addressed by your current efforts?	
3. If you don't currently achieve some of the *Foundations* recommendations—for example, you have strong safety and antibullying procedures, but lack a schoolwide conflict resolution program—consider prioritizing that area for improvement.	

Presentation 1: Keeping Students Safe From Physical and Emotional Harm

PRESENTATION

Two

Attributes of Safe and Unsafe Schools

CONTENTS

Introduction

Task 1: Understand the Attributes of Safe and Unsafe Schools
For the Foundations Team, school safety team (if one exists), school resource officer, and school psychologist

Task 2: Assess Emergency Preparedness
For the Foundations Team, school safety team (if one exists), school resource officer, and school psychologist

Task 3: Teach Lessons to Increase Connectedness and Safety
For the Foundations Team, school safety team (if one exists), school resource officer, and school psychologist

DOCUMENTS*

- Attributes of Safe and Unsafe Schools and Associated Protective and Risk Factors (E-15)
- Understanding the Attributes of Safe and Unsafe Schools (E-03)
- Assessing Emergency Preparedness (E-04)
- Red Card (E-16)
- Evaluation Form: Lessons to Increase Connectedness and Safety (E-05)
- Increasing Connectedness and Safety Lesson Outlines

* See Appendix C for information on accessing these documents.

INTRODUCTION

This presentation discusses the complex topic of school safety. Some of the factors that schools need to consider are:

- Risks from outsiders who enter school grounds
- Risks from alienated students
- Risks of students being injured on the playground, in the parking lot, and in the pickup and drop-off areas
- Risks from natural disasters

School shootings have become an all-too-real possibility for any school, and every school needs to guard against outsiders and alienated students coming onto campus with weapons. But don't narrow your focus on safety to thinking exclusively about these disastrous kinds of events. Playground injuries outnumber attacks on students by a large margin. High school parking lots and elementary school pickup and drop-off areas can be risky locations. Be sure to work on eliminating these more common risks at least as much as you work on preventing school shootings and preparing for natural disasters.

We present three tasks related to school safety with the goal of helping you think about safety in a comprehensive and broad way and integrate it into your other school improvement efforts. As you read the tasks, think about ways to coordinate *Foundations* safety efforts with the efforts of others in your school. If a school safety team already exists, for example, you don't want to duplicate or confuse what that team has already implemented. You might choose to leave school safety initiatives to the existing safety team and recommend that they review this presentation. In addition, ensure that others, such as the school resource officer and school psychologist, have access to the safety information in *Foundations*. They might find some useful ideas that no one on the safety team has considered yet.

Task 1: Understand the Attributes of Safe and Unsafe Schools provides information about risk factors and protective factors that contribute to unsafe and safe schools in order to help you assess your own school. This information will also help you identify how the different parts of *Foundations* can directly and positively affect the safety of students.

Task 2: Assess Emergency Preparedness describes how to evaluate staff preparation for dealing with emergencies such as natural disasters, intruders in the school, medical situations, and problematic student behavior. We also suggest policies and procedures for dealing with student behavior emergencies.

Task 3: Teach Lessons to Increase Connectedness and Safety offers suggestions for teaching essential information about safety-related issues in a context that enhances school connectedness and a sense of belonging. Students, staff, and parents need to know in advance about zero-tolerance policies and any policies that require specific responses from staff. We provide seven sample lessons on safety topics that can serve as models for the structure and content of lessons for your students.

TASK 1
Understand the attributes of safe and unsafe schools

Much of the information presented in this task has been adapted, with permission, from the following resources:

- Institute on Violent and Destructive Behavior website (ivdb.uoregon.edu), and personal communications with the codirectors, Drs. Hill Walker and Jeffrey Sprague
- Sprague, J. R., & Walker, H. M. (2010). Building safe and healthy schools to promote school success: Critical issues, current challenges, and promising approaches. In M. R. Shinn, H. M. Walker & G. Stoner (Eds.), *Interventions for achievement and behavior problems in a three-tier model including RTI* (pp. 225–258). Bethesda, MD: National Association of School Psychologists.
- Sprague, J. R., & Walker, H. M. (2005). *Safe and healthy schools: Practical prevention strategies.* New York, NY: Guilford Press.

The purpose of this task is to present information about factors that contribute to unsafe and safe schools so that you can identify and address the risk factors present in your own school.

Understand the attributes of unsafe schools.

Unsafe schools are often characterized as chaotic, stressful, disorganized, poorly structured, ineffective, high risk, lacking cohesion, lacking clear behavioral and academic expectations, and having high rates of gang activity and violent incidents.

Risk factors that contribute to unsafe conditions in schools include:

- Poor design and use of school space
- Overcrowding
- Lack of caring-but-firm, consistent disciplinary procedures

- Insensitivity to and poor accommodation of multicultural factors and diversity issues
- Student alienation
- Rejection of at-risk students by teachers and peers
- Anger and resentment at school routines and demands for conformity
- Poor supervision

Understand the attributes of safe schools.

Safe schools are characterized by an overarching positive structure and philosophy. They are structured for student success and promote the acceptance of all students. Their students feel safe from physical and psychological harm, and they cultivate a nurturing, caring, and protective atmosphere.

Drs. Walker and Sprague of the Institute on Violent and Destructive Behavior identified the following protective factors that contribute to safe conditions in schools. These factors should sound familiar—they form the central theme that runs throughout *Foundations*. We list the *Foundations* presentations where each factor is more specifically addressed. If you have already fully implemented the Action Steps for a particular module, you can be confident that your staff is making a conscientious effort to create a school culture that fosters safety.

Positive school climate and atmosphere. Addressed by *Foundations* in:

- Module B, Presentation 4: Effective Supervision, Part 1—Protect, Expect, and Connect
- Module B, Presentation 6: Supervising Common Areas and Schoolwide Policies—for All Staff
- All of Module C: Conscious Construction of an Inviting School Climate

Clear and high performance expectations for all students. Addressed by *Foundations* in:

- Module B, Presentation 3: Teaching Expectations to Students
- Module C, Presentation 2: Guidelines for Success
- Module D, Presentation 3: Staff Responsibilities for Responding to Misbehavior
- Module D, Presentation 4: Administrator Responsibilities for Responding to Misbehavior
- Module D, Presentation 5: Preventing the Misbehavior That Leads to Referrals and Suspensions

Inclusive values and practices throughout the school. Addressed by *Foundations* in:

- Module C, Presentation 2: Guidelines for Success

- Module C, Presentation 5: School Connectedness—Meeting Basic Human Needs
- Module C, Presentation 6: Programs and Strategies for Meeting Needs
- Module E, Presentation 2, Task 3: Teach Lessons to Increase Connectedness and Safety
- Module F, Presentation 3: Articulating Staff Beliefs and Solidifying Universal Procedures

Strong student connections to the school environment and the schooling process. Addressed by *Foundations* in:

- Module C, Presentation 4: Improving Attendance
- Module C, Presentation 5: School Connectedness—Meeting Basic Human Needs
- Module C, Presentation 6: Programs and Strategies for Meeting Needs
- Module B, Presentation 4: Effective Supervision, Part 1—Protect, Expect, and Connect
- Module B, Presentation 6: Supervising Common Areas and Schoolwide Policies—for All Staff

High levels of student participation and parent involvement in schooling. Addressed by *Foundations* in:

- Module C, Presentation 4: Improving Attendance
- Module C, Presentation 5: School Connectedness—Meeting Basic Human Needs
- Module C, Presentation 6: Programs and Strategies for Meeting Needs
- Module C, Presentation 7: Making a Good First Impression—Welcoming New Staff, Students, and Families

Opportunities for students to learn social skills and develop socially. Although *Foundations* does not include a formal social skills curriculum, we provide several lessons that give students opportunities to develop socially. In addition, the instructional correction techniques that we recommend involve teaching students expectations for socially appropriate behavior. Addressed by *Foundations* in:

- Module B, Presentation 3: Teaching Expectations to Students
- Module D, Presentation 3: Staff Responsibilities for Responding to Misbehavior
- Module D, Presentation 5, Task 3: Teach Students the Expectations for Interacting Appropriately With Adults
- Module E, Presentation 2, Task 3: Teach Lessons to Increase Connectedness and Safety

Schoolwide conflict resolution strategies. Addressed by *Foundations* in Module E, Presentation 3: Teaching Conflict Resolution

Presentation 2: Attributes of Safe and Unsafe Schools

Figure 2a summarizes the attributes of safe and unsafe schools.

Another source, the U.S. Department of Education report *Safeguarding Our Children: An Action Guide* (2000), lists these qualities of safe and responsible schools (the report is available at www.ed.gov/admins/lead/safety/actguide/index.html). Again, the concepts emphasized in *Foundations* correspond quite closely with these ideals.

- The school has strong leadership, caring faculty, student participation in the design of programs and policies, and family and community involvement, including law enforcement officials and representatives of community-based organizations.

- The physical environment of the school is safe, and schoolwide policies are in place to promote and support responsible behaviors.

- Prevention and intervention programs are sustained, coordinated, and comprehensive.

Figure 2a Attributes of safe and unsafe schools and associated protective and risk factors graphic (E-15). Adapted from Sprague and Walker, Safe and healthy schools: Practical prevention strategies, *2005, p. 3.*

SAFE SCHOOLS

Safe schools are characterized by an overarching positive structure and philosophy. They are structured for student success and promote the acceptance of all students. Their students feel safe from physical and psychological harm, and they cultivate a nurturing, caring, and protective atmosphere.

The following protective factors contribute to safe conditions in schools. These factors should sound familiar—they form the central theme that runs throughout *Foundations*.

- Positive school climate and atmosphere
- Clear and high performance expectations for all students
- Inclusive values and practices throughout the school
- Strong student connections to the school environment and the schooling process.
- High levels of student participation and parent involvement in schooling.
- Opportunities for students to learn social skills and develop socially.
- Schoolwide conflict resolution strategies.

UNSAFE SCHOOLS

Unsafe schools are often characterized as chaotic, stressful, disorganized, poorly structured, ineffective, high risk, lacking cohesion, lacking clear behavioral and academic expectations, and having high rates of gang activity and violent incidents.

Risk factors that contribute to unsafe conditions in schools include the following:

- Poor design and use of school space
- Overcrowding
- Lack of caring-but-firm, consistent disciplinary procedures
- Insensitivity to and poor accommodation of multicultural factors and diversity issues
- Student alienation
- Rejection of at-risk students by teachers and peers
- Anger and resentment at school routines and demands for conformity
- Poor supervision

- Interventions are based on careful assessment of student needs.
- Evidence-based approaches are used.
- Staff are provided with training and support to help them implement programs and approaches.
- Interventions are monitored and evaluations are conducted to ensure that the programs are meeting measurable goals and objectives.

Improve safety, and climate will improve, too.

Figures 2b and 2c illustrate how two schools effectively addressed safety issues with arrival and dismissal. Not only did the physical safety of the students improve (they were kept further away from moving traffic), but the overall climate of the bus loading area improved, too, contributing to less chaos and conflict between students.

Figure 2b shows a photo from an elementary school in Hawaii. About ten buses arrive at the school just as students are being dismissed or slightly after, when hundred of students are gathered on the relatively narrow sidewalk. The fence keeps students away from the moving buses as they pull in and out from the curb. The L-shaped gates define exactly where students are to line up and the direction the line will go, and there is ample signage to clarify which bus goes where. Imagine trying to supervise young students in this area when there was no fence! One playful shove could have sent a child into the path of a bus. Now, because students are protected and the lines are orderly, supervisors can calmly patrol the area and interact pleasantly with students.

An elementary school in Wichita had a problem with the area in front of the school that was used by walkers and bus riders as well as parent drivers who dropped off and picked up their children. The school didn't have the budget to install fencing, but the Foundations Team made it a priority to work on clarifying the

Figure 2b Bus loading area at a large elementary school in Hawaii

area with great signage and striping in the parking lot and walkway areas (Figure 2c). These relatively simple structural changes turned an area that had been chaotic and dangerous into one that is very orderly, safe, and respectful.

Figure 2c   *Drop-off and pickup area at an elementary school in Wichita, Kansas*

Find information about school safety assessments.

A school safety assessment can be a valuable tool to help you focus your safety efforts. You can have a qualified assessor come to your school, or you can conduct your own assessment. Your local fire and police departments might be good resources. Many states and school districts also offer assessment tools and guidance. Some states require periodic safety audits.

The National School Safety Center (www.schoolsafety.us/services/school-safety-site-assessments) is a terrific resource. Its school site assessments include:

- Facilities audit
- Review of the school's comprehensive safe-school plan
- Review of existing plans for crisis response and disaster mitigation
- Review of student codes of conduct
- Analysis of district policies related to student safety and management issues and their compliance with federal and state law
- Analysis of crime prevention through environmental design efforts (CPTED)
- Student input
- Discussions with key administrative personnel and local law enforcement
- Review of recent media activity
- Analysis of recent school crime and disorder incidents
- Commendations for effective practices and programs

A great example of how important just one of these suggested assessment items can be comes from a high school that had been working on implementing *Foundations*. The school resource office was on the Foundations Team, and he heard us (*Foundations* trainers) talk about the value of seeking student input through informal conversation as well as more formal student focus groups. So the resource officer asked some students to participate in a focus group about school safety. He knew these students because they were troublesome and he interacted with them frequently. As the focus group calmly discussed some of the potentially dangerous areas of the school, the students voluntarily revealed some unexpected information: When they were in the front office waiting for disciplinary action, they sat where they could view the security camera monitors. By watching the monitors, the students had figured out which areas of the school were not monitored—and they went to those areas when they didn't want to get caught breaking the rules.

If this school resource officer hadn't been seeking student input in a calm, relaxed setting, he would not have discovered this important information. The school modified the security camera arrangement and office procedures to ensure that students could no longer get information about monitoring efforts.

Resources for School Safety Assessment

National School Safety Center (www.schoolsafety.us/services/school-safety-site-assessments)

National Association of School Psychologists—School Safety and Crisis Resources (www.nasponline.org/resources/crisis_safety/schoolsafety.aspx)

National Crime Prevention Council (www.ncpc.org/resources/files/pdf/school-safety/11964-School%20Safety%20Toolkit%20final.pdf)

Assess your safety factors.

In the Action Steps, we suggest that you assess safety factors—both risk and protective—in your school by completing the form Understand the Attributes of Safe and Unsafe Schools (Form E-03 shown in Figure 2d). We suggest that each team member complete a form individually, then the group can discuss each item and reach consensus on a final score. Those scores can help you establish priorities for improving safety in your school.

Plan to conduct this short exercise annually. Archive a copy of the form that shows the group consensus scores so you can compare them with forms you will complete in future years.

Figure 2d *Understanding the Attributes of Safe and Unsafe Schools (E-03)*

Understanding the Attributes of Safe and Unsafe Schools

Team Member: _____ Date: _____

Directions: Please rate how the following protective and risk factors affect the safety of your building.

RATING GUIDE:

1 = Not a problem
2 = Minor problem
3 = Moderate problem
4 = Serious problem

Part 1—Protective Factors and Characteristics of Safe Schools

1. Positive school climate and atmosphere	1	2	3	4
2. Clear and high performance expectations for all students	1	2	3	4
3. Inclusive values and practices throughout the school	1	2	3	4
4. Strong student connections to the school environment and the schooling process	1	2	3	4
5. High levels of student participation and parent involvement in schooling	1	2	3	4
6. Opportunities for student to learn social skills and develop socially	1	2	3	4
7. Schoolwide conflict resolution strategies	1	2	3	4

Maximum Points _____ Score _____ Percentage _____

Part 2—Risk Factors and Characteristics of Unsafe Schools

1. Poor design and use of school space	1	2	3	4
2. Overcrowding	1	2	3	4
3. Lack of caring-but-firm, consistent disciplinary procedures	1	2	3	4
4. Insensitivity to and poor accommodation of multicultural factors and diversity issues	1	2	3	4
5. Student alienation	1	2	3	4
6. Rejection of at-risk students by teachers and peers	1	2	3	4
7. Anger and resentment at school routines and demands for conformity	1	2	3	4
8. Poor supervision	1	2	3	4

Maximum Points _____ Score _____ Percentage _____

 See Appendix C for printing directions.

Task 1 Action Steps & Evidence of Implementation

Action Steps	Evidence of Implementation
1. Have each team member complete Understanding the Attributes of Safe and Unsafe Schools (Form E-03), then as a group discuss the items and reach a consensus score for each. Complete a form that shows the consensus scores. Use the information to establish priorities for improving safety in your school.	Foundations Process: Safety
2. Meet with any staff members and groups currently working on school safety issues. • Identify any content covered in Tasks 2 and 3 of this presentation that duplicates efforts already underway. • Coordinate efforts on any content not currently being addressed—that is, determine who will be responsible for what.	Foundations Process: Meeting Minutes, Safety
3. Determine whether your school has had a safety assessment within the last 3 years. • If there has been a safety assessment, determine whether and how the recommendations are being addressed. • If there has not been a safety assessment, decide whether to assign someone on the team to research the feasibility of conducting one.	Foundations Process: Meeting Minutes, Safety

TASK 2

Assess emergency preparedness

In this task, we discuss preparation for natural disasters, emergencies that require school lockdown, medical emergencies, and out-of-control students.

Prepare for natural disasters and emergencies that require school lockdown.

Identify the natural disasters that might affect your school, such as fire, tornadoes, hurricanes, floods, and earthquakes. If your region of the country has never experienced a hurricane, for example, you don't need to spend time preparing for one. But you do need to plan for any disasters that can potentially occur in your area. For example, school districts near Mount Rainier, an active volcano in Washington state, have plans for evacuating the schools in the event of mudslides.

You also need to plan for school lockdowns in response to intruders and coordinate these efforts with local law enforcement. Be sure to periodically train and review all emergency procedures. A school we worked with developed a procedure for informing staff when a lockdown was required. Someone would announce over the all-call, "There will be an impromptu staff meeting after school today in _____." The location indicated where an intruder was in the building. This procedure was designed to avoid creating panic among students and to avoid giving the intruder information about actions the school was taking. However, when the announcement was used for an actual emergency (because a nearby bank had been robbed), half of the staff didn't remember the plan. Instead of locking down their rooms, they grumbled about having to attend a staff meeting! So be sure that emergency procedures are reviewed frequently.

It's important to develop detailed written plans for responding to all the natural disasters and man-made emergencies you identify as reasonably possible in your area. Most schools have excellent, established plans for what to do in case of fire. Your fire emergency plan can serve as a model for your plans for other natural disasters. Follow these important steps when planning for emergencies:

- Write detailed instructions for specific actions that staff members should take.
- Map escape routes specific to areas of the school for students and staff members.

- Clarify lockdown procedures and include plans for where staff and students should go if they are in common areas or restrooms when lockdown is implemented.

- Coordinate your plans with relevant community agencies, such as police, fire, and medical emergency responders.

- Ensure that staff members receive information and training on all emergency plans.

- Arrange for periodic drills and practice of all emergency plans so all staff and students know what to do.

To review and retrain emergency procedures, get creative! Staff will remember the procedures better when a variety of review methods are used. For example, during a staff meeting, review safety procedures by staging a 10-minute quiz show based on the *Jeopardy!* format. Or use a *Survivor* theme and pit the men against the women. Announce the competition in advance so staff will be motivated to study the procedures, and ensure that the review is light and fun, but comprehensive. Another approach is to divide the staff into subgroups, such as grade levels or departments, and have each subgroup prepare a 1-minute commercial about a specific safety or emergency procedure. Each group presents a commercial during a staff meeting once or twice during the school year.

Adequate preparation and training are key to keeping everyone as safe as possible in an emergency. For many people, it's difficult to think clearly in stressful situations. Enough practice can enable staff and students to automatically follow through on the emergency plans even in the face of the fear and urgency of a real natural disaster.

Prepare for medical emergencies.

Identify medical emergencies that might arise in your school, such as playground injuries, sports injuries, and health emergencies (serious asthma attacks, diabetic crises, reactions to insect bites and stings, allergic reactions to foods, collapse, and the like).

Ensure that your school has a detailed written plan for responding to all possible medical emergencies. Your plan should include the following elements:

- Master list of staff members who are trained in first aid and CPR so it's easy to find the nearest person who can help

- Written plans for responding to the medical needs of identified students (these plans should be provided to staff members who are responsible for those students)

- Primary and backup communication procedures staff members are to use to call for medical assistance, such as:
    - Walkie-talkies
    - Cell phones (smartphones)
    - Intercom
    - Red Card System

Organize emergency communication procedures for common area supervisors in advance, and make sure you have both a basic and a backup plan. Walkie-talkies, smartphones for calling and texting, intercom systems, and internal telephone systems are commonly used for the basic emergency communications plan. These technologies are wonderful, but like anything that depends on batteries or electricity, they can become useless instantly without power. You should have a backup plan.

Consider establishing a Red Card System. Every supervisor carries a laminated card of brightly colored paper that may say something like "Emergency" (see Figure 2e for a sample). Students are instructed, perhaps as part of regular fire drill or lockdown instruction, what to do if an adult hands them a card. In a situation where a supervisor needs help and can't use the main communication system or leave the situation, she can hand the card to a student. The student runs to the office or the nearest staff member, shows the card, and tells the adult what happened.

> **❧ FOUNDATIONS RECOMMENDATION ☙**
>
> *Consider establishing a Red Card System as a backup emergency communication procedure. This low-tech system requires no batteries or electricity.*

Figure 2e *Sample Red Card (E-16)*

RED CARD
EMERGENCY—NEED HELP IMMEDIATELY!
Location: _____
____ Fighting out of control. Send help.
____ Serious injury. Call 911.
____ Student hurt. Send trained personnel.
____ Stranger on the playground.
____ Student left the campus.
____ Abduction. Call 911.
____ Other _____
EMERGENCY—NEED HELP IMMEDIATELY!

This true story illustrates the importance of emergency communication procedures. The playground was supervised by a single staff member, who had no walkie-talkie or telephone, when a student collapsed. The supervisor immediately checked for pulse and respiration and determined that the student needed CPR. Between rescue breaths he said to the shocked students, "Go get help." A few minutes later he realized that no student had gone for help, so he then addressed a specific student and said, "Elaine, go to the office and tell them to call 911."

Elaine ran to the school building, burst into the office, and began to speak. "On the playground, something hap . . ." The secretary said, "Wait a minute. I'm on the phone," and made the student wait. Elaine was a polite, tractable child, and she waited.

The child died of a brain embolism. The staff members' actions did not affect this inevitable outcome, but think about how the secretary and the playground supervisor felt about their roles in the situation.

So consider establishing this low-tech backup system to your main communication systems. All staff can be trained: If you see a child with this card, you need to help the child because he or she is the communication link to an adult with an emergency situation. This simple, clear procedure can add a level of comfort to your common area supervisors, teachers, and all adults on the campus.

Prepare for student behavior emergencies.

Two main categories of student behavior emergencies are:

- Student threats
- Out-of-control students

Student threats. Have a detailed written plan for responding to students who threaten suicide or violence toward others. When a student says something like, "I'm going to bring a gun to school and . . . ," you are obligated to evaluate the credibility of the statement. We suggest that you organize building-based and district-based threat assessment teams to consider all threats made by students. The building-based team might consist of an administrator, a school counselor, the school psychologist, and one or two experienced teachers, all of whom should have training in how to respond to threats. The district-based team might comprise both district and building personnel, along with law enforcement and mental health professionals. Check with your district and regional service centers or state agencies for recommended threat assessment processes.

Note: In the book *Interventions: Evidence-Based Behavioral Strategies for Individual Students,* "Intervention G: Managing Physically Dangerous Behavior and Threats of

Targeted Violence" provides guidance on how to set up threat assessment teams. *Interventions* is available from Ancora Publishing, ancorapublishing.com.

Staff should be trained to immediately report any threat to the building-based team. The team will then get together and discuss the situation:

- Do we need to take this threat seriously?
- What kind of history do we have with this student?
- Has this student displayed any other signs or symptoms of worrisome behavior?
- What do we know about the student's home situation?

Then appropriate action can be taken. The building-based team should be trained to determine whether the threat is credible and dangerous enough to report to the district-based team or whether they can take action at the building level. No *individual* staff member should have the responsibility of deciding whether a threat is credible.

We also suggest that you establish a relationship with a district- or community-based threat assessment team, if possible. This team might consist of representatives from the police and the school district, along with a mental health expert who can offer expert advice and insight.

Some schools have zero-tolerance policies that treat every threat as equally serious and implement predetermined consequences—usually harsh ones, such as suspension and expulsion—for every threat. These policies do succeed in removing difficult students from school, and they send clear, consistent messages that the behavior is not tolerated at school. According to NASP (2001, para. 1), however, "research indicates that, as implemented, zero-tolerance policies are ineffective in the long run and are related to a number of negative consequences, including increased rates of school dropout and discriminatory application of school discipline practices."

A policy that requires police or mental health agency involvement has the potential not only to overburden the mental health workers, but also to create a "boy-who-cried-wolf" scenario, wherein multiple false-alarm threats make it more difficult to perceive a student who is serious about his threat. A kindergartner who tells a friend about his father's gun should probably not receive the same consequence as a bullied 12-year-old who threatens to kill his tormentors. Prudent, careful judgment needs to be exercised in all cases. A team approach at both the school and community level distributes the pressure of making these difficult decisions.

Out-of-control students. Have a detailed written plan for dealing with one or more out-of-control students, especially when the behavior puts the student or anyone else at risk of injury—for example, a student who is banging on or throwing things at glass windows or two students who are fighting.

The first intervention staff should try is verbal—give a clear instruction to the student to move to a different location. "McKenzie, go stand by my desk." When two students are arguing or fighting, tell them to separate. "Alex, go to the door. Bethany, stand by the window." If the students comply, the teacher has gained instructional control and can give directions that move the students toward their normal routine or the consequences you need to assign for their actions.

The plan should address communication among staff members. If verbal intervention doesn't work, staff need to be able to quickly get help from other staff members. You should have established primary and backup procedures for every school setting—walkie-talkies, cell phones, intercom systems, and Red Card Systems, for example (see "Prepare for Medical Emergencies" above for information about the Red Card System). Whenever a staff member is on cafeteria duty, supervising the bus loading area, or in her classroom, she should be able to think to herself, "In this setting, I can call for help by _____. If that doesn't work, I can get help by _____."

The plan should specify that more than one adult must be present when a student is out of control. There are several reasons why it's important that staff call for assistance when students are out of control:

- Two people will be able to make better decisions about how to proceed, and they can act as witnesses for each other about what took place.

- While one staff member is monitoring the out-of-control student, the other can supervise (and possibly lead away from the scene) the students who are not involved in the incident.

- Individual staff members should not attempt to break up fights between students. When one well-meaning adult pulls and holds one student away from a fight, the adult is making that student an easy target for the other student, and the adult might get hurt as well. Two adults have a better chance of halting a fight—but always consider the relative size and strength of the students and staff members. An exception to the two-adults rule might be, for example, that one adult can probably safely break up a fight between a couple of kindergartners.

- There should always be an adult witness to situations that involve physical restraint. Note that restraint may include any situation in which an adult physically holds or moves a student. If parents or authorities question the use of restraint, a witness can help clarify the behavior the student displayed and why it was necessary to restrain the student.

The plan should address the need for documentation and staff follow-up. Staff need to write detailed descriptions of all incidents and report them to the principal, and the documentation needs to be securely archived in your database system. Key school personnel need to work together to identify how to prevent future incidents and, as needed, improve future adult responses.

The plan should address each of the only two possible immediate adult responses to out-of-control behavior: room clear and physical restraint.

Room clears can be used instead of physical restraint whenever the room clear would pose an equal (or less) risk of injury. One staff member stays with the out-of-control student while another staff member removes the other students from the room and takes them to a predetermined area, such as the library, common area, or auditorium. The area can be stocked with activities—coloring books, puzzles, games—the students can use until it's OK to return to class.

An advantage of room clears is that they allow a student the time and space to get himself under control; he can learn self-control. Also, if the student is seeking attention, room clear reduces the amount of attention he gets. On the other hand, **physical restraint** can teach a student that he needs others to protect him from himself and to provide control, and some students find it reinforcing.

However, room clears are not always appropriate or possible. For example, if a student on the autism spectrum with significant cognitive delays is pounding on untempered glass windows and "Jeremy, go stand by the door" does not work, you need to move Jeremy away from those windows. Or if you have two students fighting, you certainly can't say, "Everybody clear the room and we'll come back when there's a winner." There are times when physical intervention is necessary.

Whenever an adult uses a hands-on approach to stop a fight or ensure that a child is safe, it is considered restraint. Unfortunately, children have been injured and killed as a result of restraint and seclusion. Consequently, the federal government has developed recommendations (and your state probably has some, too) to ensure that educators use restraint judiciously and properly.

Following is the U.S. Department of Education (2012, p. 3) position on restraint. Many states frame their recommendations around this policy.

> Restraint or seclusion should not be used as routine school safety measures; that is, they should not be implemented except in situations where a child's behavior poses imminent danger of serious physical harm to self or others and not as a routine strategy implemented to address instructional problems or inappropriate behavior (e.g., disrespect, noncompliance, insubordination, out of seat), as a means of coercion or retaliation, or as a convenience.

The key words in that paragraph are *imminent danger*. Putting your hands on a student should be your last resort, and only when the student is at immediate risk of hurting herself or others. All staff should know that if they use restraint, they are required to debrief with the administrator and document the following:

- Actions that preceded the incident
- Attempts to verbally de-escalate the student
- Amount of time that restraint was used
- Type of hands-on procedure used

Restraint and Seclusion in School

The Council for Exceptional Children (2009) has published a wonderful position paper that you might want to share with staff as you work on issues involving restraint and seclusion. CEC supports the following principles related to the use of physical restraint and seclusion procedures in school settings:

- Behavioral interventions for children and youth must promote the right of all children and youth to be treated with dignity.

- All children and youth should receive necessary educational and mental health supports and programming in a safe and least restrictive environment.

- Positive and appropriate educational interventions, as well as mental health supports, should be provided routinely to all children and youth who need them.

- Behavioral interventions should emphasize prevention and positive behavioral supports.

- Schools should have adequate staffing levels to effectively provide positive supports to children and youth, and should be staffed with appropriately trained personnel.

- All staff in schools should have mandatory conflict de-escalation training, and conflict de-escalation techniques should be employed by all school staff to avoid and defuse crisis and conflict situations.

- All children and youth whose pattern of behavior impedes their learning or the learning of others should receive appropriate educational assessment, including Functional Behavioral Assessments. These should be followed by Behavioral Intervention Plans that incorporate appropriate positive behavioral interventions, including instruction in appropriate behavior and strategies to de-escalate their own behavior.

Even breaking up a fight between kindergartners requires the use of verbal intervention first, then physical intervention if necessary, and documentation of the incident if restraint was used.

Finally, ensure that staff members receive information and training on all aspects of your plan for dealing with out-of-control students. All staff members should have specific training in restraining children. Your district or regional service center should have training resources approved by your district.

Assess your emergency preparedness.

In the Action Steps, we suggest that the team assess your school's emergency preparedness by completing Assessing Emergency Preparedness (Form E-04). See Figure 2f on the next page. Plan to conduct this short exercise annually, and archive the form so you can compare it with forms you will complete in future years. By completing this form and archiving it along with evidence that actions have been taken, you are documenting that your staff actively tries to make the school as safe as possible.

Task 2 Action Steps & Evidence of Implementation

Action Steps	Evidence of Implementation
1. As a group, complete the Assessing Emergency Preparedness form (Form E-04). Use the information to establish priorities for improving safety in your school.	Foundations Process: Safety
2. Identify all possible emergency situations (natural disaster, man-made, medical, and student behavior) for which your school should have written response plans.	Foundations Process: Safety
3. For each identified emergency situation, determine whether your school has established a written response plan. For each emergency situation that requires a plan but does not currently have one, develop a plan.	Foundations Archive: Safety Policies Staff Handbook: Policies and Procedures in Place Student and Parent Handbook: Policies and Procedures (as appropriate)
4. Set up a system to ensure that all school emergency plans are reviewed and updated annually.	Foundations Process: Planning Calendar

Presentation 2: Attributes of Safe and Unsafe Schools

Figure 2f *Assessing Emergency Preparedness (Form E-04)*

Assessing Emergency Preparedness

Questions for Assessing Emergency Preparedness	Y	N
1. Have you identified the possible natural disasters that might affect your school building?	☐	☐
If so, does the school have a detailed *written* plan for responding to all identified **natural disasters** that:		
a. Outlines exactly what staff members are to do?	☐	☐
b. Specifies designated escape routes for students and staff members?	☐	☐
c. Is coordinated with relevant community agencies?	☐	☐
d. Ensures that staff members receive information and training on all emergency plans?	☐	☐
e. Requires periodic practice and drills of all emergency plans so all staff and students know what to do?	☐	☐
2. Does the school have a detailed *written* plan for actions to take in case of **intruders** in the school that:		
a. Outlines exactly what staff members are to do?	☐	☐
b. Specifies designated escape routes and shelter-in-place strategies for students and staff members?	☐	☐
c. Is coordinated with local police and emergency responders?	☐	☐
d. Ensures that staff members receive information and training on all emergency plans?	☐	☐
e. Requires periodic practice and drills of all emergency plans so all staff and students know what to do?	☐	☐
3. Have you identified all the potential medical emergencies that might arise in your building?	☐	☐
If so, does the school have a detailed *written* plan for responding to possible **medical emergencies** that includes:		
a. A master list of everyone on campus who is trained in first aid and CPR?	☐	☐
b. Written plans for responding to the medical needs of *identified students* that have been provided to staff members who are responsible for those students?	☐	☐
c. Communication procedures for staff members to use to all for medical assistance (including a procedure to use when technology is not available)?	☐	☐
4. Does the school have a detailed *written* plan for responding to **behavioral emergencies** that includes:		
a. Responding to student threats, such as threats of violence or suicide?	☐	☐
b. A Threat Assessment Team that is responsible for making judgments about the credibility of threats?	☐	☐
c. A procedure for dealing with out-of-control students, with provisions for communicating with staff members in every school setting (e.g., cafeteria, gym, playground)?	☐	☐
d. The requirement that more than one adult be present to ensure adequate supervision, support, and adult witnesses?	☐	☐
e. Required documentation and staff follow-up—staff write reports on all incidents and give them to the administrator; campus staff have an opportunity to identify preventive strategies to help avoid future crisis incidents?	☐	☐
f. When it is appropriate for school staff to implement physical restraint and when they should use room clears?	☐	☐
g. Procedures for ensuring that staff members receive information and training on all emergency plans?	☐	☐

 See Appendix C for printing directions.

TASK 3

Teach lessons to increase connectedness and safety

Schools have a responsibility to provide students with important safety-related information. Students and parents need to know—*in advance*—what behavior at school will result in mandatory serious consequences.

Everyone who travels by air these days knows that comments about guns or bombs made to anyone at an airport will result in a full search of your body and bags, interrogation by authorities, and possibly detainment. A few decades ago, students could joke about guns and bombs and no one took it seriously. Since Columbine and other school shootings, however, schools must take every mention of violence seriously, just like airport security does. Similarly, because of increased awareness of bullying and the serious damage it can do to children and adolescents, including move them to commit suicide, many schools assign serious consequences for bullying and harassment. A few years ago, bullying was considered just a typical part of childhood. At the same time, you don't want to emphasize security so much that your efforts to create an inviting and inclusive school climate are compromised.

The safety information that parents and students need to know before school begins each new year includes:

- Federal and district policies
- Any zero-tolerance policies your school enforces
- Policies and laws on racial and sexual harassment
- How the school will respond to threats of violence and suicide
- Policies on bullying and harassment
- Personal power and control (students have control over allowing bullying to take place, for example)
- How all students have shared responsibility for the emotional and physical safety of everyone in the school

Well-designed lessons are an effective means of providing this safety information in a context that enhances school connectedness and a sense of belonging. We provide seven sample lessons on safety topics that can serve as models for the structure and content of lessons for your students. Outlines of the lessons follow this task (Figures 2h–2t). Lesson outlines and student worksheets, along with one fully scripted lesson for those who would like to read what a lesson might sound like in detail, are provided in the reproducible materials. Modify the lessons to suit your needs:

- The lessons are written for middle school students. You can modify the vocabulary and examples within the lessons so they are more age appropriate for the grade levels you teach.

Presentation 2: Attributes of Safe and Unsafe Schools

- Ensure that the lessons are compatible with current federal, state, and district laws and policies.

> In addition to this set of lessons on increasing connectedness and safety, we also provide lessons on conflict resolution (discussed in Presentation 3) and bullying prevention (discussed in Presentations 4 and 5) .

IMPORTANT! All the information and sample documents in the model lessons are generalized information and presented as examples only. The lessons and any supporting materials are intended as resources that you should review and adapt—with the advice of the school district's attorney—to meet all federal, state, and local needs and legal requirements. Any content of a legal nature should be reviewed and cleared by the school district's attorney or legal department.

Lessons for Increasing Connectedness and Safety

Following are brief descriptions of each sample lesson.

Lesson 1: Basic Social Interactions Between Students

This lesson emphasizes the importance of basic polite behavior. Students learn appropriate greetings and responses as well as when and how to say please, thank you, and excuse me. The whole school benefits when all students know that differences can be negotiated peacefully and that they will be treated respectfully both physically and emotionally.

Lesson 2: Basic Social Interactions With Staff and Other Adults in Authority

Students learn some key features of basic social interactions with staff and others in authority, such as greeting and responding appropriately, showing respect, maintaining social boundaries, and seeking help or assistance.

Lesson 3: Everyone Belongs in This School/This School Belongs to Everyone

Every student, regardless of family income, racial and ethnic background, strengths and disabilities, sexual orientation, gender identity, and gender has an equal right to be at school, to feel a sense of purpose and belonging to the school, and to succeed.

Lesson 4: Everyone Has the Right To Express an Opinion/Everyone Has the Right to Be Treated Respectfully

Lesson 4 helps students understand how everyone has the right to express an opinion, but that opinion cannot infringe on or disrupt the right that every person has to be safe and to be treated respectfully at school. Respectfully expressing an opinion involves using respectful words, tone, voice level, body language, and facial expressions.

Lesson 5: Threats Will Be Taken Seriously

Lesson 5 gives students information about the kinds of behaviors that are considered threatening and why and how the school must respond when a student engages in threatening behavior. Threats must be taken seriously, even when a student later says he or she was joking. When students understand why all threats must be taken seriously, they can avoid exhibiting threatening behaviors.

Lesson 6: Everyone Has the Right To Be Safe/Everyone Has the Responsibility to Contribute to Safety

Students learn that with the right to be safe in school comes a responsibility to contribute collectively to school safety. Many school shooters told other students about their plans, yet those students did not report the potential violence that ultimately occurred at their schools. Students need to know that reporting threats of violence, suicide, or weapons at school is not tattling or squealing; it is social responsibility, just like calling the fire department when a house is on fire.

Lesson 7: Help Is Available When You Need It

Students learn who in the school and in the community can help with a variety of minor and major issues. You will essentially advertise the school's services to support students—for example, "For help with academics, we have peer tutoring and an after-school homework room. This is how these programs work . . . For help with a peer conflict, see Mr. O'Connor or Mrs. Wheeler. We have several ways to deal with these issues . . ."

Consider using some or all of these lessons, either as is or modified for your needs. Also consider how the lessons will be delivered. Initial lessons can be taught by homeroom teachers, a team (or teams) that go to all classrooms, or prepared video. After lessons are taught to all students initially, ensure that they are reviewed or taught to the following students:

- New students who enter the school midyear
- Returning students at the beginning of each school year
- Students who violate the rules frequently

Module B, Presentation 3, "Teaching Expectations to Students" gives detailed information about organizing and planning for teaching, launching, and re-teaching expectations. This information applies to lessons on safety, conflict resolution, and bullying prevention, too.

In the Action Steps, we suggest that you complete the Evaluation Form: Lessons to Increase Connectedness and Safety (Form E-05 shown in Figure 2g on the next page). Plan to conduct this short exercise annually. Archive the form so you can compare it with forms you will complete in future years.

Task 3 Action Steps & Evidence of Implementation

Action Steps	Evidence of Implementation
1. As a group, complete the Evaluation Form: Lessons to Increase Connectedness and Safety (Form E-05). Use the information to establish priorities for improving safety in your school.	Foundations Process: Safety
2. Identify all the important safety-related information your students (and parents) should be informed about each year.	Foundations Archive: Safety Policies Student and Parent Handbook: Policies and Procedures
3. Decide on an appropriate way (such as lessons) to provide that information to students.	Foundations Process: Safety
4. If you decide that student lessons are appropriate: • Determine whether to review and modify the *Foundations* lessons, use existing lessons, purchase published lessons, or create new lessons. • Develop a plan that addresses how initial lessons will be taught and when and how essential content will be delivered after the initial lessons.	Foundations Archive: Lesson Plans for Teaching Safety Expectations Foundations Process: Planning Calendar

Figure 2g *Evaluation Form: Lessons to Increase Connectedness and Safety (E-05)*

Foundations: A Proactive and Positive Behavior Support System

REPRODUCIBLE FORM
E-05

Evaluation Form
Lessons to Increase Connectedness and Safety

Questions to Evaluate Student Lessons to Increase Connectedness and Safety	Y	N
1. Does the school have a written plan for presenting lessons on specific safety information? Do the lessons cover the topics below? • Basic Social Interactions Between Students • Basic Social Interactions With Staff and Other Adults in Authority • Everyone Belongs in This School/This School Belongs to Everyone • Everyone Has the Right to Express an Opinion/Everyone Has the Right to Be Treated Respectfully • Threats Will Be Taken Seriously • Everyone Has the Right to Be Safe/Everyone Has the Responsibility to Contribute to Safety • Help Is Available When You Need It	☐ ☐ ☐ ☐ ☐ ☐ ☐ ☐	☐ ☐ ☐ ☐ ☐ ☐ ☐ ☐
2. Does the written plan include where and when to deliver the initial lessons?	☐	☐
3. Does the plan cover how to deliver essential content from the lessons to new students, returning students, and students who are frequent violators of school safety rules?	☐	☐

© 2014 Ancora Publishing • For use by purchasing school only

 See Appendix C for printing directions.

Presentation 2: Attributes of Safe and Unsafe Schools

Figure 2h *Increasing Connectedness and Safety, Lesson 1 Outline*

Module E, Presentation 2

Lesson Outline

Page 1 of 3

Increasing Connectedness and Safety
Lesson 1

Basic Social Interactions Between Students

OBJECTIVES

- Students will explain why appropriate basic social interactions are beneficial inside and outside of school.
- Students will describe the key features of basic social interactions.

MATERIALS

- Document camera, overhead projector, or interactive whiteboard to display the worksheet and student responses
- Student copies of the Student Worksheet for Lesson 1

Introduction

1. Introduce the lesson and provide rationale.

2. Have students complete the following activity using the Lesson 1 Student Worksheet.

   Put students into groups or partners. Give half of the groups Scenario A, and half Scenario B. Tell the groups to read the scenario and answer the follow-up questions. They should be prepared to share their answers with the whole class.

   Create a T-chart on the board or document camera with Scenario A on one side and Scenario B on the other.

   Without reading the scenario out loud, have students who read Scenario A share their responses to the questions. List responses on the board. As the A group students share, tell students from the B group to think about Scenario B and predict some of the things that were different in Scenario A.

   Have students who read Scenario B share their responses. List them on the board. As the B group students share, tell students from the A group to think about Scenario A and predict some of the things that were different in Scenario B.

   Read the two scenarios (or have students read them out loud).

3. Explain that this lesson will be about basic social interactions between students, and how all students can work to create a positive and safe environment, similar to the school in Scenario B.

© 2014 Ancora Publishing • For use by purchasing school only   *Foundations: A Proactive and Positive Behavior Support System*

 See Appendix C for printing directions.

Figure 2h (continued)

Module E, Presentation 2

Lesson Outline
Page 2 of 3

Increasing Connectedness and Safety
Lesson 1 • Basic Social Interactions Between Students

Lesson Body

1. Introduce these key features of basic social interactions among students:

    a. Providing appropriate greetings and responses
    b. Including others
    c. Negotiating differences
    d. Staying safe

2. For each feature, have students discuss, brainstorm, or participate in your explanation of why the attribute is important and how they can demonstrate it.

    Providing appropriate greetings and responses

    a. Have students list appropriate greetings (smile, nod, shake hands, wave, say "Good morning" or "How's it going?").
    b. Have students discuss why appropriate greetings are important.

    > When someone greets you, it is important to respond with a similar greeting or other appropriate response. All students in the school should feel safe from being rejected if they greet someone. Even if you don't know or don't particularly like the person, you have a responsibility to respond in an appropriate and kind way if that person greets you.

    c. Have students create a T-chart with appropriate responses and inappropriate responses to another person's greeting:

Appropriate	Inappropriate
Say "hi" back	Ignore
Smile	Roll eyes
Nod	Tell the person not to talk to you
Shake hands	Respond and then make fun of the person to someone else
Wave	

    Explain that part of providing appropriate greetings and responses is using basic skills such as saying "please" when you need something, "thank you" when you get something or someone does something for you, and "excuse me" when you need to get someone's attention. Have students discuss how these basic interactions create a more polite, pleasant, and safe atmosphere.

© 2014 Ancora Publishing • For use by purchasing school only

Foundations: A Proactive and Positive Behavior Support System

Figure 2h (continued) Increasing Connectedness and Safety, Lesson 1 Outline

Module E, Presentation 2

Lesson Outline
Page 3 of 3

Increasing Connectedness and Safety
Lesson 1 • Basic Social Interactions Between Students

For each of the remaining features, have students participate as you introduce the rationale and these key points:

Including others

Reach out to people you don't know well, avoid gossip, avoid bullying behavior, and avoid cliquish behavior.

Negotiating differences

Resolve problems calmly and respectfully.

Staying safe

Maintain physical safety and boundaries with all other students.

Conclusion

Have students complete an exit ticket. Have them set a goal for one aspect of basic social interactions that they will work on improving and explain how they think this goal will benefit themselves, other students, and the school.

Conclude by emphasizing that these basic social interactions between students help contribute to a physically and emotionally safe environment for all students. The whole school benefits when all students know they will be included and treated with respect both physically and emotionally and when differences can be negotiated peacefully.

Possibilities for Follow-Up

Have students keep a log of their appropriate interactions with other students during the coming week. Have individual students set goals for the number of times they greet students with whom they don't typically interact and the number of times they make efforts to include others. Also have each student record examples of negotiating differences and staying safe.

© 2014 Ancora Publishing • For use by purchasing school only   *Foundations: A Proactive and Positive Behavior Support System*

 See Appendix C for printing directions.

Figure 2i *Increasing Connectedness and Safety, Lesson 1 Student Worksheet*

Presentation 2: Attributes of Safe and Unsafe Schools

Figure 2j *Increasing Connectedness and Safety, Lesson 2 Outline (page 1 only)*

Module E, Presentation 2

Lesson Outline
Page 1 of 4

Increasing Connectedness and Safety
Lesson 2

Basic Social Interactions With Staff and Other Adults in Authority

OBJECTIVES

- Students will explain why appropriate basic social interactions with staff and other adults in authority are beneficial inside and outside of school.
- Students will describe key features of basic social interactions with staff.

MATERIALS

Document camera, overhead projector, or interactive whiteboard

---

Introduction

1. Have students brainstorm on their own or in partners or groups responses to the following:

   Imagine you are driving on the highway and a police officer pulls you over for speeding.

   Give some examples of appropriate basic social interactions you might have with the police officer—appropriate ways to greet the officer, appropriate responses to his or her questions or requests, and appropriate responses to consequences if given.

   What might happen as a result of these interactions?

   Give examples of inappropriate social interactions—inappropriate greetings, inappropriate responses to questions or requests, and inappropriate responses to consequences.

   What might happen as a result of these interactions?

   Have students share their responses to each question.

2. Introduce the lesson and rationale. Say something like:

   This lesson will help you understand and develop skills for basic social interactions with staff members at school and other authority figures. Your skill with basic interactions can lead to positive results or negative results, as demonstrated in the previous example.

© 2014 Ancora Publishing • For use by purchasing school only   *Foundations: A Proactive and Positive Behavior Support System*

 See Appendix C for printing directions.

Figure 2k   *Increasing Connectedness and Safety, Lesson 3 Outline (page 1 only)*

Module E, Presentation 2

Lesson Outline

Page 1 of 3

Increasing Connectedness and Safety
Lesson 3

Everyone Belongs in This School/
This School Belongs to Everyone

OBJECTIVES

- Students will identify the mission of the school.
- Students will explain why all students have an equal right to be at school, to feel a sense of purpose and belonging within the school, and to be successful.
- Students will identify those aspects of the school that contribute to and those that interfere with their own sense of physical and emotional safety at school.

MATERIALS

- Document camera, overhead projector, or interactive whiteboard to display the worksheet and student responses
- Student copies of the Student Worksheet for Lesson 3

Introduction

1. Have students complete Item 1 on their worksheet by copying the school's mission statement. Review the mission statement with students.

   If the mission statement is not already posted in the room, write it on the board.

   If the school does not have a mission statement, consider using the following:

   We, the staff of _____ School, are committed to helping every student become a lifelong learner and achieve his/her fullest potential.

2. Emphasize to students that every student, regardless of family income, racial/ethnic background, strengths, disabilities, sexual orientation, gender identity, and gender, has an equal right to be part of the school.

   Make sure students understand that no one in the school has the right to do things that interfere with anyone else's right to be successful in school.

   Explain that anyone who feels they have more of a right to be in the school than anyone else is WRONG.

3. Tell students that the school staff is committed to making the school a place where every student feels a sense of purpose and belonging—a place where all students can strive to reach their fullest potential.

© 2014 Ancora Publishing • For use by purchasing school only   *Foundations: A Proactive and Positive Behavior Support System*

Figure 21 *Increasing Connectedness and Safety, Lesson 3 Student Worksheet*

Module E, Presentation 2
Student Worksheet
Page 1 of 2

Increasing Connectedness and Safety
Lesson 3

Name _____ Class/Teacher _____ Period ___

Everyone Belongs in This School/ This School Belongs to Everyone

Item 1: Fill in the name of your school and its mission statement.

_____ School's Mission Statement

_____
_____
_____
_____

Item 2

Goal: Everyone at _____ School will feel physically and emotionally safe at school.

Respond to the following questions, listing as many ideas as possible. If you run out of room to write, continue on the back of the page.

- Why is it important that everyone feel physically and emotionally safe at our school?
- Why do people need to feel physically and emotionally safe in order to be successful, learn, and reach their fullest potential?

© 2014 Ancora Publishing • For use by purchasing school only

Module E, Presentation 2
Student Worksheet
Page 2 of 2

Increasing Connectedness and Safety
Lesson 3 • Everyone Belongs in This School/This School Belongs to Everyone

Item 3

Conditions that Contribute to Physical or Emotional Safety	Conditions that Interfere With Physical or Emotional Safety

Exit Ticket:

1. Three things at school that help me and others feel physically and emotionally safe are:

  - _____
  - _____
  - _____

2. Three things at school that interfere with my physically and emotionally safety are:

  - _____
  - _____
  - _____

© 2014 Ancora Publishing • For use by purchasing school only   *Foundations: A Proactive and Positive Behavior Support System*

See Appendix C for printing directions.

Figure 2m *Increasing Connectedness and Safety, Lesson 4 Outline (page 1 only)*

Module E, Presentation 2

Lesson Outline
Page 1 of 5

Increasing Connectedness and Safety
Lesson 4

Everyone Has the Right to Express an Opinion/ Everyone Has the Right to Be Treated Respectfully

OBJECTIVES

- Students will identify when it is appropriate to express an opinion and when it is inappropriate.
- Students will demonstrate how to express an opinion in a respectful manner.
- Students will explain and demonstrate how to respect the opinions of others by agreeing to disagree.

MATERIALS

- Document camera, overhead projector, or interactive whiteboard to display the worksheet and student responses
- Student copies of the Student Worksheet for Lesson 4

Introduction

1. Review the previous lesson. Have students share reasons why everyone should feel physically and emotionally safe at school and factors that contribute to or take away from feelings of safety at school.

2. Introduce the lesson. Say something like:

    This lesson will help you understand how people have the right to their opinions, but their opinions cannot infringe on or disrupt the right that every person has to be safe and be treated respectfully at school.

Lesson Body

1. Introduce and have students fill in the missing words for Item 1, the definition of *opinion*: A view or <u>judgment</u> formed about something, not necessarily based on <u>fact</u> or <u>knowledge</u>.

© 2014 Ancora Publishing • For use by purchasing school only   *Foundations: A Proactive and Positive Behavior Support System*

Presentation 2: Attributes of Safe and Unsafe Schools

Figure 2n Increasing Connectedness and Safety, Lesson 4 Student Worksheet

Module E: Improving Safety, Managing Conflict, and Reducing Bullying

Figure 20   *Increasing Connectedness and Safety, Lesson 5 Outline (page 1 only)*

Module E, Presentation 2

Lesson Outline

Page 1 of 3

Increasing Connectedness and Safety
Lesson 5

Threats Will Be Taken Seriously

OBJECTIVES

- Students will explain why school personnel must take action when they become aware of threatening comments or behavior.
- Students will identify the types of verbal or written statements that could be interpreted as threats.
- Students will identify the range of consequences that school personnel and law enforcement agencies can apply for making threats.

MATERIALS

- Document camera, overhead projector, or interactive whiteboard to display the worksheet and student responses
- Student copies of the school Policy on Threats (see the Sample Policy for Lesson 5). Your policy should be developed ahead of time with help from the school district's attorney or legal department. Specific content should reflect your school and district policies.

Introduction

Introduce the lesson. Say something like:

> This lesson gives you information about the kinds of behavior that are considered threatening and why and how the school must respond when a student engages in threatening behavior. We all have to take threats very seriously, even if a student later says he or she was joking. This lesson will teach you why threats are considered so serious and why all students should avoid threatening behaviors.

Lesson Body

1. Give each student a copy of the school Policy on Threats.
2. Have students read the first section ("Threats are no joking matter!") on their own or in partners, or have the whole class choral or cloze read the section.
3. Have students discuss why "I was only joking" is not an acceptable explanation or defense. Have them respond to the question: What would happen at an airport if

© 2014 Ancora Publishing • For use by purchasing school only   *Foundations: A Proactive and Positive Behavior Support System*

Presentation 2: Attributes of Safe and Unsafe Schools

Figure 2p *Increasing Connectedness and Safety, Lesson 5 Student Worksheet*

Module E, Presentation 2
Sample Policy
Page 1 of 2

Increasing Connectedness and Safety
Lesson 5

Threats Will Be Taken Seriously

We have read and discussed the information in the "Policy on Threats."

_____   _____
Parent/Guardian Signature   Date

_____   _____
Student Signature   Date

© 2014 Ancora Publishing • For use by purchasing school only   *Foundations: A Proactive and*

Module E, Presentation 2
Sample Policy
Page 2 of 2

Increasing Connectedness and Safety
Lesson 5 • Threats Will Be Taken Seriously

SAMPLE DOCUMENT: A document similar to this should be developed by staff ahead of time with help from the school district's attorney or legal department. Specific content should reflect your school and district policies.

POLICY ON THREATS

In the interest of ensuring that _____ School is a safe place for everyone, all threats will be taken seriously. Please read and discuss the information on this page with your student. Then sign the document and have your student return it by _____. If you have any questions or concerns about this policy, feel free to contact a school administrator.

1. **Threats are no joking matter!**

   In the past, if someone said something like, "I am going to shoot those teachers and students who give me a hard time," it might have been treated as a joke or an idle threat. The rules and expectations regarding language related to threats of violence have changed. Due to violent incidents that have taken place in schools, any statement of this type must now be taken very seriously.

   "I was only joking" is not a reasonable explanation or defense. This type of comment will be treated as seriously in our school as it would be in an airport.

2. **Behavior that will be considered threatening include:**

   - Stating that you have a weapon or bomb in your possession at school.
   - Stating that you plan to bring a weapon or bomb to school.
   - Stating that you plan to cause physical harm to a student or staff member.
   - Making a false statement that there is a bomb or other destructive device at school.
   - Any written or verbal indication that you intend to harm any person or damage property.

   Note: Physically threatening behaviors are also considered very serious and are subject to consequences.

3. **In addition to parental notification, outcomes and consequences that may be imposed for making a threat include:**

   - Further investigation by school personnel
   - Detention
   - Suspension
   - Expulsion
   - Further investigation by law enforcement
   - Prosecution for Disorderly Conduct, Criminal Mischief, or Menacing

© 2014 Ancora Publishing • For use by purchasing school only   *Foundations: A Proactive and Positive Behavior Support System*

See Appendix C for printing directions.

Figure 2q *Increasing Connectedness and Safety, Lesson 6 Outline (page 1 only)*

Module E, Presentation 2

Lesson Outline

Page 1 of 4

Increasing Connectedness and Safety
Lesson 6

Everyone Has a Right to Be Safe/Everyone Has the Responsibility to Contribute to Safety

OBJECTIVES

- Students will learn that they have both a right to feel safe in school and a responsibility to help keep the school safe.
- Students will verbalize that their responsibilities include:
  - Reporting any knowledge of weapons or a person's plans to engage in actions that could cause physical injury or death.
  - Never fabricating a report of threatening or unsafe behavior as a joke or to cause problems for another student.
  - Never promising another student that they will keep anything related to physical safety a secret.

MATERIALS

- Document camera, overhead projector, or interactive whiteboard to display the worksheet and student responses
- Student copies of the Student Worksheet for Lesson 6

Introduction

1. Introduce the following concepts:
   - Learning cannot take place if a person does not feel safe.
   - Adults alone cannot ensure school safety—everyone in the school has a role.

2. Introduce the lesson. Say something like:

   This lesson identifies rights and responsibilities that you have at school. All students have the right to be safe at school, and all students and staff have responsibilities to help ensure that everyone's right to safety is respected. It's a collective effort.

© 2014 Ancora Publishing • For use by purchasing school only   *Foundations: A Proactive and Positive Behavior Support System*

Presentation 2: Attributes of Safe and Unsafe Schools

Figure 2r *Increasing Connectedness and Safety, Lesson 6 Student Worksheet*

Module E, Presentation 2

Student Worksheet
Page 1 of 2

Increasing Connectedness and Safety
Lesson 6

Name _____ Class/Teacher _____ Period ____

Everyone Has a Right to Be Safe/Everyone Has the Responsibility to Contribute to Safety

Right 1

All _____ have the right to feel _____ at school.

Responsibility 1

Each student and staff member has the responsibility to immediately _____ any knowledge of weapons possession or any person's _____ to engage in actions that could result in physical injury or death.

Item 1. Situations that should be reported include:
- _____
- _____
- _____
- _____
- _____
- _____

Item 2. List adults in the school to whom you can report any of the above situations:
- _____
- _____
- _____

Item 3.

Ratting or tattling is done to get someone _____ potentially dangerous situation is like someone calling the _____ _____ if you see a _____. It is y...

© 2014 Ancora Publishing • For use by purchasing school only   Foundations: A Proactive and...

Module E, Presentation 2

Student Worksheet
Page 2 of 2

Increasing Connectedness and Safety
Lesson 6 • Everyone Has a Right to Be Safe/Everyone Has the Responsibility to Contribute to Safety

Right 2

The identity of any student making a report will be kept _____.

Responsibility 2

To _____ a report as a joke or to cause problems for another student.

Responsibility 3

To never promise another student that you will keep anything related to physical safety _____.

Your friend plans to commit suicide or enact violence against another person and asks you to keep the plan secret.	
Consequences of telling the secret	Consequences of keeping the secret

Exit Ticket:

To uphold everyone's right to safety at school, I pledge to follow the responsibilities listed below:

- To report my knowledge of weapons or a person's plans to engage in actions that would cause physical injury or death.
- To never fabricate a report of threatening or unsafe behavior as a joke or to cause problems for another student.
- To never promise another student that I will keep anything related to physical safety a secret.

_____
First and last name

_____   _____
Signature   Date

© 2014 Ancora Publishing • For use by purchasing school only   Foundations: A Proactive and Positive Behavior Support System

---

See Appendix C for printing directions.

Figure 2s   *Increasing Connectedness and Safety, Lesson 7 Outline (page 1 only)*

Module E, Presentation 2

Lesson Outline

Page 1 of 4

Increasing Connectedness and Safety
Lesson 7

Help Is Available When You Need It

OBJECTIVES

- Students will identify those staff members who are available to help them with a variety of problems and situations.
- Students will identify community agencies who are available to help them deal with a variety of problems and situations.

MATERIALS

- Document camera, overhead projector, or interactive whiteboard to display the worksheet and student responses
- Student copies of the "Help Is Available" booklet (see Materials Preparation below)

MATERIALS PREPARATION

In advance of the lesson, prepare a "Help is Available" booklet. Use the Lesson 7 Template (see Appendix C) or create your own. If the whole school or multiple classrooms will deliver this lesson, create one master booklet for all to use.

Tip: Replace a few critical words or phrases with blanks so that students can fill in information as each page is discussed during the lesson. This will help keep students engaged.

1. Identify staff members to list in the booklet. Recommended staff include:

    a. Counselor(s)
    b. Administrator(s)
    c. School Resource Officer(s)
    d. School Nurse
    e. Social Worker

2. For each staff member, collect the information needed to complete a Staff Member page:

    a. Picture
    b. Contact information: location in the school, email, phone number
    c. Issues the person is qualified or trained to address
    d. Issues for which the person can serve as an advocate to link the student with appropriate supports
    e. The best method of contacting and reporting to the staff member
    f. Personal statement offering support to those who need it

© 2014 Ancora Publishing • For use by purchasing school only   *Foundations: A Proactive and Positive Behavior Support System*

Figure 2t *Increasing Connectedness and Safety, Lesson 7 Student Worksheet*

Module E, Presentation 2

Student Booklet

Page 1 of 2

Increasing Connectedness and Safety
Lesson 7

Help Is Available When You Need It

STAFF MEMBER

Name: ____________________

Title: ____________________

Location: ____________________

Email: ____________________

Phone number: ____________________

Issues I am qualified or trained to address:

Issues for which I can be an advocate and help link you to appropriate supports:

My preferred method for initial contact is:

Personal statement:

Module E, Presentation 2

Student Booklet

Page 2 of 2

Increasing Connectedness and Safety
Lesson 7 • Help Is Available When You Need It

COMMUNITY AGENCY

Name: ____________________

Address: ____________________

____

Directions from school: ____________________

____

Email(s): ____________________

____

Phone number(s): ____________________

Services provided:

Additional information:

See Appendix C for printing directions.

PRESENTATION

THREE

Teaching Conflict Resolution

CONTENTS

Introduction

Task 1: Determine Whether STP Meets the Needs of Your Students
For the Foundations Team or special task force working on conflict resolution

Task 2: Develop an STP Program in Your School
For the Foundations Team or special task force working on STP

Task 3: Educate Parents About STP
For the Foundations Team or special task force working on STP

DOCUMENTS*

- Stop–Think–Plan negative and positive strategies poster (E-18)
- Parent handout on STP (E-19)
- Lessons on Conflict Resolution (STP)

*See Appendix C for information on accessing these documents.

> If your school body already has a conflict resolution process that all staff and students are using successfully and that creates a common language among students and staff, you probably don't need to switch to the approach we recommend, Stop–Think–Plan (STP). There's no need to fix what isn't broken. However, really think about whether you have a common language—that's the key to an effective schoolwide strategy. If you don't have a schoolwide approach to identifying and resolving conflict, consider the strategies we suggest in this presentation. STP integrates well with other *Foundations* initiatives, such as safety, improving climate, and reducing bullying.
>
> Students in grades K–9 can use STP successfully. High school students can also find it useful, although it may be too simplistic for some older students. The accompanying lessons are written at about the middle school level and may be modified to fit the ages of your students

INTRODUCTION

In this presentation, we suggest that you teach all students a conflict resolution strategy. Why is it important for students to have skills for resolving conflict peacefully? Violence is a major health hazard, as we discussed in the introduction, and conflict between students *in school* is a part of that hazard.

The U.S. Department of Health and Human Services (2012) reports that in 2011, in a representative sample of high school students in grades 9–12, 16% of males and 7.8% of females reported being in a physical fight on school property in the 12 months preceding the survey. And almost 6% of students did not go to school on 1 or more days in the 30 days preceding the survey because they felt unsafe at school or on the way to or from school.

In surveys administered to staff, conflict and violence are leading concerns. Conflict, even when it falls short of violence, can significantly disrupt the learning process. For example, squabbles and conflicts on the playground between elementary students frequently spill over into subsequent classroom instruction. At the secondary level, a conflict between two students during a 5-minute passing period can heighten the energy and tension of all students in the area, and the students bring that tension into the classroom.

"Somebody ought to do something!" is a common refrain about violence and conflict in schools. Factors outside the school certainly contribute to the violence problem, but school personnel have some control over what happens in the building. Strong preventive actions that educators can take are to teach strategies for reducing conflict and violence and to develop a consistent approach among staff for dealing with conflict when it does happen. For this approach to be effective, everyone—teachers, administrators, common area supervisors, students, and parents—must be on the same page, implementing a common strategy and talking a common language.

*E*xample From the Field

> In the mid-1980s I was working with a district in which all schools were working on *Foundations* processes and having great success. During an inservice with the faculty of one school, the staff reported that they still had issues with conflict among students even though they had implemented a conflict resolution program. I asked them to describe the program to me. They said it was a ten-step process, but they couldn't agree on what the ten steps were. They were able to verbalize about six of the ten steps.

> I realized that if a conflict resolution process is so complex that the teachers can't remember it, there is no hope that the students will remember it or be able to proceed through ten steps, particularly in a tense, potentially violent situation. The staff and I decided to simplify their program. After some discussion and brainstorming, we identified the three most critical elements of conflict resolution as:
>
> - **Stop** what you are doing (de-escalate your emotions).
> - **Think** about your options for resolving the conflict.
> - Develop a **plan** for resolving the conflict that all parties can agree to.
>
> We came up with the Stop–Think–Plan program, or STP. The school taught it to students and found it very effective for calmly resolving many different kinds of conflicts. Since then, STP has been available through Safe & Civil Schools, and we are including it in this third edition of *Foundations*. —R.S.

We recommend a simple conflict resolution process called STP, which stands for Stop–Think–Plan. In this presentation, we outline the strategies in the process and provide sample STP lessons for students. The first skill students learn is how to discriminate between a simple disagreement (for example: I like dogs—you like cats) and a more serious conflict that needs to be resolved. Students then learn to slow the conflict down to create both time and psychological room to think about alternative actions and positive ways to end the conflict. A conflict can be a little like a tennis match, with the players slamming the ball across the net so fast that there is no time to think about what's really happening. A key concept in STP is creating time for cognition. When a person involved in a conflict can stop and think, he or she is more likely to develop a positive plan, work with the other person to reach consensus, and resolve the conflict peacefully.

The STP approach has some features that, to our knowledge, other conflict resolution strategies lack:

- It's simple. Students focus on three basic steps: Stop, think, and plan. (There's also a pre-step and a post-step—see below.) Students can generalize the simple process in stressful situations.
- It teaches students to distinguish between simple disagreements and conflicts.
- It emphasizes the need for at least one involved person to begin de-escalating the conflict by stopping what he or she is doing, without any requirement to make the other person stop.
- All students, not just a few mediators, are taught the strategies.

- All staff know the strategies.
- Parents are encouraged to learn STP so that students get consistent feedback and corrections at home and at school.
- Students can relate to the lessons because they consist largely of role-plays based on the students' experiences.

The process is so simple that we can describe it in five brief steps.

Step 1: Identify whether a disagreement is simple or a conflict that needs to be resolved.

Step 2: If it is a conflict, begin STP. Stop what you are doing to ensure that you don't get into a fast-paced argument that makes it difficult to think.

Step 3: Think about your options for handling the situation.

Step 4: Prepare to propose a plan to the other person, and listen to the other person's proposal about how to resolve the conflict.

Step 5: Decide on an action and follow through.

Consider implementing STP if you don't already have a schoolwide process and common language for resolving conflict. The Foundations Team or a special task force can guide implementation of the STP process by working through the planning steps in Tasks 1, 2, and 3. Some or all members of the team or task force should read or view this entire presentation. All staff, teachers, paraprofessionals, and administrators should be represented on the team or task force to ensure consistency and follow-through. Also decide whether parent and student representatives should participate in planning for STP implementation. When people are involved in planning and implementing the program, they develop a greater sense of ownership.

Task 1: Determine Whether STP Meets the Needs of Your Students guides the Foundations Team in determining whether STP is right for your students. If it is, the team will review the content of the seven lessons and adapt them as needed to fit the needs of your school.

Task 2: Develop an STP Program in Your School helps the team or task force develop an STP plan that includes initial teaching and also ensures ongoing implementation.

Task 3: Educate Parents About STP provides information on educating parents about STP and encouraging them to use the strategy when they see conflicts happening in their homes.

TASK 1

Determine whether STP meets the needs of your students

The Foundations Team (with the administrator) should review the three tasks and the lesson outlines in this presentation and think about whether the Stop–Think–Plan (STP) process will meet the needs of your students. If so, the administrator should decide whether implementation of a schoolwide conflict resolution strategy will be a staff decision or an administrative decision. If it will be a staff decision (that is, you will proceed through the Improvement Cycle steps), the staff should also get to decide whether the school will implement STP or another approach. The team should prepare a presentation to staff about STP. The presentation should cover what will be expected from all staff and from individual staff members, including how staff will teach the lessons.

Outlines of the lessons appear at the end of this task. The outlines, along with a sample scripted lesson, are provided in the reproducible materials. The lessons introduce the concept that STP is a process for teaching students to calmly resolve many conflicts. With STP, students can slow things down and take time to think about their options for more appropriate ways to resolve any conflict.

We provide seven STP lessons as well as ideas for additional lessons that you may wish to provide as extension. The lessons follow a basic *tell–show–practice* format. Much of the lesson content is devoted to role-plays based on actual conflicts from students' lives. The role-plays make the lessons directly relevant to your students.

It's important to repeat the lessons often and provide a variety of practice opportunities so that students achieve mastery of the STP steps. With mastery, they will be able to generalize the steps into other settings outside the lessons.

Note that you should integrate these lessons with other existing programs at your school. STP can be used in conjunction with peer mediation and restorative justice or with curricula such as bullying prevention, social skills training, and social-emotional learning. You don't want staff and students to groan, "Oh no, *another* program we have to learn!" Present STP as an extension of complementary programs you are already implementing.

Outlines of the conflict resolution lessons follow this task (Figures 3b–3m), and the outlines and one sample scripted lesson are provided in the reproducible materials.

Lessons on Conflict Resolution (STP)

The seven lessons cover the following topics related to conflict resolution and the Stop–Think–Plan (STP) process.

Lesson 1: What Is a Disagreement?/What Is a Conflict?

Lesson 1 helps students see that a disagreement is not bad or wrong. Disagreement is defined as failure to agree or a difference of opinion. Disagreements are natural and healthy. However, they can become unhealthy when they escalate and lead to negative outcomes—that is, when they become conflicts. The STP strategy can help keep disagreements from snowballing into conflicts.

Lesson 2: Reading Social Cues to Avoid Conflict

Reading social cues can help prevent disagreements from escalating into conflicts and can help end conflicts that do arise. Students learn to recognize verbal and nonverbal cues, or signs, that another person is getting upset and angry. They also consider their own personal cues when they get angry.

Lesson 3: Conflict and Electronic Communications/Social Media
(Optional: For secondary schools or whenever this issue becomes problematic)

Communicating through social media, email, or texting can lead to conflict because most of the social cues described in Lesson 2 are not available. Misunderstandings are more likely because people can't hear each other's tone or see their facial expressions. People may also say and do things they wouldn't do when interacting in person. Students brainstorm things to do and not do to avoid conflict when using electronic communications and social media.

Lesson 4: Stop–Think–Plan: A Strategy to Resolve Conflict (Stop)

The fourth lesson introduces the Stop step. Conflicts often escalate because people react emotionally, without thinking. Stop gives those involved in a conflict time and space to calm down and think rationally.

Students brainstorm positive and negative ways to resolve conflicts and develop a T-chart. Using the T-chart, students discuss the possible results of using the positive and negative plans. A sample T-chart (E-18) appears in Figure 3a on the next page and is available in the reproducible materials.

Students then learn ways of slowing or stopping a conflict. They brainstorm examples of conflicts and use those examples to role-play use of the Stop step.

Figure 3a *Stop–Think–Plan negative and positive strategies poster (E-18)*

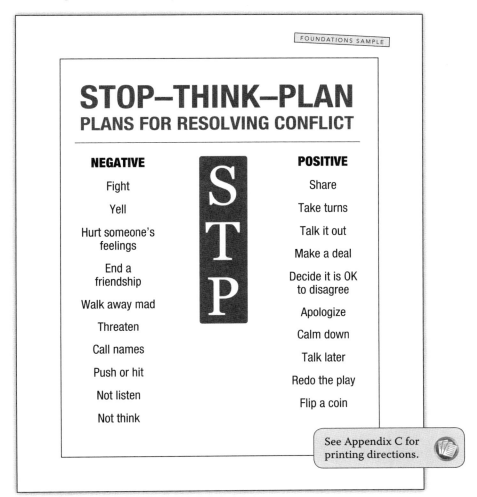

Lesson 5: Stop–Think–Plan: A Strategy to Resolve Conflict (Think)

Next, students learn the Think step. Once they slow things down (Stop), they should think about staying calm, what they want, and what the other person wants. Students learn strategies for staying calm and questions to ask themselves to identify what they (and the other person) want. They then role-play using the Stop and Think steps in scenarios they brainstormed during a previous lesson.

Lesson 6: Stop–Think–Plan: A Strategy to Resolve Conflict (Plan)

Lesson 6 covers the third element in STP: Develop a plan. Once students think about what they want and what their options are, they propose a plan. They also listen to the other person's plan, then work with that person to come up with a solution that works for both of them. The STP chart (E-18) introduced in Lesson 4 lists potential positive plans on the right side.

Lesson 7: Determine Whether You Need Help

If their plan to resolve a conflict doesn't work, students must identify for themselves whether they need help. Though STP provides a great set of conflict resolution strategies, in a bullying situation just having the two parties talk more about it may not be productive (situations like this will be discussed further in Presentations 4 and 5). Students discuss times when it may be necessary to seek help from someone in authority and identify people they could approach for help.

Remember that all of these lessons can be modified to fit the needs of your student body.

Task 1 Action Steps & Evidence of Implementation

Action Steps	Evidence of Implementation
1. Foundations Team (with the administrator): Review the tasks and sample lessons in this presentation and decide whether STP seems appropriate for your school.	Foundations Process: Safety, Presentations/ Communications With Staff, Meeting Minutes
2. Administrator: Decide whether implementing STP or another schoolwide conflict resolution strategy will be a staff-based decision or an administrative decision.	
3. Foundations Team: If staff will decide whether to use STP, prepare a presentation to introduce the STP process to the staff. (The Presentation 3 PowerPoint provided in the reproducibles will be useful for this task.) Clarify how using role-plays of conflicts from students' lives can make the content of the lessons directly relevant to your students.	
4. Conduct a staff vote on whether to adopt STP as the schoolwide conflict resolution strategy.	

Figure 3b *Lessons on Conflict Resolution (STP), Lesson 1 Outline*

Module E, Presentation 3

Lesson Outline

Page 1 of 4

Conflict Resolution (STP)
Lesson 1

What Is a Disagreement?/What Is a Conflict?

OBJECTIVES

- Students will define *disagreement* and *conflict*.
- Students will explain how disagreements can escalate into major conflicts that have negative outcomes.
- Students will identify when a disagreement turns into a conflict.

MATERIALS

- Document camera, whiteboard, or interactive whiteboard
- Copy of Lesson 1 Student Worksheet for each student

Introduction

Introduce the lesson and provide the rationale for why addressing the issue of conflict resolution is important.

Lesson Body

1. Provide the definition for *disagreement* and have students fill in the blanks in Item 1 on their worksheets.

    disagreement /disə-ə'grēmənt/ Failure to agree, or a difference of opinion.

    Explain that disagreements are natural. They can be healthy and lead to positive outcomes.

    Provide examples and have students provide examples of healthy disagreements:

    - When people in a business disagree about the best way to do something and are able to calmly and respectfully discuss pros and cons, they often find an even better solution than the original ideas—it's the "two heads are better than one" concept.

    - In some families, some members are affiliated with one religion and others believe in a completely different religion. They have lively discussions and disagreements, but whenever things become tense or someone becomes upset, they agree to disagree and move on to another topic.

    - When friends disagree about what they should do, they calmly discuss and work together to come up with a solution that works for both people—they compromise.

© 2014 Ancora Publishing • For use by purchasing school only   *Foundations: A Proactive and Positive Behavior Support System*

 See Appendix C for printing directions.

Presentation 3: Teaching Conflict Resolution

Figure 3b (continued)   *Lessons on Conflict Resolution (STP), Lesson 1 Outline*

Module E, Presentation 3

Lesson Outline
Page 2 of 4

Conflict Resolution (STP)
Lesson 1 • What Is a Disagreement?/
What Is a Conflict?

Explain that disagreements can become unhealthy, escalate, and lead to negative outcomes—this is when a disagreement becomes a conflict.

2. Provide the definition for *conflict*, and have students fill in the blanks in Item 1 on their worksheets.

    conflict /ˈkän-flikt/ a strong or serious disagreement that is not easily solved. Conflict is often long and angry, and results in negative outcomes.

    Explain that some conflict is natural, but when disagreements escalate in intensity and turn into serious conflicts, they are usually unhealthy and can even be dangerous.

    Provide examples and have students provide examples of disagreements that escalate and turn into unhealthy conflicts.

    - In some families, disagreements about political views, lifestyle choices, or other issues can quickly turn into heated arguments and conflict. In these families, people may not want to spend time together because there is too much conflict.

    - Two small children may have a disagreement about sharing a toy. Because they don't have strategies to deal with this disagreement, they escalate to a conflict with pushing and yelling.

3. Model the conflict situation provided at the end of the lesson on page 4 or create your own. If possible, have a coteacher or other adult play Person 1, but if necessary choose a mature, responsible student to role-play. Before modeling, display and read the questions below. Ask students to be prepared to respond to the questions in Item 2 on their worksheet:

    a. At what point do you think the situation moved from a disagreement to a conflict?

    b. What did you see in this example that makes you think it was a conflict?

    c. How can you tell when you or someone else is in a conflict situation? How does it look? Sound? Feel?

    d. What signs can you see and hear to identify when a disagreement becomes a conflict?

    Give students time to write responses to the questions in Item 2 and share with a partner or small group. Then hold a class discussion about students' responses.

4. Discuss the question: When does a disagreement become a conflict?

© 2014 Ancora Publishing • For use by purchasing school only   *Foundations: A Proactive and Positive Behavior Support System*

 See Appendix C for printing directions.

Figure 3b (continued)

Module E, Presentation 3

Lesson Outline

Page 3 of 4

Conflict Resolution (STP)
Lesson 1 • What Is a Disagreement?/
What Is a Conflict?

5. Explain that having a strategy for dealing with conflict can help a person. Introduce the idea of a *snowball effect*—what starts as minor quickly snowballs into something more serious without strategies to slow down and stop the momentum. One of the most important aspects of a conflict resolution strategy is to slow down the momentum of escalation. Introduce the STP strategy and have students fill in the blanks for Item 3 on their worksheet:

- Stop (say it aloud or to yourself)

- Think (think about staying calm, what you want, and what the other person wants)

- Plan (identify a possible solution and discuss it with the other person, be open to other possibilities, and stay calm until you find a mutually acceptable plan)

Conclusion
Have students complete an exit ticket, answering the question, "Why would it be helpful to use the STP strategy when in a conflict?" Provide a few examples:

- It might help people stay friends.

- It slows down the momentum of the conflict.

Explain that without strategies for keeping disagreements calm and respectful, conflicts escalate, ruining friendships and sometimes becoming dangerous. The next lessons will help students understand how to use the simple strategy to resolve conflict—Stop, Think, Plan.

© 2014 Ancora Publishing • For use by purchasing school only   *Foundations: A Proactive and Positive Behavior Support System*

Figure 3b (continued) Lessons on Conflict Resolution (STP), Lesson 1 Outline

Module E, Presentation 3

Lesson Outline
Page 4 of 4

Conflict Resolution (STP)
Lesson 1 • What Is a Disagreement?/
What Is a Conflict?

Conflict Scenario for Modeling

Setting the scene: Neighbor 1 is practicing electric guitar with the window open. Neighbor 2 is trying to get ready for a really important presentation and is having trouble concentrating with the practice next door. Neighbor 2 walks over to Neighbor 1's house and knocks on the door.

Neighbor 2: *(Use calm body language and a pleasant voice and facial expression)* Hi. I'm sorry to bother you, but could you please close your window? I'm trying to work and am having trouble focusing because I can hear you practicing.

Neighbor 1: *(Use calm body language and a pleasant voice and facial expression)* Oh, sorry. I just painted the house and need the window open so the fumes aren't too bad. Maybe you could close your window?

Neighbor 2: *(Start showing minor signs of agitation—small change of tone and facial expression)* I can't do that because I don't have air conditioning and it's really hot today. Could you just practice in another room, then?

Neighbor 1: *(Start frowning)* I really can't. My equipment is here, and I don't have time to move it all.

Neighbor 2: *(Show frustration and agitation—voice a little louder, sharper gestures, frown)* Listen, I'm sure you don't really need to have the music this loud. I really need to concentrate and can't with your music blaring. Why don't you turn the sound down?

Neighbor 1: *(Show frustration and agitation—sarcastic or annoyed facial expression and tone)* If it's really this much of a problem, why don't you go to the library? It will be quiet there.

Neighbor 2: *(Show frustration and agitation—talk faster, angry tone, frowning)* I don't have time to move all over the place. This presentation is really important. I'm sure it's more important than your tinkering around on the guitar. Can't you just take a break for a few hours?

Neighbor 1: *(Show frustration and agitation—voice louder, angry tone, frowning)* I'm getting ready for a show tonight. My practicing is just as important as your presentation. You don't have any right to come over here and tell me my business. Maybe you would get more done if you would just tell yourself to focus instead of trying to tell other people what to do.

Neighbor 2: *(Step forward and point aggressively at the other person's face, use an angry tone and yelling voice level)* This isn't a problem I have with focusing. Who could focus with that awful scratching you are doing? What's your problem? I made a polite request and you are being totally unreasonable.

Neighbor 1: *(Also step forward, angry tone and yelling voice level)* Don't tell me I'm being unreasonable. You are the one with the problem. Please leave.

Neighbor 2: *(Aggressively point at the other person's face)* Not until you tell me you are going to stop playing that obnoxious guitar.

Neighbor 1: I don't have to do anything you tell me, you selfish jerk. Get out of my face. *(Lightly push the other person)*

Ending the scene: Obviously, this could end badly if things continue to escalate. This started out as a disagreement. It's now a serious conflict.

© 2014 Ancora Publishing • For use by purchasing school only   *Foundations: A Proactive and Positive Behavior Support System*

 See Appendix C for printing directions.

Figure 3c   *Lessons on Conflict Resolution (STP), Lesson 1 Student Worksheet*

Module E, Presentation 3

Student Worksheet
Page 1 of 2

Conflict Resolution (STP)
Lesson 1

Name _____ Class/Teacher _____ Period ____

What Is a Disagreement?/What Is a Conflict?

Item 1
Disagreement: failure to _____, or a difference of _____.

Conflict: a _____ or _____ disagreement that is not easily solved.
Conflict is often long and angry, and results in _____ outcomes.

Item 2
After viewing the conflict role-play, answer the following questions.

a. At what point do you think the situation moved from a disagreement to a conflict?
   _____
   _____
   _____
   _____

b. What did you see in the example that makes you think it was a conflict?
   _____
   _____
   _____
   _____

Module E, Presentation 3

Student Worksheet
Page 2 of 2

Conflict Resolution (STP)
Lesson 1 • What Is a Disagreement?/
What Is a Conflict?

c. How can you tell when you or someone else is in a conflict situation? How does it look? Sound? Feel?
   _____
   _____
   _____

d. What signs can you see or hear to identify when a disagreement becomes a conflict?
   _____
   _____
   _____
   _____

Item 3
To slow down the momentum of a conflict, use the following strategy:
- _____
- _____
- _____

Exit Ticket
Why would it be helpful to use the STP strategy when in a conflict? Give at least two reasons.
   _____
   _____
   _____
   _____
   _____
   _____
   _____

Presentation 3: Teaching Conflict Resolution

Figure 3d *Lessons on Conflict Resolution (STP), Lesson 2 Outline (page 1 only)*

Module E, Presentation 3

Lesson Outline
Page 1 of 3

Conflict Resolution (STP)
Lesson 2

Reading Social Cues to Avoid Conflict

OBJECTIVES

- Students will explain why stopping conflict is more important than proving a point.
- Students will identify social cues they can use to know when it is necessary to stop doing or saying something in order to avoid conflict.

MATERIALS

- Document camera, whiteboard, or interactive whiteboard
- Copy of Lesson 2 Student Worksheet for each student

Introduction

1. Review key features that distinguish a disagreement from a conflict. Have students recall factors they identified in the modeled scenario from Lesson 1. Also explain that these lessons will help students use a strategy called Stop–Think–Plan to deal with conflicts in appropriate and positive ways.

2. Discuss how stopping conflict is more important than proving a point. If you are having a disagreement that escalates into a conflict, it is better to walk away or change the subject than for the conflict to escalate.

   For Item 1 on their worksheets, have students identify negative outcomes that can occur if conflict escalates. For example:

   - It could turn into a physical fight.
   - Someone could get hurt—physically or emotionally.
   - People say things they regret later.
   - It can ruin a relationship.

   Explain that these are all reasons to avoid conflicts. A person may want to prove a point and continue arguing, but if it could lead to these negative outcomes, it would be better just to agree to disagree or wait to have a discussion when both people are calm.

© 2014 Ancora Publishing • For use by purchasing school only   *Foundations: A Proactive and Positive Behavior Support System*

 See Appendix C for printing directions.

Figure 3e   *Lessons on Conflict Resolution (STP), Lesson 2 Student Worksheet*

Module E, Presentation 3

Student Worksheet
Page 1 of 1

Conflict Resolution (STP)
Lesson 2

Name _____ Class/Teacher _____ Period ____

Reading Social Cues to Avoid Conflict

Item 1
List negative outcomes that can occur if conflict escalates:

- _____
- _____
- _____
- _____
- _____

Item 2

Ways People Communicate	Social Cues That Someone Else Is Upset	Personal Cues When I Am Upset
Words		
Tone		
Voice Level		
Facial Expression		
Body Language		
Actions		

© 2014 Ancora Publishing • For use by purchasing school only   *Foundations: A Proactive and Positive Behavior Support System*

Presentation 3: Teaching Conflict Resolution

Figure 3f *Lessons on Conflict Resolution (STP), Lesson 3 Outline (page 1 only)*

Module E, Presentation 3

Lesson Outline
Page 1 of 3

Conflict Resolution (STP)
Lesson 3

Conflict and Electronic Communication/ Social Media

OBJECTIVES

- Students will explain how electronic forms of communication can lead to conflict—through misunderstandings or by people saying and doing things they would not normally do.

- Students will identify ways to remain free from conflict when using electronic forms of communication.

MATERIALS

Document camera, whiteboard, or interactive whiteboard

Introduction

1. Review:

    - Why it is important to remain free from conflict.

    - How to identify when a disagreement is turning into a conflict by reading social cues such as:
        - Words
        - Tone
        - Voice level
        - Facial expression
        - Body language
        - Actions

    - Why reading social cues is an important step in being able to stop a conflict before it escalates.

2. Introduce the lesson topic: It can be even more difficult to deal with potential conflicts when communicating with others through social media or other electronic means because the only clue to someone's meaning is that person's words—the other social cues are not available. This lesson will help students learn how to act appropriately when they communicate with others using electronic methods like e-mail, social media, and texting. It will also help them understand how to deal with potential conflicts when they are unable to see social cues other than words.

© 2014 Ancora Publishing • For use by purchasing school only   *Foundations: A Proactive and Positive Behavior Support System*

 See Appendix C for printing directions.

Figure 3g *Lessons on Conflict Resolution (STP), Lesson 4 Outline (page 1 only)*

Module E, Presentation 3

Lesson Outline
Page 1 of 4

Conflict Resolution (STP)
Lesson 4

Stop–Think–Plan: A Strategy to Resolve Conflict (Stop)

OBJECTIVES
- Students will explain the importance of the word *Stop* in dealing with conflicts.
- Students will demonstrate stopping a variety of conflicts.

MATERIALS
- Document camera, whiteboard, or interactive whiteboard
- Copy of Lesson 4 Student Worksheet for each student
- Copy of Stop–Think–Plan Plans for Resolving Conflict (Form E-18) to display

---

Introduction

1. Review highlights from previous lessons:
    - Conflict can escalate.
    - A strategy like Stop–Think–Plan can be very useful for dealing with conflict.
    - It is important to read cues—other people's and your own—that indicate conflict is occurring (how it looks, sounds, feels).

2. Introduce the lesson's focus on the most important step of the Stop–Think–Plan strategy: Stop. Students will learn how to slow the momentum of a conflict so that they have time to think about positive solutions, rather than just react emotionally and in negative ways.

© 2014 Ancora Publishing • For use by purchasing school only   *Foundations: A Proactive and Positive Behavior Support System*

Figure 3h *Lessons on Conflict Resolution (STP), Lesson 4 Student Worksheet*

Module E, Presentation 3

Student Worksheet

Page 1 of 1

Conflict Resolution (STP)
Lesson 4

Name _____ Class/Teacher _____ Period ____

Stop–Think–Plan: A Strategy to Resolve Conflict (Stop)

Item 1
The most important step of the Stop–Think–Plan strategy is _____ .

Item 2
Brainstorm negative and positive ways of dealing with conflict.

PLANS FOR RESOLVING CONFLICT	
Negative	**Positive**

Item 3
Suggestions for stopping or slowing the momentum of a conflict:

- Ask the person: _____
  _____

- Tell the person: _____
  _____

- Tell yourself: _____
  _____

© 2014 Ancora Publishing • For use by purchasing school only

Foundations: A Proactive and Positive Behavior Support System

 See Appendix C for printing directions.

Figure 3i *Lessons on Conflict Resolution (STP), Lesson 5 Outline (page 1 only)*

Module E, Presentation 3

Lesson Outline
Page 1 of 3

Conflict Resolution (STP)
Lesson 5

Stop–Think–Plan: A Strategy to Resolve Conflict (Think)

OBJECTIVES
- Students will identify key elements of the Think step of STP.
- Students will demonstrate thinking through conflict situations in rational ways.

MATERIALS
- Document camera, whiteboard, or interactive whiteboard
- Copy of Lesson 5 Worksheet for each student

Introduction
1. Review highlights from previous lessons:
   - Conflict can escalate and lead to negative outcomes
   - Why the Stop step is the most important part of Stop–Think–Plan, and strategies and examples of stopping the momentum of a conflict
   - Stop can be under your control regardless of the other person
   - Stop can mean slow down and take a few seconds to remind yourself to be calm
2. Introduce this lesson and its focus on the Think step of the Stop–Think–Plan strategy. Students will practice thinking through conflict situations after they have used their Stop strategies to slow the momentum of a conflict.

Lesson Body
1. Display and explain the key elements of the Think step of STP. Have students fill in the blanks for Item 1 on their worksheet.
    1. Think about staying <u>calm</u>.
    2. Think about <u>what you want</u>.
    3. Think about the <u>other person</u> and what <u>he or she wants</u>.

© 2014 Ancora Publishing • For use by purchasing school only   *Foundations: A Proactive and Positive Behavior Support System*

Presentation 3: Teaching Conflict Resolution

Figure 3j *Lessons on Conflict Resolution (STP), Lesson 5 Student Worksheet*

See Appendix C for printing directions.

Module E: Improving Safety, Managing Conflict, and Reducing Bullying

Figure 3k *Lessons on Conflict Resolution (STP), Lesson 6 Outline (page 1 only)*

Module E, Presentation 3

Lesson Outline

Page 1 of 4

Conflict Resolution (STP)
Lesson 6

Stop–Think–Plan: A Strategy to Resolve Conflict (Plan)

OBJECTIVES
- Students will explain how to develop a plan for resolving conflict.
- Students will demonstrate talking about and finding a plan with the other person.

MATERIALS
- Document camera, whiteboard, or interactive whiteboard
- Copy of Lesson 6 Student Worksheet for each student
- Type up and number the examples of conflict that students generated in previous lessons and any other examples you or other staff members identify. Provide a copy of the Conflict Scenarios for each student

Introduction
1. Display the Stop–Think–Plan chart (Form E-18; see Appendix C) and have students follow on their worksheets. Review that STP is designed to help people avoid the negative plans and outcomes that are on the left side of the page. Also review how to stop and think during a conflict.
2. Introduce this lesson and its rationale: It will help students understand the range of options they have when developing a plan to deal with conflict and teach them how to talk calmly and rationally with the other person until they find a solution that works for both of them.

Lesson Body
1. Tell students that there are many options for resolving a conflict. The ideas on the right side of the STP chart are some of the possibilities. With students, read the positive plans on the right side of the chart.
2. For the first several positive plans on the STP chart, provide examples of types of conflicts that might be resolved using these strategies. Explain that different types of conflicts require different types of solutions. For example:
    - **Share:** If two children are fighting over who gets the last piece of cake, a logical and positive plan would be to cut the cake in half and share it.
    - **Take turns:** If two siblings both want to use the computer at the same time, they could agree to take turns and each use it for a set amount of time.

© 2014 Ancora Publishing • For use by purchasing school only   *Foundations: A Proactive and Positive Behavior Support System*

Figure 3l *Lessons on Conflict Resolution (STP), Lesson 6 Student Worksheet*

Module E, Presentation 3
Student Worksheet
Page 1 of 1

Conflict Resolution (STP)
Lesson 6

Name _____ Class/Teacher _____ Period ____

Stop–Think–Plan: A Strategy to Resolve Conflict (Plan)

STOP–THINK–PLAN
PLANS FOR RESOLVING CONFLICT

NEGATIVE
- Fight
- Yell
- Hurt someone's feelings
- End a friendship
- Walk away mad
- Threaten
- Call names
- Push or hit
- Not listen
- Not think

POSITIVE
- Share
- Take turns
- Talk it out
- Make a deal
- Decide it is OK to disagree
- Apologize
- Calm down
- Talk later
- Redo the play
- Flip a coin

© 2014 Ancora Publishing • For use by purchasing school only

Foundations: A Proactive and Positive Behavior Support System

 See Appendix C for printing directions.

Figure 3m Lessons on Conflict Resolution (STP), Lesson 7 Outline (page 1 only)

Module E, Presentation 3

Lesson Outline

Page 1 of 4

Conflict Resolution (STP)
Lesson 7

Determine Whether You Need Help

OBJECTIVES
Students learn when and how to seek outside help in resolving a conflict.

MATERIALS
Document camera, whiteboard, or interactive whiteboard

Introduction

1. Review the Stop–Think–Plan strategy. Points to cover include:
   - Ways to stop or slow the momentum of a conflict
   - Key elements of the Think step: 1) think about staying calm, 2) think about what you want, 3) think about what the other person wants
   - The range of positive plans that can be used to resolve a conflict, and how to communicate when discussing a plan

2. Explain that sometimes a conflict cannot be resolved by the individuals who are involved. In those cases, it is important to get help from someone in authority or someone outside of the situation. This lesson will help students identify whether they need help and who they might approach for help in resolving a conflict.

Lesson Body

1. Read the following scenario:

   > Justin and Paul are in the same PE class, and they don't get along very well. One day, Justin goes to his locker and discovers that his phone is missing. He thought he saw Paul near his locker putting something in his pocket, so he goes to Paul and asks where his cell phone is.
   >
   > Paul tells Justin he hasn't seen it and didn't take it. Justin doesn't believe Paul and says, "Give me back my phone." Paul starts to become angry and denies it again. Justin isn't listening and doesn't believe him. Paul's voice rises as he says, "Get out of my face. I didn't take your phone." Justin steps forward and yells, "You're a thief and a liar!"

© 2014 Ancora Publishing • For use by purchasing school only   *Foundations: A Proactive and Positive Behavior Support System*

TASK 2

Develop an STP program in your school

This task presents a series of steps to guide the Foundations Team or STP task force in planning the rollout of the STP conflict resolution process in the school and ensuring that staff and students actively use it.

> Suggestions for how individual teachers can implement STP is available in *Teacher's Encyclopedia of Behavior Management: 100+ Problems/500+ Plans* (2nd ed.) by Randy Sprick, in "Arguing—Students With Each Other." This book is available through Ancora Publishing.

STEP 1. Ensure that staff members, especially teachers, are aware of the major steps in STP.

If the decision to implement STP was administrative and staff did not vote to adopt it, you will need to give all staff members information about the program. The major steps in the STP process are:

Step 1. Identify whether a disagreement is simple or a conflict that needs to be resolved.

Step 2. If it is a conflict, **stop** what you are doing.

Step 3. **Think** about your goals and your options for resolving the conflict.

Step 4. Propose a **plan** to the other person and listen to the other person's plan.

Step 5. Try the plan and see if both parties are satisfied.

Even if you have already presented STP to staff as a precursor to a vote to adopt the program (as we suggest in the Task 1 Action Steps), you might want to add more details to the presentation and review it with all staff. The PowerPoint slides provided in the reproducible materials will be useful for this purpose, and you may customize them as needed. Also ensure that staff members know that there is potential for bullying and imbalance of power when conflict occurs repeatedly. Although STP is a great set of strategies, it will not solve all issues related to bullying, which is usually a more complex problem.

STEP 2. Design schoolwide lessons and a plan for teaching them.

Review and modify the seven sample lessons. Keep in mind that, as part of the first lesson, students generate lists of disagreements and conflicts that they have experienced. The lists will be important components of all subsequent lessons. Consider age-appropriate vocabulary and community and cultural norms as you modify the lessons. Remember that a key goal is to introduce and embed a common language among students and staff about how to resolve conflicts.

An effective teaching plan is essential—in fact, it's the hub of the entire STP program. All staff need to know that every student has had the same lessons about conflict resolution, and all staff need to have the same understanding of how STP works. When teaching has been consistent, staff can give appropriate positive or corrective feedback when students use the process. If students do not use STP, staff can guide them to do so. When all staff—administrators, counselors, teachers, playground supervisors, cafeteria supervisors, and campus security—are using the same steps and the same language to describe those steps, it sends a powerful message to students about the importance of using STP and resolving conflicts. Consider the following aspects of teaching STP.

Time requirements. For middle school through ninth grade, schedule the lessons for about 15 to 20 minutes, perhaps during advisory periods. For primary students, you may want to split the lessons and teach each one in two sessions of 5 to 10 minutes each. Your primary teachers can help you with appropriate lesson format, design, and length for young children.

How to teach the strategies. We recommend you consider a team of two coteachers—for example, a counselor and a paraprofessional or an administrator and a teacher on special assignment who can travel from classroom to classroom. The classroom teachers can also participate in the teaching, but a core group of traveling coteachers will help ensure that all classrooms get consistent information. Consistent information and teaching methods will help ensure that everyone in the school uses the same language and has the same understanding of the STP concept.

Another benefit of coteaching is that it allows modeling of conflict situations that is not possible with just one teacher. It's important for the adults to model positive ways (as well as poor ways) to handle conflict. It's also tremendously beneficial for students to see their classroom teachers actively participate in the lessons and support students as they learn and practice these skills. So even if you have a core group that visits the classrooms, encourage the teachers to participate in the lessons.

When to teach the strategies. Consider conducting some lessons during a school assembly or perhaps grade-level assemblies. You might have older students create video lessons (with adult assistance) on how to apply the STP strategies. The videos can be shown in classrooms and in schoolwide assemblies.

If your plan is for all teachers to teach the STP lessons to their own classes, be sure to provide training so that all classes receive the same content.

Presentation 3: Teaching Conflict Resolution

Staff training. Review the STP process and details of its implementation, such as the teaching schedule, with staff. Be sensitive to time issues and the potential of overburdening staff with too much to teach. Emphasize that the minutes spent learning and helping students learn the process can save lots of time later by reducing the frequency of conflict in the school.

> **◈ FOUNDATIONS RECOMMENDATION ❧**
>
> *To teach STP, use a core group of coteachers who travel from classroom to classroom. Consistent information and teaching methods will help ensure that everyone in the school uses the same language and shares the same understanding of the STP concept. Coteachers can also model conflict situations.*

STEP 3. Determine how supervisors will be trained.

Common area supervisors, campus monitors, and the like need training in using the STP process to correct conflict situations and reinforcing students when they use STP. Determine whether your classified staff should read or view all or part of the introduction and Tasks 1 and 2 of this presentation to enhance their sense of ownership in carrying through with these processes.

STEP 4. Consider possible areas of staff resistance to implementing STP and prepare to deal with them effectively.

The greatest resistance you will encounter will likely be related to the time required to prepare the lessons. A good plan for using coteachers, assemblies, and other methods will reduce the preparation teachers have to do, although some instructional time will be lost. Be sure to explain the benefits of reducing violence in children's lives and addressing conflict situations that lead to emotional turmoil. An effective schoolwide conflict resolution program is also a great precursor to reducing bullying in the school.

STEP 5. Decide on and teach schoolwide procedures for dispersing from a conflict.

Establish a verbal cue, such as "Everyone move along." Teach students that when they hear those words, they are to immediately disperse from the scene of the conflict. Staff might say, "Everyone move along and go past Room 9," but the common language that students recognize and react to is, "Everyone move along." Another verbal cue might be, "Everyone follow this direction. You all need to go to _____." Secondary schools might use a sentence such as, "Everyone disperse and go to _____." The key is common language used by all staff and recognized by all students.

Tell students that if they choose not to move away from a conflict when given a direction to do so, they may receive consequences for not following that direction. When students in a conflict see and hear other students around them, listening and possibly heckling them or cheering them on, it's difficult to stop, think calmly, and develop a rational plan.

Lesson 4 in the STP lessons at the end of Task 1 includes a section on teaching students to disperse from conflicts. You might teach your procedures as part of that lesson or as a separate extension lesson. Also consider incorporating your dispersal procedure into the Increasing Connectedness and Safety lessons in Presentation 2 and the lessons on Bullying Prevention in Presentation 4.

STEP 6. Inform staff about the content of any extension lessons.

You might want to expand on some of the concepts covered in the lessons included with this presentation. If so, develop lesson outlines modeled on the lesson plans in Task 1. For example, when discussing negative outcomes of conflict in Lesson 4, you might want to insert an additional lesson to discuss how conflict can affect friendships and other relationships and look at ways to repair relationships that have been damaged by conflict.

If you teach Lesson 3 on electronic communications and social media, you might want to incorporate an additional lesson or two on Internet safety.

Another concept that may be worth exploring in more depth is how to stay calm in a conflict by using strategies such as deep, even breathing; positive self-talk; and visualizing oneself as strong and calm. These techniques are briefly discussed in Lesson 4, but students might benefit from more in-depth instruction and practice.

Students might also benefit from more information about how to get help when needed, the subject of Lesson 7.

Consider teaching students, particularly intermediate and secondary students, about the concept of assault. If a conflict gets physical and someone is hurt, it might be considered assault and lead to legal consequences, even if there was no intent to cause harm.

As part of Step 6, we suggest you review the Lessons on Increasing Connectedness and Safety (Module E, Presentation 2) and Lessons on Bullying Prevention (Module E, Presentation 5) to see how the STP processes can be integrated with those lessons. All lesson outlines are available in the reproducible materials.

Presentation 3: Teaching Conflict Resolution

STEP 7. Establish feedback loops so that information about actual conflicts goes to the people who teach the lessons.

The role-plays in the lessons are based on conflicts that have occurred in your school. Your common area supervisors and campus security personnel will be great resources for conflict scenarios because they probably deal with most of them. Make sure they know that when they deal with a conflict that students have trouble resolving, they should relay that information to the people who are preparing the lessons. The conflicts will make good examples for review lessons. When you create the role-plays, be sure to modify the conflicts so that the actual people involved are not recognizable.

> When you create the role-plays, be sure to modify the conflicts so that the actual people involved are not recognizable.

STEP 8. Decide how to involve parents.

Inform parents about the school's initiative to establish STP as a schoolwide conflict resolution strategy. Post an announcement and information on the school website or newsletter, and discuss it at a parent-teacher association (PTA) meeting. STP can be used to help parents of chronic offenders learn strategies for dealing with conflicts at home. The next task explains how to educate parents about STP.

Note: Task 3 in this presentation explains how to involve parents in the STP process.

As you think about involving parents, try to anticipate any philosophical or cultural objections that might be raised about the STP process. Think about how you can deal with any objections in advance or modify the lessons to be sensitive to those issues.

STEP 9. Develop a plan to get students to generalize the STP strategy.

Common language used by staff is the key to getting students to generalize STP so they can use it in actual conflict situations. Staff should correct students who do *not* use the STP process and prompt them to stop, think, and plan, but should not take responsibility for resolving the conflict for the students. Staff should intervene and stop a conflict if it's escalating and students haven't stopped. "Hey, you two, I see that you're starting to get into a little bit of an argument. Think about the steps. What's the first step? Right—S. What does that mean? Right, it means stop. That gives you time to think. If you need my help, I'll be right over here."

That last sentence, "If you need my help, I'll be right over here," is important so students don't think they are completely alone. One of the students might be naturally more domineering or aggressive, and smaller students might be afraid of larger students. Staff can return and help students with the process, if necessary, and give suggestions for resolution, but the students should resolve the conflict. So the goal is that everybody uses the same language to prompt the same process.

Reinforcing students for using STP will also help them generalize the process. "Ben, how did you resolve the problem with Juan? That sounds like a good compromise. You did a good job of remembering to stop, think, and plan." If you find that the resolution the students agreed on was unfair to one student, remind the students that they don't have to immediately accept the other person's proposal. An older or more aggressive student might suggest an unfair resolution. If this behavior is repeated, it begins to meet the definition of bullying. "LaShawn, you agreed to stop playing basketball to resolve the conflict with Andrea. Are you happy with that plan? You don't have to go along with Andrea's suggestions. Let's get together with her and talk about a better way to solve the problem."

 Common language used by staff when they correct and reinforce STP is the key to getting students to generalize the process so they can use it in actual conflict situations."

STEP 10. Discuss how you will evaluate the effectiveness of the STP implementation.

You can use objective data sources to evaluate whether STP is working to reduce conflicts that result in adult correction and consequences. Compare pre- and post-intervention data on the frequency of office referrals from your common areas and on the frequency of fights, for example. Have common area supervisors track how many conflicts they intervene with on the playground or in the cafeteria—are the weekly numbers trending up or down?

Subjective data can also be useful. Have teachers and supervisors informally report whether students are using the STP strategies and resolving conflicts successfully on their own.

STEP 11. Develop emergency procedures so that if STP fails, all staff know what to do.

All staff should know the following procedures:

- How and why to call for help when a physical fight occurs. It can be dangerous for one person to try to break up a fight. (See Module E, Presentation 2 for information about main and backup communication procedures and the dangers of breaking up a fight.)

- How and why to disperse onlookers to a conflict. Peer onlookers can increase the likelihood that a conflict will escalate to a physical fight (see Step 5 earlier in this list.)

- How and why to keep records of incidents that required emergency procedures. You might need to re-create the situation for legal reasons, and you don't want to rely on memories. You can also analyze the situations and perhaps learn how to prevent them from happening again.

STEP 12. Develop long-range procedures for dealing with students who chronically fight or exhibit aggressive behavior.

Stop–Think–Plan (STP) is likely to help many students, but students who have problems with anger management and rage or lack social skills will probably need more intensive lessons in how to handle conflict appropriately. These students may benefit from remedial lessons taught during structured recess in elementary school or lunchtime detention in a middle school. These lessons should not be presented as punishment, but as additional opportunities to practice the skills needed to deal with conflict. A skilled paraprofessional or school counselor might conduct these lessons. If this strategy is not successful, you will probably have to move into contracts, self-monitoring, or other individual behavior support plans for these students. More information about individual behavior support plans appears in Module F, Presentations 4, 5, and 6.

Conflict resolution is a worthwhile endeavor, but making a difference requires ongoing lessons, instructional corrections that re-teach the process, encouragement procedures, and reinforcement for using the process.

Task 2 Action Steps & Evidence of Implementation

Action Steps	Evidence of Implementation
The Foundations Team or STP task force should work through these steps in developing a Stop–Think–Plan (STP) program in the school. • Ensure that staff, especially teachers, are aware of the major steps in STP. • Design schoolwide lessons and a plan for teaching them. • Determine how supervisors will be trained. • Consider possible staff resistance. • Decide on schoolwide procedures for dispersing from a conflict. • Inform staff of any extension lessons. • Establish feedback loops so that information about actual conflicts goes to the people who teach the lessons. • Decide how to involve parents. • Develop a generalization plan. • Evaluate the effectiveness of the STP implementation. • Develop emergency procedures in case STP fails. • Develop long-range procedures for students who chronically fight or exhibit aggressive behavior.	Foundations Process: Safety, Presentations/Communications With Staff Foundations Archive: Lesson Plans for Teaching Safety Expectations, Safety Policies Staff Handbook: Policies and Procedures Student and Parent Handbook: Polices and Procedures

Presentation 3: Teaching Conflict Resolution

TASK 3
Educate parents about STP

Plan to conduct a communication campaign for parents. Tell them about STP and encourage them to prompt their children to use the process at home. You might present STP during a PTA meeting or at back-to-school night, or post information about it on the school website. The suggested information below is available in the reproducibles as a handout for parents (Sample E-19 shown in Figure 3n on the next page).

Introduction

School staff have decided to teach all students a process for dealing calmly with conflict. The program is called Stop–Think–Plan, or STP for short. We begin by telling students that disagreements and conflict are part of life, but they don't have to result in fighting, hitting, name calling, and so on. There are peaceful ways to resolve conflict. Conflict can escalate in intensity, leading to dangerous situations. Violence is a major health hazard, especially to teenage boys.

The STP poster (see Figure 3n) shows examples of negative and positive ways to handle a conflict. We encourage students to think about these types of plans and create a chart like this during the STP lessons.

What Is STP?

STP is simple. It's based on three basic steps—Stop, Think, and Plan—and easy for students to remember and use. Major emphasis is on the word Stop. Students learn that they have a right to say "Stop" and be respected, and that they also need to respect others' right to say "Stop" to slow down escalating emotions. Saying "Stop" is the most difficult step for students to generalize to actual situations because it's so easy to get sucked into the momentum of a conflict. But if they don't stop and think about what to do, they are more likely to make a poor choice, such as threaten, call names, or just walk away angry.

All students are learning this strategy in school, but school implementation alone is weak. Home implementation alone is also weak. But if students are prompted to use STP at both school and home, the program is likely to be very successful and will give students strategies that will help them throughout their lives. Parents and teachers working together can teach more effectively.

Figure 3n   Parent handout on STP (E-19)

See Appendix C for printing directions.

Presentation 3: Teaching Conflict Resolution

Students are learning the following information and skills:

- *How to recognize simple disagreements (I like cats—you like dogs; we can agree to disagree) and conflicts that need resolving.*

- *How to say **Stop** to de-escalate the conflict and rising emotions, and expect to be respected. How to respect other students' right to say **Stop**.*

- *How to **think** about options for resolving the conflict, such as compromise. Think about both students' goals.*

- *How to propose a **plan** to the other person and listen to the other person's plan.*

- *Students don't have to accept another person's plan. They have the power to negotiate and be assertive, but they should always stay calm when doing so.*

- *How to try the plan and see if both parties are satisfied.*

Staff members are trained to stop conflict when necessary, but when possible they will just remind students about the STP process and let students resolve the conflict themselves. Staff members will stay nearby to help if STP doesn't work, and they will provide positive feedback to students for using STP.

How Can Parents Help?

Parents can help with this process by talking to their children about conflicts and clarifying the advantages of handling them calmly: No one gets hurt, friendships can be maintained, and all parties can get what they want. Each child may have to compromise a bit, but everybody has a right to get something out of the resolution. Parents can also emphasize that children can stick up for themselves by being calmly assertive. Of course, parents should make decisions about what they want their children to do when self-defense is necessary, but we suggest that trying to resolve conflict with words will result in a better outcome.

Tell your children about your own experiences with resolving conflict—for example, a situation with a coworker. Talk to your children about the importance of the STP lessons that they're receiving at school. Support your children by helping them master the lessons at home. Set up expectations for dealing with conflicts in the home based on the STP process. For example, instead of intervening with sibling rivalry issues, prompt the children to use STP:

- *Emphasize the importance of Stop. Let's say a brother and sister are arguing about what to watch on television. The sister says, "Stop," but the brother grabs the remote and flips through the channels. Correct the brother for not stopping and respecting his sister instead of for taking control of the television. "Kamiel, your sister said 'Stop.' What does that mean? Right, you need to stop what you are doing and respect her by coming up with a plan that you both agree with." Then let the children resolve the problem themselves, but stay nearby in case one child bullies or intimidates to get the other to accept an unfair plan. "You two work out a plan. I'll be right over here if you need me."*

- *Be cautious about taking sides with children. If they fight chronically, both (or all) of them are probably feeding the problem.*

- *Later, follow up with a calm discussion about what Stop means. "Kamiel, you need to work on respecting others when they say 'Stop.' What do you do when someone says 'Stop?' That's right. And you have the right to say 'Stop' when you feel like you need to slow things down, too."*

- *Children need to know they have the power to say "Stop" whenever they need to slow things down and think about what to do. This sense of power becomes even more important as children grow into adolescence.*

In Conclusion

Teaching students to resolve conflict is important and worthwhile. The major points to remember from this handout are:

- *STP stands for Stop–Think–Plan:* **Stop** *what you are doing,* **Think** *about options, and develop a fair* **Plan** *that all parties can agree to.*

- *Children need ongoing support and encouragement at home to emphasize the importance of using STP and resolving conflicts peacefully.*

- *Correct children by reminding them about the STP process, not by solving the problem for them.*

- *This conflict resolution strategy can help students now and throughout their lives.*

Task 3 Action Steps & Evidence of Implementation

Action Steps	Evidence of Implementation
1. Schedule a time to present STP to parent organizations connected to your school, such as the PTA, or during back-to-school night. Plan to distribute the parent handout.	Foundations Process: Planning Calendar, Communications With Parents
2. Announce the STP initiative and provide information about it on your school website, in newsletters, in email blasts, or in other means of communication that your school uses.	Foundations Archive: Lesson Plans for Teaching Safety Expectations
3. Consider preparing a video of one or more staged home-based conflicts that demonstrates using and not using the STP process. Post the video online and ask parents to view it with their children and use it to practice STP. Post the link on your school website or newsletter.	

PRESENTATION

FOUR

Analyzing Bullying Behavior, Policies, and School Needs

CONTENTS

Introduction to Presentations 4 and 5

Task 1: Understand Bullying Issues
For the Foundations Team or bullying prevention task force, and possibly the entire staff

Task 2: Collect Data on Bullying in Your School
For the Foundations Team or bullying prevention task force

Task 3: Define and Refine Your Bullying Policy
For the Foundations Team or bullying prevention task force

Task 4: Analyze Bullying Data and Determine Priorities
For the Foundations Team or bullying prevention task force

DOCUMENTS*

- School-Based Analysis of Bullying Data (E-06)
- Bullying Incident Report (E-07)
- Schoolwide Bullying Incident Log (E-08)
- School-Based Analysis of Bullying Policies (E-09)
- Range of Consequences and Interventions for Bullying (E-20)
- Statement Regarding a Balanced Approach to Consequences and Supports for Bullying Intervention (E-21)
- STOIC Analysis of Universal Prevention of Bullying (E-10)

* See Appendix C for information on accessing these documents.

INTRODUCTION
Presentations 4 and 5

Bullying is a complex issue and can be difficult to address. Although recent years have seen an exponential increase in school-based efforts to address bullying problems, research on the effectiveness of these efforts has yielded mixed results. There are few strong conclusions about ways to solve the bullying problem. Many students do not even report bullying concerns because they think their school won't do anything or they're afraid the school's efforts to address the concerns will make the situation worse.

Research has revealed that bullying problems exist not in isolation but as part of larger concerns such as school climate, family and community environment and supports, peer ecology, and many other factors. Leading school and mental health organizations concur with this finding. The consensus is that preventing and intervening with bullying problems must be part of a comprehensive approach that addresses school climate and safety (covered in other parts of *Foundations*), family and community involvement, supports and interventions for students who are victimized, bystander training in intervention, and consequences and meaningful interventions and supports for those who bully.

Bullying prevention and intervention efforts cannot be one sided, short term, or small scale. They're not a one-time campaign or a brief series of lessons. You need to revisit the bullying issue frequently and review and infuse positive messages throughout the school year. Your efforts cannot simply focus on bystander intervention, although this will be one part of your comprehensive plan. You also cannot simply focus your efforts on consequences and interventions to change the behavior of students who perpetrate bullying. If consequences for bullying don't address the cause of a student's bullying behavior, the student is likely to continue doing it, although he or she may just get more sneaky, retaliate in a stronger way, or otherwise escalate the behavior.

You need to develop a long-term, systematic approach to understand all of the factors that contribute to bullying behavior in your school and provide multi-tiered efforts to address these concerns. These efforts will probably take many different angles and approaches to bullying prevention and intervention.

Presentations 4 and 5 are designed to help your Foundations Team or bullying prevention task force develop a long-term, systematic approach in coordination with your other *Foundations* climate and safety efforts. If you are beginning *Foundations* with these two presentations and have not worked on other parts of the process, your bullying prevention efforts are less likely to have a real and long-lasting effect on student behavior. We recommend that you focus on the issue of bullying as a follow-up to and continuation of your efforts to address other safety and climate concerns. As the team works to address bullying, recognize that the issue of bullying is never truly solved. You will not neatly complete the tasks and check them off your list, never to revisit them. This work requires continual effort, much like vacuuming your carpets or addressing students who are running in the halls. You'll always need to invest energy into ensuring active supervision and monitoring. Likewise, you'll never be done teaching students how to treat each other respectfully, and you'll never finish giving students meaningful, positive, and corrective feedback.

> ### ❦ FOUNDATIONS RECOMMENDATION ❧
>
> *Focus on the issue of bullying as a continuation of your efforts to address other safety and climate concerns. If you are beginning* Foundations *with these two presentations and have not worked on other parts of the process, your efforts to prevent bullying are less likely to have a real and long-lasting effect on student behavior. If another group or task force is leading bullying prevention and intervention efforts, be sure that the Foundations Team's work on climate and behavior is coordinated with the bullying prevention work.*

The four tasks in Presentation 4 will help you understand bullying, collect information about bullying at your school, and determine your priorities for addressing school issues.

Task 1: Understand Bullying Issues provides information that will help school personnel understand bullying and the variables they can manipulate to reduce problems with bullying. This information will also help staff respond effectively when bullying does occur.

Task 2: Collect Data on Bullying in Your School guides the team in collecting meaningful data on bullying to identify immediate priorities within your school. It also covers long-term reporting, documenting, and monitoring procedures. This task is most useful for the Foundations Team or bullying prevention task force, although data collected should be shared regularly with staff, students, and families.

Task 3: Define and Refine Your Bullying Policy helps the team examine existing policies related to bullying to determine whether they meet state and district requirements and address specific concerns revealed in the schoolwide data.

Task 4: Analyze Bullying Data and Determine Priorities guides the team in analyzing schoolwide data and determining priorities for addressing bullying issues.

In Presentation 5, the four tasks focus on implementation of schoolwide bullying efforts.

Task 1: Train Staff to Respond to and Prevent Bullying provides suggestions for training staff members about bullying issues. Topics include getting all staff on board with addressing bullying problems and training staff members to respond appropriately when they witness or receive a report about a bullying incident. This task also explains how adult modeling of positive behavior is critical to building a climate that does not support bullying behavior among students.

Task 2: Help Students Prevent Bullying identifies information about bullying that you should communicate to students and a range of methods you can use to teach about bullying. The goal is to infuse the antibullying message and positive expectations about peer behavior into the school climate.

Task 3: Partner With Families to Prevent Bullying suggests activities for training families about bullying prevention, including rules, policies, and responsibilities. It provides specific suggestions on how to communicate important information to families on such topics as avoiding cyberbullying and educating children about responsible technology use.

Task 4: Actively Engage Students to Prevent Bullying expands on the information presented in Module C on engaging students. Student engagement is one of the best ways to reduce bullying because it can both prevent it and provide students with resiliency when it does occur. This task covers schoolwide and individual strategies that increase student engagement and connectedness.

TASK 1
Understand bullying issues

All schools need to address bullying, not only because most states have laws in place that require schools to address bullying and harassment issues, but also because students who are involved in bullying situations tend to have negative outcomes. This task provides information to help school personnel understand bullying issues and the variables they can manipulate to reduce bullying problems and respond effectively when bullying occurs.

Research indicates that students who are bullied:

- Tend to experience increased levels of insecurity and low self-esteem.
- Often experience depression, anxiety, sadness, and loneliness.
- May experience a loss of interest in activities that they previously enjoyed.
- May have increased difficulty in school, including lower participation, worse attendance, lower GPAs, and increased likelihood of dropping out.
- Tend to have more health complaints and physical and mental health symptoms.

Students who bully others are more likely to:

- Drop out of school.
- Abuse alcohol and drugs.
- Fight.
- Engage in delinquent activities and have criminal convictions
- Engage in early sexual activity.
- When they're adults, be abusive to partners, spouses, or children.

Students who both bully and are bullied have the greatest risk factors for all of the above issues, and they have the poorest psychosocial functioning of any students who are involved in bullying.

Bystanders—students who witness bullying—also experience negative effects such as:

- Increased risk of depression, anxiety, and other health problems
- Increased risk of absenteeism and truancy issues
- Increased likelihood of alcohol and drug use

The stakes are high. No one wants children to be bullied, yet bullying issues are widespread. The American Psychological Association estimates that 40% to 80% of children experience bullying at some point during their time in school and that 10% to 15% of students either bully or are bullied chronically (Graham, 2014). The National

Association of School Psychologists highlights research that suggests that 70% to 80% of students bully, are bullied, or witness bullying (or some combination of those three roles) at some time during their school careers (Rossen & Cowen, 2012).

So bullying is a problem that affects huge numbers of students and leads to many negative effects. Increased attention and efforts to address bullying are certainly steps in the right direction. However, people tend to bring emotion into the bullying discussion, and this can be counterproductive to bullying prevention and intervention efforts by increasing over-the-top, reactive procedures. Proactive and positive approaches are more likely to create real behavioral change and improve outcomes for all students who are or might be involved in bullying. In this presentation and the next, we take some of the emotion out of the topic of bullying and present practical strategies that can make a difference for many students. We focus on moving schools and their students, staff, and families to a more instructional and solution-based approach to dealing with bullying situations instead of a reactive, emotional, and punitive approach.

Avoid labeling students.

As part of these efforts to increase productive decision making and dialogue around bullying issues, we encourage you to avoid referring to students as *bullies* or *victims*, even in discussions among staff. Research indicates that students are rarely static within one role. Roles may change in different situations and at different times in students' school careers. For example, imagine a popular eighth-grade girl and her seventh-grade sidekick. In their middle school, these two students engage in frequent verbal and relational bullying of sixth- and seventh-grade students. They're supported by a group of eighth-grade girls who also participate in the bullying by spreading rumors and laughing when the two ringleaders bully others.

Now imagine it's the following year, and the eighth graders have all moved on to high school. The younger girl no longer has her friend and the group who put her in the position of power. This girl is now relentlessly bullied, called names, ostracized, and victimized in other ways, mainly by the students she bullied during the previous year. The torment is so bad that eventually she tries to move to a different school district.

Because the girl was labeled a *bully* in seventh grade, she may have been less likely to change her behavior that year because she and others, including school staff, saw her as fixed in that role. In eighth grade, the *bully* label made her less likely to seek and get help when her role shifted to *victim*.

Labeling students as *bullies* and *victims* can be damaging because it fixes students in those roles—others may think, "Once a bully, always a bully," or "Once a victim, always a victim." That kind of thinking can damage the students' and others' perceptions that the students can change their behavior or mature beyond bullying in the future. It also tends to paint a simplistic picture of bullying situations in which they always have single distinct perpetrators and targets. The reality is that bullying situations are often complex interactions that include several students (involved to varying degrees), the school staff, and the general school environment. Interventions should address all of these factors, not just a bully and a victim.

We encourage you to replace the term *bully* with *the student who bullied* or *the student who engaged in bullying behavior* and the term *victim* with *the student who was bullied* or *the student who was targeted*. This practice is similar to other person-first language you're likely already using—for example, *the student with emotional disturbance* rather than *the emotionally disturbed student*, or *the child who stutters* rather than *the stutterer* or *the stuttering child*. You identify the student first, then the characteristic, disability, or behavior.

Avoid overstating the relationship between bullying and violent acts.

Avoid oversimplifying or overstating the relationship between bullying and suicide or bullying and school shootings. Bullying and violent acts have been conflated; heightened media attention to certain catastrophic events in schools has even led to terms like *bullycide*. Although bullying has been a factor or a trigger in some of these catastrophes, a complex mix of factors always contributes to the student's actions. These factors may include:

- Mental health issues, such as depression and anxiety
- Mood disorders or emotional disturbance
- Environmental factors such as access to weapons
- Family support and parenting style, as well as the general home and community environment
- The student's peer and adult support systems
- The conditions and climate of the general school environment

For every student who commits suicide after a bullying incident and for every student who engages in an act of school violence and cites bullying as the cause, countless other students have experienced similar bullying issues without resorting to or even considering these extremes. Oversimplifying the relatively few extreme examples serves only to heighten unproductive emotional responses to bullying problems.

Define bullying behavior and understand the factors that contribute to it.

An essential part of your efforts to address bullying is developing a clear understanding of what bullying is and some of the factors that contribute to bullying situations in schools.

Presentation 4: Analyzing Bullying Behavior, Policies, and School Needs

Bullying is a subset of aggressive behavior. It involves negative or unwanted actions by one or more people directed at another person. These acts are characterized by a marked imbalance of power between the person who perpetrates and the person who is targeted. The acts are repeated or are likely to be repeated over time. Some definitions state that bullying also entails an intent to cause distress or harm, and an unequal display of emotion; for example, the student who bullies experiences either neutral or positive emotions about the events, and the student who is targeted experiences distress. Essentially, bullying has two key features:

- The actions are repeated over time, which means a one-time offense would not be considered bullying (although it should still be addressed if it is serious).

- The actions involve an imbalance of power between the student who bullies and the student who is targeted.

> ### DEFINITION OF BULLYING
>
> *Bullying behavior is aggressive behavior that involves negative or unwanted actions by one or more people directed toward another person.*
>
> *The actions involve a real or perceived imbalance of power between the student or students who bully and the student who is targeted.*
>
> *The actions are repeated or are likely to be repeated over time.*

The imbalance of power distinguishes bullying from conflict. Conflict is back-and-forth aggression between students who have equal status or power. In a bullying situation, one student is in a weaker position, so even if he attempts to defend himself or retaliate after the initial act of aggression, he usually can't gain or regain power. The power imbalance can take many forms.

Physical. A physically stronger student targets someone who is smaller, has less strength, or has a physical disability. Physical strength is often what springs to mind when one thinks of bullying, although the imbalance is usually not *just* physical.

Emotional. For example, a dominant student targets a student who is depressed or anxious, or has other serious emotional stressors.

Social. The student who is targeted has few friends, is disliked by other students, or isn't well connected (such as a student who is new to the school).

Intellectual. The student might be targeted because she gets good grades and is known as a nerd or a geek. Or the targeted student struggles in school and is considered stupid and therefore weak.

Situational. Within a particular context, the student who is targeted is less skilled or in a weaker position for some reason. For example, the student excels in many areas but is terrible at sports, so he is teased relentlessly about his lack of athletic ability.

Both bullying and conflict need to be addressed, but the approaches will differ. For student conflicts, conflict resolution methods such as Stop–Think–Plan (discussed in Presentation 3), peer mediation, and restorative practices can be highly effective, but they are not recommended as bullying prevention strategies. According to the U.S. Department of Education (n.d.), there is *no* research to indicate that conflict resolution and peer mediation are effective with bullying situations—in fact, they can be harmful. A student who was targeted can be victimized again because the procedures assume that both students are equally to blame and need to compromise or meet in the middle to resolve the situation. This is not the case with bullying.

When you're unsure whether a situation is bullying or conflict, err on the side of caution. Don't engage in conflict resolution or peer mediation, but intervene with one of the approaches we describe later in this and the next presentation.

Who bullies?

Traditional depictions of the schoolyard bully include characters like Nelson Muntz from *The Simpsons* and Biff from *Back to the Future*—boys who are bigger and physically stronger than their peers, but not very smart. The stereotypical bully is usually not very attractive and a bit of an outcast or social misfit, but he does lead a gang of slightly subordinate male characters, also social outsiders, who follow him around and reinforce him for his bullying behavior. The stereotypical bully might also have social skill or other deficits and some self-esteem issues. He engages in mostly physical bullying, such as shoving students into their lockers and verbally threatening and intimidating others.

Although our stereotypical description might fit some students who bully, in reality the range of what bullying looks like and who is involved is much broader and more complex. For example, another possible picture of a student who engages in bullying behavior is a student who is highly connected. This student has a variety of friends and many recognizable strengths. He or she is a popular kid who uses power and control to gain status and popularity. Pellegrini, Bartini, and Brooks (1999) found that bullying actually enhanced the status and popularity of students who were transitioning to middle school. While all students were struggling to find their places in the new social hierarchy of middle school, bullying was one clear way to assert oneself in the social order.

So there is no single picture of what a student who bullies looks like. Ensure that your staff, students, and families understand that any child can be involved in bullying as a student who bullies, as a student who is bullied, as a bystander, and as any combination of these three roles.

Understand the forms of bullying.

Everyone also needs to understand that bullying can take many forms:

Physical: pushing, hitting, kicking, physically intimidating, and taking or damaging another student's materials or items, for example.

Verbal: threatening, name calling, teasing, and making inappropriate gestures, for example.

Relational: spreading rumors, excluding others, making friendship conditional, and staring in an intimidating way, for example.

Cyberbullying: using electronic means such as texting, email, social media, and online videos to tease, threaten, call someone names, spread rumors, gossip, and embarrass others.

The four forms can be either direct or indirect.

Direct: physical or verbal acts directed at a student, either in person or via technology. Direct bullying is usually easier to detect because it's more blatant.

Indirect: covert behaviors that occur around a student, such as looks, gossip, and exclusion. Indirect bullying can be very difficult for adults to detect, even with good supervision and monitoring.

In general, direct forms of bullying are more common among younger students, and bullying can start as early as kindergarten. As students get older, physical and more overt forms of bullying tend to be replaced by more covert and indirect forms, such as spreading rumors and cyberbullying. There is often a marked increase in harassment, especially sexual harassment, when students enter high school. Bullying peaks in the middle school years. Research indicates that it's especially problematic in the first year of middle school, which might be sixth or seventh grade, depending on the school. And, while physical bullying tends to be more common with boys and relational bullying more common with girls, all forms are exhibited across gender lines.

What can schools do?

Susan Swearer, a leading researcher and expert on bullying behavior in school, says that there is no bully profile to use to identify the students who are engaging in bullying (American Psychological Association, 2010). She recommends analyzing bullying from a socioecological or sociointeractional perspective. Bullying doesn't occur in isolation. It's the result of complex interactions between the individual student and his or her family, peer group, school community, and societal norms (Espelage & Swearer, 2004). This principle is true for both students who engage in bullying behavior and students who are targeted.

As you analyze how to reduce bullying in your school, it is important to be aware of and consider how you can affect factors at each of these levels: individual student, family, peer group, school community, and society. The following are examples of how schools might intervene at each of these levels if the school identifies specific factors that are contributing to bullying behavior.

Individual students. Conditions such as depression and anxiety can be major factors in whether an individual student is bullied. These mental health concerns can affect the development of friendships, and the presence or absence of friends is also a major factor in whether a student is targeted for bullying. The student's mental health and social situation also affect whether the student has the resiliency to bounce back from bullying problems.

What can schools do if they determine that these factors are playing into bullying problems for students with depression or anxiety? They can:

- Establish schoolwide support systems to help all students develop resiliency, self-confidence, and self-advocacy skills.

- Investigate supports available within the school and community for students with depression and anxiety.

- Ensure that students with internalizing issues are identified and connected with appropriate supports.

- Help individual students who are victimized make friends, engage with the school community, and develop a relationship with a trusted adult who supports them in school.

Here's another example of how a school can make a difference for an individual student. Imagine a student who engages in bullying others and has some conduct problems. The student is prone to anger and lacks anger management and coping skills. The student also struggles with hostile attribution bias—that is, he interprets ambiguous social cues as hostile. For example, if another student accidentally bumps him in the hallway, the student with hostile attribution bias assumes it was an intentional push rather than an accident. His aggression is in part related to his malevolent interpretations of others' unintentional slights. Hostile attribution bias has been found to be a common feature among students who bully or exhibit other aggressive behavior, although it's not present in all students who bully.

The school can provide schoolwide social and emotional training in essential skills such as conflict resolution and stress management and in avoiding thinking errors that may be affecting large numbers of students. For individual students, the school can provide targeted small group and individual training in specific social or coping skills, link students to mental health supports, and provide additional interventions such as mentoring, Meaningful Work, and check and connect. See Module C, Presentation 6 for examples of programs and strategies for meeting students' basic needs.

Families. Inconsistent discipline and monitoring at home and punitive home environments that allow bullying are factors that can contribute to a student's bullying behavior at school. At home and at school, a major factor that influences a student's behavior is whether adults model positive forms of conflict resolution, problem solving, and prosocial skills and behaviors. Schools can do more to increase parents' awareness about parenting styles and skills that will benefit their children. On a schoolwide level, schools can work with families and staff on positive modeling of healthy and productive interactions. With individual families that are struggling, schools can collaborate and build partnerships that allow additional skill-building and parenting management and intervention strategies.

Peer groups and school community. School factors to consider and address include staff indifference and lack of awareness about bullying issues, whether rules and discipline policies effectively address bullying behaviors that occur in the school, and whether staff intervene consistently with bullying issues. Schools should also consider whether poor school engagement and lack of school connectedness among students and staff are contributing to the bullying problems. Poor supervision, unsafe or chaotic climates, and primarily punitive or negative climates are additional factors associated with higher incidences of bullying behaviors.

Society. Students may be receiving messages—consciously or unconsciously—that encourage bullying and other aggressive behavior. Although many people believe there is no clear evidence that violence in movies, TV programs, and video games is related to increased aggression in children, there is strong consensus to the contrary among the public health community. The "Joint Statement on the Impact of Entertainment Violence on Children" (2000) was signed by six of the main health and mental health organizations in the United States: the American Academy of Pediatrics, the American Academy of Child and Adolescent Psychiatry, the American

Psychological Association, American Medical Association, American Academy of Family Physicians, and the American Psychiatric Association.

This joint statement is based on research from well over 1,000 reputable studies that all point overwhelmingly to a connection between media violence and aggressive behavior in some children. The statement explains that when entertainment media showcase violence, particularly in a context that glamorizes or trivializes violence, the lessons learned can be destructive.

Children who see a lot of violence are more likely to view violence as an effective way of settling conflicts, and they are more likely to assume that acts of violence are perfectly acceptable ways to behave. Entertainment violence has also been shown to lead to emotional desensitization, and it decreases the likelihood that a person will take action on behalf of a victim when they witness violence or aggression in real life. In addition, children who are exposed to violent programming at a young age have a greater tendency for violent and aggressive behavior later in life than those who are not exposed (American Academy of Pediatrics, 2000).

This information is especially troubling when we consider statistics indicating that the average American student spends 4.5 hours a day in front of a television—that's a combination of watching TV programming, watching movies, and using a game console. More than 70% of children aged 8 to 18 have a TV in their bedroom (Rideout, Foehr, and Roberts, 2010), so much of this entertainment consumption is probably unsupervised. Another study indicates that the average American child will see 200,000 violent acts and 16,000 murders on TV by age 18 (Senate Committee on the Judiciary, 1999).

What can schools do to counteract some of the negative impact of violent entertainment media? Schools may not be able to change the fact that students will be exposed to violent acts in the media and to aggressive characters they might regard as role models. However, they can make a difference by helping students understand how entertainment is different from reality and by guiding families to information and better practices related to entertainment media. School staff can teach students lessons about the realities of the TV shows, movies, and online videos they are watching and video games they are playing—how they do and do not reflect real life, good role models, effective conflict resolution, and so on.

Schools can help families be aware of the negative impacts of certain forms of entertainment. They can provide options for enforcing limits on viewing and having meaningful discussions with children about the media they are watching. They can suggest to all families that a logical consequence for a student who engages in acts of aggression at school or at home is to lose the privilege of watching violent entertainment or playing violent video games until the student has shown that he or she is responsible enough to handle consuming these forms of entertainment.

CONCLUSION

The preceding brief examples show how schools can tackle issues that contribute to bullying at the individual, family, peer group, school community, and social levels. There are many possibilities for reducing the likelihood that some students bully, that others are targeted, and that the long-term effects of any bullying that does occur will be detrimental. These opportunities for helping students are strongly within the bounds of what a school can reasonably do.

In this presentation's next tasks and in Presentation 5, we move from relatively general information to more specific actions you can take to proactively address bullying in your school. You will learn to identify the factors related to bullying that need to be addressed within your school community. These tasks provide a range of strategies and procedures your school can implement to target your identified priorities for improvement. Each task is presented as a series of questions and considerations your team can use to evaluate whether your school has already addressed the concern, has addressed it somewhat (but additional efforts are still needed), or has not addressed it.

Task 1 Action Steps & Evidence of Implementation

Action Steps	Evidence of Implementation
1. Decide whether any information from this task will be useful for your staff as you embark on your plan for addressing bullying. If so, determine how to communicate the information. You might: • Have all staff read or view the task. • Present a summary of key information during a staff meeting or professional development opportunity. Use the PowerPoint presentation provided in the reproducibles as a starting point. • Prepare written information and distribute it to staff. 2. Determine whether the entire team will read or view the remaining tasks in Presentations 4 and 5 or whether subsets of the team will take on different portions to summarize for the entire team.	Foundations Process: Meeting Minutes, Presentations/ Communications With Staff

TASK 2

Collect data on bullying in your school

In Task 2, we present a series of guided questions that the Foundations Team can use to determine steps for collecting data on bullying. These questions correspond to School-Based Analysis of Bullying Data (Form E-06), which appears in Figure 4a on the next page and can be printed (see Appendix C). You might wish to have a copy of this document to review and make notes on as you work through the task. You (the Foundations Team or bullying prevention task force) will answer each of the questions as the Action Steps for this task.

The task guides your team in collecting initial data to determine the extent of bullying issues in your school and identify specific areas of concern and priorities for improvement. We also discuss several different methods that students, staff, and families might use to report bullying issues, and we explain some straightforward systems your school can use to continually monitor bullying incidents. Data collection is an important first step to making informed decisions about bullying policies and other preventive efforts that will benefit your school.

The items in bold correspond to items on Form E-06 (provided in the reproducibles).

1. **Who will lead your bullying prevention and intervention efforts?**

   The Foundations Team may be in charge of implementing the tasks outlined in Presentations 4 and 5, or you may form a special task force to deal with bullying issues. Your decision will depend in part on the extent of the bullying problem in your school and on how many other priorities the Foundations Team is working on.

   More information about forming and working with special task forces is provided in Module A, Presentation 3, Task 2.

   If you decide to form a task force, be sure that task force members communicate frequently and coordinate schoolwide efforts with the Foundations Team because the bullying prevention initiatives will likely overlap with other school climate and safety efforts. The task force should include representatives from all factions of the school community—administrators, school psychologists and counselors, teachers, and classified staff members. Be sure to include representatives of areas that have considerable problems with bullying. For example, if bullying on school buses is a problem, ask a bus driver or transportation supervisor to join the group. If playground bullying is especially problematic, ask a playground supervisor to lend her expertise. Consider including parents, students,

Presentation 4: Analyzing Bullying Behavior, Policies, and School Needs

Figure 4a *School-Based Analysis of Bullying Data (Form E-06)*

School-Based Analysis of Bullying Data (p. 1 of 2)

Directions: Use the questions below to determine how you will collect data on bullying. (Review Presentation 4, Task 2 before using this form.)

1. Who will lead your bullying prevention and intervention efforts?

2. Does your school collect data on bullying? If so, what data are collected?

3. Do your current data collection methods allow you to analyze (check if Yes):
   - ☐ How much bullying occurs?
   - ☐ Where in the school bullying occurs?
   - ☐ Locations where bullying is most problematic?
   - ☐ Times and activities during which bullying is most likely to occur?
   - ☐ Types of bullying that occur and types that are most prevalent?
   - ☐ Whether students target other students because of certain characteristics—for example, weight, socioeconomic status, or sexual orientation?
   - ☐ Names of students who are most frequently involved, including those who bully, those who are victimized, and bystanders?
   - ☐ How students who are victimized typically respond?
   - ☐ How peers who witness bullying incidents typically respond?
   - ☐ How adults who witness bullying incidents typically respond?
   - ☐ Percentage of bullying incidents that are reported to staff?
   - ☐ Any discrepancies in how staff, students, and families view the bullying problems in your school?

4. Do students, staff, and family members have multiple ways to report bullying incidents and concerns? Describe.

 See Appendix C for printing directions.

Figure 4a (continued)

School-Based Analysis of Bullying Data (p. 2 of 2)

5. Do most initial reports about bullying give you all the information you need to form a fairly clear picture of what occurred?

6. Are minor incidents reported and monitored along with major bullying incidents?

7. How do you monitor bullying incidents across time and analyze trends that may be emerging in the schoolwide data?

8. Does your school have or need other reporting mechanisms? Describe.

9. When will your team analyze schoolwide data from multiple sources and report these data to staff, students, and families?

10. Create a schedule and plan for sharing bullying data with students, staff, and families at regular intervals throughout the year.

Presentation 4: Analyzing Bullying Behavior, Policies, and School Needs

and possibly other community stakeholders in your meetings at times when individual student issues and staff members will not be discussed.

The Foundations Team should already represent the entire staff, but if the team will be handling bullying prevention as a priority, you might want to ask people with firsthand experience with bullying—such as the bus driver and playground supervisor—to join the team for work on this improvement priority.

The team or task force should meet as frequently as needed to keep the momentum of the bullying prevention efforts going and to sustain them over time. The team will conduct bullying assessments and review other schoolwide data sources, work to develop and refine schoolwide policies and rules related to bullying, and train staff, students, and families in these rules and policies. They will also plan other bullying prevention and intervention efforts, such as modifying supervision and structure in problematic locations, creating social-emotional learning lessons and activities, and developing antibullying campaigns and themes throughout the school year.

The team will not address bullying issues with individual students. However, as part of ongoing data management, the team may be in charge of ensuring that multi-tiered systems are in place, identifying individual students who engage in bullying behavior or are targeted, and connecting these students to appropriate supports and interventions in the school. Of course, discussions about such issues should occur when parents and students are not present.

Module F explains in more detail how to develop and sustain Multi-Tiered Systems of Support.

2. **Does your school collect data on bullying? If so, what data are collected?**

Susan Swearer, a leading researcher and author who deals with bullying issues in schools, says that one of the first questions she asks students, parents, and educators who are interested in preventing bullying is this: What are the conditions in the school, family, or community that allow bullying to occur? (American Psychological Association, 2010) The answers to that question tell you the areas you need to address with intervention. For example, school conditions that can contribute to bullying include inadequate supervision, lack of commitment by staff to address bullying behavior, and adults who model bullying behavior in their interactions with each other or with students. Your data should allow you to identify factors that contribute to bullying in your student population.

While one school may need to focus more time and energy on problems with physical bullying, others may need to focus on relational bullying. One school may need to prioritize prevention efforts in the hallways because of ineffective supervision or overcrowding, while another school may identify classrooms as the most problematic locations and so focus on addressing bullying issues there. And in some schools, certain subgroups of students may be targeted at much higher rates than other students. You need to be aware of these kinds of trends in your data as you craft your schoolwide priorities. Collecting data specifically on bullying allows you to perceive and track those trends.

3. **Do your current data collection methods allow you to analyze:**

    - **How much bullying occurs?**
    - **Where in the school bullying occurs ?**
    - **Locations where bullying is most problematic?**
    - **Times and activities during which bullying is most likely to occur?**
    - **Types of bullying that occur and types that are most prevalent?**
    - **Whether students target other students because of certain characteristics—for example, weight, socioeconomic status, or sexual orientation?**
    - **Names of students who are most frequently involved, including those who bully, those who are victimized, and bystanders?**

Examine general percentages schoolwide. For example, what percentage of your students experience no bullying compared with those who are targeted a few times a year, a few times a month, or a few times a week? To reveal trends that may be occurring for students who engage in bullying and students who are targeted, break down the schoolwide data into categories such as grade level; racial and ethnic demographics; socioeconomic status; students who receive special education services; students who identify as gay, lesbian, bisexual, transsexual, or questioning; and students who receive English language services. If you hypothesize that other subgroups of students may be responsible for a lot of bullying or are targeted more frequently, ensure that your data collection methods allow you to analyze data for those categories of students.

Your data collection methods should also allow you to answer the following questions:

- **How do students who are victimized typically respond?**
- **How do peers who witness bullying incidents typically respond?**
- **How do adults who witness bullying incidents typically respond?**
- **What percentage of bullying incidents are reported to staff?**
- **Are there discrepancies in how staff, students, and families view the bullying problem in your school?**

In some schools, for example, staff members think that very few students are targeted frequently, while students indicate that a much higher percentage of students are targeted frequently. To gather this kind of specific information about bullying, you may need to use multiple data collection methods, such as surveys, student self-reports, teacher reports, structured observations, focus groups, and discipline data.

Sometimes your preliminary data collection will indicate that more data are needed to get a clearer picture of what's going on; an additional data collection method is often very useful for this purpose. For example, when a schoolwide survey indicates that the playground is especially problematic, conduct interviews and observations to determine the specific locations where the bullying occurs—the blacktop, field, or play structures, for example. Similarly, multiple methods of data collection can help you identify whether factors such as inadequate or poorly assigned supervision or unclear expectations for students are contributing to your high rates of bullying.

A good way to begin collecting data on bullying is to administer anonymous surveys. You can have all students and staff take them, or use random samplings of students who represent the school's demographics. Students may be more likely to honestly report their involvement in bullying in anonymous surveys than with more personal methods such as focus groups or self-reports, so surveys can yield some of the most useful information. Teacher reports and structured observations probably provide only partial data because much bullying is covert and occurs when adults are not present or actively observing.

Discipline data, while very useful, will also give just a partial picture of the school's problem because most research indicates that only a small portion of bullying incidents are reported to school staff, especially when the school doesn't have effective systems in place to address bullying. Many incidents may not be dealt with through disciplinary procedures that leave a paper trail.

Several questions in the Safe & Civil Schools Climate & Safety Surveys are relevant to bullying—for example, "Does this school have a problem with students bullying other students?" Answers to this question will give you a general sense of the degree to which students perceive that bullying is a problem and whether there are discrepancies in staff, student, and parent perceptions of bullying in the school. The Climate & Safety Surveys can also help you determine how safe students feel in various locations in the school and how respectfully students treat each other in various areas. These responses are indicators of how frequently bullying might occur in these locations. In the survey reports you can drill down to see whether different genders, race/ethnicity groups, and grade levels perceive bullying to be more prevalent. Other Climate & Safety Survey questions that relate to bullying are:

- Does this school have a problem with students physically hurting (e.g., hitting, pushing, grabbing, kicking) other students?"

- Does this school have a problem with students picking on (or teasing in a mean way) other students?
- Is it easy for students to make friends?
- Are student cliques (i.e., students excluding other students) a problem at this school?

The logistics of giving surveys and the Safe & Civil Schools Climate & Safety Surveys are discussed in detail in Module A, Presentation 4, Task 2.

If your school doesn't use the Climate & Safety Surveys, or you need to gather more specific information related to bullying—for example, the responses that students and staff typically give when they witness bullying incidents—consider designing a short supplementary survey that asks questions such as:

When a bullying incident occurs, students who are bullied usually

a. Try to fight back or retaliate
b. Say "Stop"
c. Walk away and ignore it
d. Tell an adult
e. Cry or show they are upset in another way

A question like this can help your team decide whether additional training is needed for all students on how to respond if they are targeted.

Several commercial online bully surveys are available. See http://www.hhpublishing.com/_assessments/BULLY-SURVEY/index.html for information about Susan Swearer's Bully Survey.

Plan to administer surveys a month or two into the school year. Graph the results to create a picture of the scope and nature of the bullying behaviors. At a minimum, review survey data and other data that relate to bullying during your quarterly data reviews. If possible, administer the survey again sometime during the second half of the school year so that you can compare the results with your earlier survey and determine whether your schoolwide efforts are effective and whether you need to reevaluate your priorities for improvement.

Survey results and other bullying data should be used throughout the year to inform staff, students, and parents about bullying issues (include successes as well as areas that need improvement) and to motivate everyone involved in addressing bullying problems in your school.

4. **Do students, staff, and family members have multiple ways to report bullying incidents and concerns? Describe.**

   When there are several options for reporting bullying, more people are likely to report it, giving you a more accurate assessment of the frequency and type of bullying that is occurring. Some examples of reporting methods include:

   - Locked boxes at various locations throughout the school where students can insert written concerns
   - A web forum or online survey that students and parents can complete outside of school
   - An email account that students and parents can write to about bullying concerns
   - Talking directly with staff members

   Ensure that students and family members know they can always talk to staff members about bullying concerns. Frequently remind them who the appropriate staff members are (perhaps it's the counselor or a specific bullying task force member), but also remind students that they can report incidents to *any* staff member. As we mentioned previously, all staff members should make a conscious effort to build relationships with students. Students will be more comfortable reporting incidents and asking for help from staff members they trust and respect.

5. **Do most initial reports about bullying give you all the information you need to form a fairly clear picture of what occurred?**

   This is a good question to ask your administrator and other personnel who process and investigate bullying concerns. It can be frustrating to receive vague and incomplete incident reports such as "Tova was being mean to me" or "An eighth grader is bullying my child on the bus." With these kinds of reports, it's difficult to distinguish between incidents that are serious and need to be addressed immediately and incidents that are minor (or might not even qualify as bullying) and can be addressed when other, more pressing situations are taken care of.

   A standardized reporting form that is more detailed than the typical "describe what happened" form can give you more specific and useful information about incidents. It can also save time and effort for the reporters and the people who compile the data.

   Figure 4b shows a sample Bullying Incident Report (Form E-07). This form allows you to gather specific information about a bullying incident in minimal time. The checklist format makes it easier to fill out and, by guiding the adult's discussion with the reporting student, the form ensures that as much information as possible is collected. The form asks the reporter to tell who was involved in the

Figure 4b Bullying Incident Report (Form E-07)

Bullying Incident Report

Student who was targeted _____ Grade ____ ❑ M ❑ F Report # _____
Person reporting _____ Date _____

Frequency of targeting (with this perpetrator):	Frequency of targeting (with other perpetrators):
❑ First time ❑ Once a week ❑ A few times a year ❑ 2–3 times a week ❑ At least once a month ❑ At least once a day ❑ 2–3 times a month ❑ Multiple times a day	❑ First time ❑ Once a week ❑ A few times a year ❑ 2–3 times a week ❑ At least once a month ❑ At least once a day ❑ 2–3 times a month ❑ Multiple times a day

Student(s) who perpetrated (include grade level and gender) _____
_____

Frequency of reported bullying offenses:	**FOR ADMINISTRATOR USE ONLY**
❑ First time ❑ A few times a year ❑ At least once a month ❑ 2–3 times a month ❑ Once a week ❑ 2–3 times a week ❑ At least once a day ❑ Multiple times a day	Number of reported bullying offenses: _____ Behaviors described: ❑ Same target ❑ Different target

Location of incident

❑ Cafeteria   ❑ Stairway   ❑ Bus   ❑ Bus stop
❑ Hall   ❑ Classroom   ❑ Via email or instant message   ❑ Field
❑ Playground   ❑ Bathroom   ❑ Social media site   ❑ Via text message
❑ Other _____   ❑ En route to school

Activity taking place during incident

❑ Transition   ❑ Teacher-directed activity   ❑ Game   ❑ Lunch
❑ Classroom entry   ❑ Class free time   ❑ Bathroom or drinking fountain break   ❑ Recess
❑ Independent work   ❑ Classroom exit   ❑ Other _____   ❑ Break
❑ Partner or group activity

Behavior

Write a specific description of what happened—words that were said, how many times, etc. Then complete the checkboxes.

_____
_____
_____
_____
_____

1

 See Appendix C for printing directions.

Figure 4b (continued)   Bullying Incident Report (Form E-07)

Physical Aggression	Verbal Aggression
❏ Hit ❏ Pushed ❏ Kicked ❏ Took materials or items ❏ Damaged materials or items ❏ Inappropriate touching ❏ Other _____	❏ Teasing ❏ Threatening ❏ Name calling ❏ Inappropriate gesture ❏ Other _____
Relational Aggression	**Cyber Aggression**
❏ Spreading rumors ❏ Excluding ❏ Intimidating staring or looks ❏ Other _____	❏ Teasing ❏ Threatening ❏ Name calling ❏ Spreading rumors ❏ Other _____

Other Behavior Information

Words or actions expressed harassment or discrimination toward the following:

❏ Racial/Ethnic   ❏ Sexual orientation   ❏ Religious   ❏ Weight
❏ Gender identity/   ❏ Sexuality/Sex   ❏ Disability   ❏ Physical
   Expression   ❏ Other _____   ❏ Ancestral

How did the student who was targeted respond? Check all that apply.

❏ Said, "Please stop."   ❏ Physically fought back   ❏ Cried or visibly upset
❏ Walked away   ❏ Told an adult   ❏ Other _____
❏ Verbally fought back

List names of all peers who were present and near enough to witness or overhear the incident: _____
_____

How did peers respond? Check all that apply. To the right of each checked item write names, if known, of students who engaged in that behavior.

❏ Intervened
    ❏ Told the student who was bullying to stop: _____
    ❏ Told the student who was targeted to come with them: _____
    ❏ Immediately got an adult: _____
    ❏ Verbally fought back: _____
    ❏ Physically fought back: _____
    ❏ Other: _____

❏ Walked away: _____

❏ Watched but did not say or do anything: _____

❏ Watched and gave a positive response to the aggressive behavior
    ❏ Laughed: _____
    ❏ Smiled: _____
    ❏ Other: _____

❏ Joined in: _____

 See Appendix C for printing directions.

Figure 4b (continued)

How did adults who were present respond? Check all that apply. Then write names, if known, to the right of each checked item.

- ❏ Ignored: _____
- ❏ Verbal reprimand: _____
- ❏ Moved student(s) to new location: _____
- ❏ Sent to office: _____
- ❏ Ended the task or activity: _____
- ❏ Other: _____

What was the immediate result for the student who perpetrated the aggressive behavior? Check all that apply.

- ❏ Negative peer attention
- ❏ Positive peer attention
- ❏ Gained adult attention
- ❏ Gained property
- ❏ Gained technology
- ❏ Caused anger
- ❏ Caused fear or pain
- ❏ Removed from task or activity
- ❏ Gained access to activity or game
- ❏ Gained access to social group/peer attention

FOR ADMINISTRATOR USE ONLY

What follow-up measures have been or will be taken with the student who was targeted? Check all that apply, and list dates to the right of each item for when follow-up measures have or will occur.

- ❏ None at this time
- ❏ Phone call to parents
- ❏ Counselor support
- ❏ Referral to Student Support Team
- ❏ Other intervention

FOR ADMINISTRATOR USE ONLY

What follow-up measures have been or will be taken with the student who perpetrated? Check all that apply, and list dates to the right of each item for when follow-up measures have or will occur.

- ❏ None at this time
- ❏ Phone call to parents
- ❏ Staff-assigned consequences:
  _____
  _____
- ❏ Administrator-assigned consequences:
  _____
  _____
- ❏ Police notified
- ❏ Student referred to Student Support Team
- ❏ Review of case scheduled

3

incident and whether the bullying has occurred before. It lists the locations in the school so the reporter can simply check a location like cafeteria, playground, or stairway. You can tailor the locations to your school to get as specific as "third/fourth-grade girls' restroom" or "first-floor west hallway." The form prompts the reporter to indicate the activity that was taking place during the incident, the specific behaviors that occurred within the four bullying categories, and whether the words or actions expressed any discrimination against the student who was targeted. The form also allows you to gather information about the responses of the student who was targeted.

In the last section of the checklist, administrators or staff who investigate bullying incidents record the follow-up measures taken and the dates, both for the student who was targeted and the student who bullied.

One benefit of a standardized reporting form is that all staff can use it to record not only major incidents, but also minor bullying incidents that do not rise to the level of an office disciplinary referral but do need to be recorded and monitored. Minor as well as major incidents need to be noticed and addressed because they can severely affect the school climate and students' sense of well-being. This information leads us to the next question.

6. **Are minor incidents reported and monitored along with major bullying incidents?**

   Are Level 2 notifications, not just Level 3 incidents, being recorded so that you can identify bullying problems in your school before they become severe? Level 2 notifications are essentially expressions of staff concern about situations or incidents in which the staff member corrects the misbehavior or address the situation, but also wants administrators or counselors to be aware of the problem. (The three levels of misbehavior are explained in Module D.)

7. **How do you monitor bullying incidents across time and analyze trends that may be emerging in the schoolwide data?**

   Consider whether the method that you're currently using is as clear and efficient as it can be and whether it allows you to monitor both minor and major bullying incidents.

   An example of how you might monitor all schoolwide bullying incidents over time is the Schoolwide Bullying Incident Log (Form E-08), shown in Figure 4c. An Excel spreadsheet, the log corresponds to information gathered on the Bullying Incident Report (Form E-07), making it easy to monitor and analyze data over time, across incidents, and for your entire school, a feat that is notoriously difficult with bullying issues.

Figure 4c Schoolwide Bullying Incident Log (E-08)

Rpt#	Date	Time	Targeted Student	M/F	Grade	Single or Multiple Offender	Location	Activity	Bullying Behavior	Target Group	Target Student Response	Peers Present?	Peer Response	Adults Present?	Adult Response	Immediate Consequence	Target Student Follow-Up
1	10/13/14	10:05 AM	Hill, Devontae McDonald,	M	6	Multiple	Cafeteria	Lunch	Physical	Gender Ident/exprssn	Said "Please stop"	Y	Watched & positive response	Y	Moved student to new location	Removal from Task/Activity	Refer to SS Team
2	10/14/14	12:00 PM	Kevin	F	8	Single	Hall	Transition	Verbal	None	Other	N		N			None
3	10/30/14	9:30 AM	Ravell, Aisha	F	7	Single	Playground	Game	Physical	None	Told an adult	N		N			None
4	11/2/14	12:00 PM	Prince, Julia	F	7	Single	Bus Stop	Other	Cyber	None	Told an adult	N		N			None
5	11/27/14	1:00 PM	John, Lyle Williams,	M	8	Multiple	Hall	Transition	Verbal	Weight	Cried/Visibly upset	Y	Joined in	N		Positive Peer Attn Negative Peer Attn	None
6	12/5/14	2:20 PM	Dorita	F	6	Single	Hall	Break	Verbal	Sexual/Sex	Said "Please stop"	Y	Intervened	N			None
7	12/5/14	11:45 AM	Palmer, Doug Swearingen,	M	8	Single	Stairway	Other	Verbal	None	Walk away	N		N			None
8	12/17/14	9:47 AM	Amy	F	8	Multiple	Playground Social Media	Recess	Physical	None	Cried/Visibly upset	Y	Watched only	Y	Ended task/activity	Removal from Task/Activity	None
9	12/20/14	12:07 PM	Lee, Kai	M	7	Single	Site	Other	Cyber	None	Other	N		N			None
10	1/5/14	10:08 AM	Ravell, Aisha	F	7	Single	Bathroom	Recess	Verbal	None	Told an adult	N		N			None
11	1/9/14	10:52 AM	Chang, Mo	M	7	Single	Cafeteria	Lunch	Physical	None	Physically fought back	N		N			None
12	1/11/14	8:15 AM	Chin, Maureen	F	6	Single	Playground	Break	Verbal	Racial/Ethnic	Verbally fought back	Y	Joined in	N		Positive Peer Attn	None
13	1/20/14	1:39 PM	Wilson, Kit	M	8	Multiple	Bathroom	Break	Physical	Physical	Physically fought back	Y		N			None
14	2/8/14	10:05 AM	Hart, Setsuko	F	8	Single	Hall	Break	Verbal	None	Verbally fought back	N	Watched only	N			None
15	2/19/14	12:00 PM	Frost, David	M	7	Single	Hall	Exiting Class	Verbal	None	Verbally fought back	Y		N			None
16	2/19/14	9:30 AM	Stone, Emma	F	8	Multiple	Stairway	Transition	Relational	None	Cried/Visibly upset	Y	Walked away	N			None
17	2/28/14	12:00 PM	Layman, Ty	M	6	Single	Other	Other	Physical	None	Physically fought back	Y		N			None
18	3/7/14	1:00 PM	Prince, Julia	F	7	Single	Bathroom	Break	Relational	None	Verbally fought back	N		N			None
19	3/10/14	2:20 PM	Atwell, Melvin	M	7	Single	Other	Other Entering Class	Verbal	Physical	Other	N		N			None
20	3/15/14	11:45 AM	Strong, Mark	F	6	Single	Hall	Class	Physical	None	Walk away	N		N			None
21	3/17/14	9:47 AM	Orr, Anthony	M	8	Single	Stairway En Route to	Lunch	Physical	None	Physically fought back	Y	Intervened	N			None
22	4/8/14	12:07 PM	Beck, Tiffany	F	6	Single	School	Other	Cyber	None	Other	N		N			None
23	4/8/14	10:08 AM	Potter, Janie	F	6	Single	Stairway	Transition	Relational	None	Verbally fought back	N		N			None
24	4/8/14	10:52 AM	Beck, Tiffany	F	6	Single	Bus	Other	Cyber	Gender	Cried/Visibly upset	N		N			None
25	4/20/14	8:15 AM	Hill, Devontae	M	6	Multiple	Cafeteria	Lunch	Verbal	Ident/exprssn	Said "Please stop"	Y	Watched only	Y	Sent to office	Adult Attn	None
26	5/11/14	1:39 PM	Downey, Sarah	F	7	Single	Bathroom	Break Class Free	Verbal	None	Told an adult	Y	Watched only	N			Other
27	5/14/14	8:03 AM	Atwell, Melvin Gonzales,	M	7	Single	Classroom	Time	Verbal	Physical	Walk away	N		N			None
28	5/26/14	11:48 AM	Maria	F	8	Multiple	Hall	Break	Verbal	Sexual/Sex	Walk away	Y	Walked away	N			None
29	5/29/14	12:04 PM	Booker, John	M	8	Single	Bus	Other	Cyber	None	Other	N		N			None
30	6/3/14	11:14 AM	Mariota, Ann	F	7	Single	Other En Route to	Other	Cyber	None	Told an adult	Y	Watched only	N			None
31	6/3/14	10:16 AM	Olomu, Layla	F	7	Single	School	Other	Cyber	None	Other	N		N			None
32	6/5/14	1:05 PM	Beck, Tiffany	F	6	Multiple	Playground	Recess	Verbal	None	Cried/Visibly upset	N		N			None
33	6/9/14	3:05 PM	Hill, Devontae	M	6	Multiple	Cafeteria	Lunch	Verbal	None	Verbally fought back	Y	Watched only	Y	Verbal reprimand	Adult Attn	None
34	6/10/14	11:47 AM	Palmer, Dana	F	7	Single	Field	Other	Physical	None	Walk away	N		N			None

This worksheet can help you analyze trends in bullying in your school. Enter information from the Bullying Incident Report (E-07) in the Target Student Data and Offender Data sheets. Use the Charts sheet to analyze the data. Some charts have already been created to get you started. See the Bullying Incident Report Log Instructions document on the CD for more complete instructions on using this worksheet.

The data on this sheet is provided to allow you to see how the spreadsheet works. Select the top cell in any column to sort based on an item within that column. To the right of the sample data is a pie chart that shows the percentage of bullying incidents by type.

This spreadsheet is provided in the reproducible materials.

Presentation 4: Analyzing Bullying Behavior, Policies, and School Needs

Figure 4c (continued)   Schoolwide Bullying Incident Log

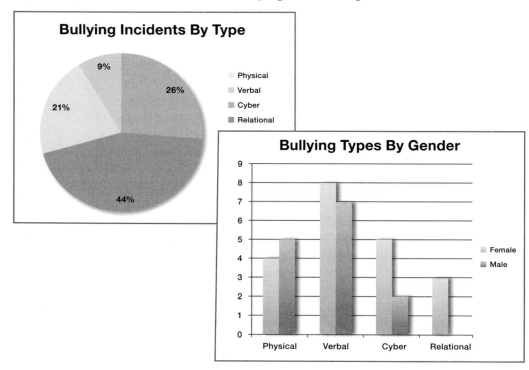

Information about each incident is entered into a row on the spreadsheet. So if the location checked is the cafeteria, select Cafeteria in the Location column. A classified staff member or other person might be assigned to enter all of the bullying incident reports each week into this spreadsheet, or staff might be granted access to a master form online so they can enter their own incident reports each week.

When you meet to review schoolwide data, you can look at trends by sorting, filtering, and graphing data. Detailed instructions for using the spreadsheet to examine schoolwide data are included in the reproducible materials.

For example, you can tabulate and compare the frequency of different bystander responses to determine whether students are being responsible when they witness bullying incidents (walking away, getting an adult, or intervening) or whether they are joining in, smiling and laughing, or watching but not doing anything. If the latter responses occur frequently, consider re-teaching appropriate responses schoolwide with an emphasis on peers' accountability to respond appropriately to bullying.

You can also use this spreadsheet to identify the students who are most frequently involved in bullying as those who bully, those who are targeted, and those who are bystanders. Use this information to connect students with appropriate support and intervention systems within your school.

8. **Does your school have or need other reporting mechanisms? Describe.**

   When someone suspects a student is being bullied or is bullying but isn't sure, how does he or she request follow-up? For example, a school nurse notices that a student frequently asks to be sent home for somatic complaints, although nothing is physically wrong with her. The attendance counselor notices that a student is frequently tardy because he misses the morning bus, and she notices that he avoids getting on the afternoon bus, too. How can these staff members report their suspicions? You should also have reporting mechanisms for teachers and counselors when they have significant concerns about a student's mental health, depression, anxiety, or conduct disorder, so the student can be evaluated and get support. In other words, ensure that staff know who they should report concerns to so that an appropriate staff member will either gather more information or begin some form of intervention.

9. **When will your team analyze schoolwide data from multiple sources and report this data to staff, students, and families?**

   Conduct data reviews quarterly (as we recommend in Module A, Presentation 3). Even if you administer surveys once a year, review those data during each quarterly review to see whether the priorities you identified have been addressed or still need work, and analyze your intervention efforts. Create a schedule for regularly looking at data collected from other sources, especially incident reports, to see if new priorities are emerging.

10. **Create a schedule and plan for sharing bullying data with students, staff, and families at regular intervals throughout the year.**

    You may return to this portion of the School-Based Analysis of Bullying Data to indicate how you plan to share the data after you've read or viewed Presentation 5, Tasks 1, 2, and 3. Those tasks are all about how to train staff, students, and families on bullying issues.

Task 2 Action Steps & Evidence of Implementation

Action Steps	Evidence of Implementation
1. Answer each of the questions on School-Based Analysis of Bullying Data (Form E-06).	Foundations Process: Meeting Minutes
2. If a procedure suggested on the form is not addressed or is not sufficiently covered in your school's current practices, plan to develop the procedure. Proceed through the Improvement Cycle if staff input is necessary.	Foundations Archive: Bullying Prevention

Presentation 4: Analyzing Bullying Behavior, Policies, and School Needs

TASK 3

Define and refine your bullying policy

School antibullying policies are underused tools. In some schools, policies don't fully address the needs of the school, or they're too generic or vague to be truly useful. In others, policies are effectively written but are rarely used by school personnel to guide practices and teach students about how to prevent and, if needed, address bullying. Your school policies should be major mechanisms for providing guidance and protection for your staff and students and for setting the stage for positive changes in the school community. This is especially true for your bullying policies.

This task focuses on defining and refining bullying-related policies within your school to ensure that everyone views your bullying policy as a working, functional document and that it's used frequently to teach and remind staff, students, and families about their roles and responsibilities in preventing bullying. This task also helps you analyze your policy each year in light of your schoolwide data and make changes as needed. When problems clearly emerge in your data, you should explicitly address them in your bullying policy.

We present this task as a series of questions that correspond to School-Based Analysis of Bullying Policies (Form E-09), which appears in Figure 4d. You might wish to have copies of this document and your current bullying and harassment policies to review and make notes on as you work through the task. You (the Foundations Team or bullying prevention task force) will answer each of the questions on the form as the Action Steps for this task.

The numbered items in this task correspond to items on Form E-09 (provided in the reproducibles).

1. **Does your bullying policy meet all state and district requirements for antibullying policies? Does it contain references to federal antidiscrimination and harassment laws?**

   Most states have at least some laws that pertain to bullying, but the requirements within the laws vary widely by state. For example, some states specifically require that policies cover cyberbullying, while others do not. Some states specify the protected classes of students that need to be named in the school's bullying policies, such as race, color, religion, ancestry, sex, sexual orientation, socioeconomic status, and physical appearance, among others.

   Many states have model policies that you can find on your state's Department of Education website or at stopbullying.gov, a federal website managed by the U.S. Department of Health and Human Services. The website has a Policies and Laws

Figure 4d *School-Based Analysis of Bullying Policies (E-09)*

School-Based Analysis of Bullying Policies (p. 1 of 2)

Directions: Use the questions below to determine whether your antibullying policies need to be revised. (Use Presentation 4, Task 3 as a guide while completing this form.)

1. Does your bullying policy meet all state and district requirements for antibullying policies? Does it contain references to federal antidiscrimination and harassment laws?

2. Does your policy include an initial statement or description of expectations for the positive behaviors that students should display?

3. Does your policy include a statement that explicitly prohibits bullying behavior between members of the school community?

4. Does your policy provide a clear definition of bullying behavior?

5. Does the definition of bullying include specific behaviors that may be considered bullying?

6. Does your policy list specific subgroups of students who are likely to be targeted?

7. Does your policy list locations where bullying will be addressed?

8. Does your policy differentiate bullying from conflict?

9. Does your policy address the repetitive nature of bullying offenses?

 See Appendix C for printing directions.

Figure 4d (continued) School-Based Analysis of Bullying Policies (E-09)

School-Based Analysis of Bullying Policies (p. 2 of 2)

10. Does your policy include clear procedures for how bullying incidents are reported and investigated? Does your policy indicate:
    - ☐ How students, staff, and families fill out an incident report?
    - ☐ Who students and families submit reports to?
    - ☐ Who staff members submit reports to?
    - ☐ That staff, students, and families are responsible for reporting bullying incidents that they witness or suspect?
    - ☐ That retaliation in any form against those who report bullying is expressly prohibited and subject to disciplinary action?
    - ☐ That knowingly submitting a false report is prohibited and subject to disciplinary action?
    - ☐ That all reported incidents, including anonymous reports, must be investigated?
    - ☐ Procedures for investigations?

11. Does your policy include the range of possible consequences and interventions for those who perpetrate bullying incidents, retaliate, or make false accusations? Does it include information about available supports for students who are bullied?

12. Does your policy call for the Foundations Team or bullying prevention task force to review schoolwide bullying data and update bullying policies and procedures at least annually?

13. Does your policy describe the school's plan for a comprehensive schoolwide approach to address bullying?

14. Does your policy indicate how the Foundations Team or bullying prevention task force will share and review policy information (at least quarterly) and reference the policies as occasions arise with staff, students, and families?

 See Appendix C for printing directions.

section (broken down by state) where you can learn more about your state's specific antibullying laws and policies.

Go to www.stopbullying.gov/laws/index.html to access information about antibullying laws and policies for each state.

Some of these state-level policies are as bare as one page of vague prohibitions against bullying behavior. Other states provide comprehensive, multistep model policies that cover each of the issues we discuss in this task. If your state's model falls into the bare-bones category, consider reviewing models from some of the other states to see whether any language and procedures are useful for addressing the needs of your school.

As we write this, there are no federal laws that deal specifically with bullying. However, numerous federal laws prohibit discriminatory harassment of protected classes of people. These laws prohibit harassment of students based on their race, color, national origin, sex, disability, or religion. If your school receives federal funding, be sure your antibullying policy refers to these federal laws that relate to harassment because some bullying situations also fit into the category of harassment. When bullying and harassment overlap, federal law requires that schools respond by:

- Providing an immediate and impartial investigation, including written documentation of all actions taken.
- Taking reasonable steps to end harassment and eliminate a hostile environment.
- Working actively to prevent retaliation or recurrence of harassment.
- Communicating with the targeted student or students about the steps the school takes and to make sure no additional harassment has occurred.

If schools do not respond appropriately, they may be found guilty of violating one or more civil rights laws.

Note that numerous court cases have ruled that harassment based on actual or perceived sexual orientation or gender identity may be recognized as a form of sex discrimination under Title IX of the Education Amendments of 1972. It's not acceptable for schools to ignore this kind of sex-based discrimination against lesbian, gay, bisexual, transgender, or questioning (LGBTQ) students, or those who are perceived to be LGBTQ. Ignoring this kind of discrimination is likely a violation of federal law, similar to ignoring race- or disability-based harassment. It violates the right of all students to be in an educational environment where they are safe and treated respectfully.

Presentation 4: Analyzing Bullying Behavior, Policies, and School Needs

The next sections of this task outline features of a comprehensive antibullying policy. Although you still must meet the minimum requirements of your state or district, it may be useful to go beyond minimal requirements and address specific concerns within your school or community.

Each remaining question on School-Based Analysis of Bullying Policies (Form E-09) asks whether your current policy contains a particular feature. If the answer is no, discuss whether including this feature will help clarify your antibullying policy, address specific concerns that occur within your school, and reduce bullying problems. Then determine whether changes to the policy need to be reviewed by the staff or district personnel before they are adopted. Note that if a district Foundations Team is working on refining district-level policies and procedures related to bullying, any recommendations from this task should go to the district or superintendent.

2. **Does your policy include an initial statement or description of expectations for the positive behaviors that students should display?**

   For example, your policy might refer to your Guidelines for Success, mission statement, or staff beliefs. Stopbullying.gov provides the following example of a student bill of rights:

   > Each student at Carver Elementary School has the right to learn in a safe and friendly place, be treated with respect, and receive the help and support of caring adults.

   The state of Washington's model policy includes the following statement in the introduction:

   > This school district strives to provide students with optimal conditions for learning by maintaining a school environment where everyone is treated with respect and no one is physically or emotionally harmed.

   This kind of positive statement keeps the focus on what is expected of all students and members of the school community, and it should be referred to frequently whenever the policies and bullying behavior are addressed.

3. **Does your policy include a statement that explicitly prohibits bullying behavior between members of the school community?**

   After your Guidelines for Success, mission statement, or other statement of positive expectations, include a statement like the following:

   > Therefore, it is a violation of school policy for students to bully others in the school community.

Some policies extend this statement to also prohibit bullying by other members of the school community. The policy might say something like:

> It is a violation of school policy for students or staff to bully others in the school community. This includes student-to-student, student-to-staff, staff-to-student, and staff-to-staff bullying.

One benefit of extending the definition to include the whole school community is that it emphasizes the importance of staff members modeling respectful behavior toward students and each other. Appropriate modeling is essential in creating a safe and respectful school community. If you expand the language of your policy beyond just student-to-student interactions, be sure to adjust the remaining portions of the policy to reflect this change.

4. Does your policy provide a clear definition of bullying behavior?

Despite the wide variety in how states define bullying behavior, most researchers and established practitioners who deal with bullying issues adopt some form of the definition that we recommend in Task 1:

- Bullying behavior is aggressive behavior that involves negative or unwanted actions by one or more people directed toward another person.
- The actions involve a real or perceived imbalance of power between the student or students who bully and the student who is targeted.
- The actions are repeated or are likely to be repeated over time.

Some policies indicate that the behavior must be intentional, but intention can be difficult to determine. Some students engage in bullying behavior because they lack certain social skills and abilities, so their behavior may be based on habit or a lack of understanding and can't really be called intentional. Because the behavior is inappropriate and needs to be addressed, however, it should be included in the antibullying policy.

5. Does the definition of bullying include specific behaviors that may be considered bullying?

The bullying policy should address both direct and indirect forms of bullying. Some policies provide specific examples of behaviors that might be considered bullying. For example, Florida state statutes say that bullying may involve behaviors such as teasing, social exclusion, threats, intimidation, stalking, physical violence, and theft, as well as sexual, religious, and racial harassment. Consider organizing your specific examples within the four types of bullying: physical, verbal, relational, and cyberbullying. For example:

Physical bullying includes, but is not limited to, the following behaviors: hitting, kicking, tripping, pushing, physical posturing, taking items or materials, intimidation, and inappropriate hand gestures.

Then provide similar examples for verbal, relational, and cyberbullying.

Also include in the four categories examples of bullying behaviors that occur with relative frequency in your school. For example, if you have a problem with binder checking (students slam other students' binders to the floor, causing materials to spill), list binder checking under physical bullying.

6. **Does your policy list specific subgroups of students who are likely to be targeted?**

Certain subgroups of students are at higher risk for targeting, including students with mental or physical disabilities, students who are racial or ethnic minorities, students who identify with a certain religion or have shared ancestral characteristics with a religion, students from lower socioeconomic situations or whose family source of income is scorned, and students who are perceived to be LGBTQ, among others.

Listing these subgroups in your antibullying policy emphasizes that targeting students because of these characteristics is expressly prohibited and will be dealt with according to the procedures outlined in the policy. It also emphasizes to staff members that they must intervene when they witness bullying that targets these subgroups, regardless of their own personal views or beliefs. This addition to the policy highlights that everyone deserves to be respected and safe within the school.

The more common a discrimination issue is within your school, the more likely it should be specifically addressed in your antibullying policy. If your school data from surveys and bullying incident reports indicate that, for example, students who are Muslim or Sikh are frequently targeted, update your bullying policy to list these specific groups.

Here's an example of how you might update your policies to address concerns that arise over time. A new reality TV show portrayed Italian American stereotypes, and the show even used the term *guido* in its initial advertisements. Many reputable Italian American groups found this term highly offensive and requested that the show be canceled. The network didn't cancel the show, however, and continued to advertise using the term *guido*. Because the show became quite popular, many students probably use the term *guido* and don't realize that it's offensive to others.

If your school found that students were using this term frequently and that Italian American students were being bullied about their Italian heritage, characteristics, or stereotypes, it would be appropriate to include bullying due to racial or ethnic heritage in your antibullying policy. You might also parenthetically include Italians and Italian Americans with other racial and ethnic groups that are listed as protected. Then you would implement lessons, verbal reprimands, and other efforts to eliminate the use of the term *guido* and associated bullying behaviors among the students.

Another example of how policies need to be updated relative to risk is illustrated through the 2011 National School Climate Survey of students who identify as lesbian, gay, bisexual, or transgender (LGBT). Data from this nationwide survey indicate that almost 90% of students heard the word *gay* used in a negative way frequently or often, 71.3% heard other homophobic remarks frequently or often, and an astonishing 56.9% of students heard homophobic remarks from their teachers and other staff (Kosciw, Greytak, Bartkiewicz, Boesen, and Palmer, 2012). That last statistic is especially troubling. We address this type of concern in Presentation 5, Task 1, where we discuss adult modeling of positive and negative behaviors.

In the 2011 National School Climate Survey, 63.5% of LGBT students indicated that they felt unsafe because of their sexual orientation and 43.9% felt unsafe due to gender expression. Over 80% of LGBT students were verbally harassed and almost 40% were physically harassed because of their sexual orientation (Kosciw et al., 2012). Given that the survey was nationwide in scope, the data probably indicate that bullying due to actual and perceived sexual orientation, gender identity, and conformity to gender and sexual stereotypes is problematic in most schools and should be explicitly listed in a bullying policy. If your data are even remotely similar to these nationwide data for specific subgroups and indicate that students in certain groups experience high rates of bullying, your policy should include language to expressly prohibit targeting of these students.

If your policy does list specific groups to which it applies, also be sure to state that the antibullying policy is not limited to those specific groups so that no one will assume that bullying that doesn't fit within the listed categories won't be addressed.

7. **Does your policy list locations where bullying will be addressed?**

Many policies identify the locations that fall under the jurisdiction of the school—that is, locations where the school will address bullying behaviors according to policy procedures. Common locations include school grounds, any school-sponsored activity, bus stops, and on school transportation vehicles. Consider including bullying that occurs through school-owned technology.

A gray area that you'll need to discuss is bullying that occurs outside of school but creates a hostile environment in school. For example, many cyberbullying incidents take place through texting or social media interactions that are initiated in students' homes during nonschool hours. However, spillover from these acts can drastically interfere with the education of students who are targeted.

You'll need to look at your state and district guidelines to determine whether to include incidents that occur off campus in your policy. An increasing number of states are passing legislation that allows schools to address bullying that occurs off school grounds, especially cyberbullying. Consider your data on off-campus incidents. Are high numbers of incidents being reported? Do these incidents contribute to a hostile climate at school? One possible way to address this situation is to include language like that suggested by Oregon Revised Statue (ORS) 339.351 in your antibullying policy:

> "Harassment, intimidation, or bullying" means any act that (a) substantially interferes with a student's educational benefits, opportunities, or performance; (b) takes place on or immediately adjacent to school grounds, at any school-sponsored activity, on school-provided transportation, or at any official school bus stop; (c) has the effect of (A) physically harming a student or damaging a student's property; (B) knowingly placing a student in reasonable fear of physical harm to the student or damage to the student's property; or (C) creating a hostile educational environment, including interfering with the psychological well-being of a student . . .

Language like this may increase the number of incidents the school needs to address. It can also provide guidance for students about what it means to be part of the school community and provide protections for students that allow you to maintain a safe and respectful environment.

8. Does your policy differentiate bullying from conflict?

Include language and examples in your policy that explain how bullying and conflict are different, with a focus on the imbalance of power. It can also be useful to emphasize that retaliatory behavior (fighting back) by students who are bullied can muddy the waters and make it difficult for school personnel to determine whether they're dealing with bullying or conflict. This distinction can change the nature of intervention.

9. Does your policy address the repetitive nature of bullying offenses?

The policy should differentiate bullying from one-time aggressive offenses. While one-time incidents should be addressed according to their severity, they're not considered bullying unless the behaviors are repeated or are likely to be repeated, such as when the student who bullied has directed similar offenses at other students.

10. **Does your policy include clear procedures for how bullying incidents are reported and investigated?**

    - Does your policy indicate how students, staff, and families fill out an incident report? (Refer to the procedures that you developed in the previous task.)
    - Does your policy indicate who students and families submit reports to? Who staff members submit reports to?
    - Does your policy indicate that staff, students, and families are responsible for reporting bullying incidents that they witness or suspect?

    We recommend that your policy specify that staff members are required to report any incident they witness or hear about—this may be a state requirement. Consider including a statement strongly recommending (but not requiring) that students, families, and community members report all incidents. Reporting bullying is everyone's responsibility to the school community to maintain a safe and respectful environment.

    - Does your policy include a protection clause stating that retaliation in any form against those who report bullying is expressly prohibited and subject to disciplinary action?
    - Does your policy indicate that knowingly submitting a false report is prohibited and subject to disciplinary action?
    - Does your policy indicate that all reported incidents, including anonymous reports, must be investigated? Does it outline the procedure for investigations?

    Items to consider for the investigation portion of your policy include:

    - Reports will be kept confidential and private.
    - Although reports can be made anonymously, students cannot be formally disciplined based solely on an anonymous report.
    - The investigation will proceed in a timely manner, depending on the severity of the incident. A reasonable timeline for each investigation will be developed.
    - Identify who will be in charge of the investigation.

Presentation 4: Analyzing Bullying Behavior, Policies, and School Needs

- Identify the documentation that will be kept on investigative procedures.

- Students will be interviewed individually. The school will never put the student who was bullied and the student who bullied in the same room during investigation procedures or follow-up.

- The school will notify the parents of the student who was targeted and the student who bullied whenever an investigation indicates that bullying occurred.

- Law enforcement will be notified, if appropriate. Provide examples of when this notification might occur.

11. **Does your policy include the range of possible consequences and interventions for those who perpetrate bullying incidents, retaliate, or make false accusations? Does it include information about available supports for students who are bullied?**

Within the range of possible consequences, include minor consequences, such as verbal reprimands, through severe consequences, such as expulsion, for repeated and egregious acts. Also include a range of possible interventions that may reduce bullying, such as anger management training, increased supervision or structure, reinforcement systems for respectful behavior, check and connect, and any other interventions that might apply.

Staff, students, and families need to be aware that purely consequence-based approaches, especially zero-tolerance approaches, are ineffective, according to research. Many studies indicate that zero-tolerance policies actually increase negative outcomes in many cases. Therefore, you should apply appropriate consequences to incidents of bullying behavior, but also take a proactive and positive approach to help students learn more prosocial forms of behavior.

Figure 4e shows a sample document that you might include in your policy to show the range of consequences and interventions for a variety of bullying behaviors and severities. Figure 4f shows a sample statement of how the school will provide a balanced approach of consequences and supports for intervening with bullying behavior. Both documents are available in the reproducible materials.

Figure 4e *Range of consequences and interventions for bullying (E-20)*

FOUNDATIONS SAMPLE

Range of Consequences and Interventions for Bullying

	EXAMPLES OF BULLYING BEHAVIORS	POSSIBLE CONSEQUENCES	POSSIBLE INTERVENTIONS
Level 1 Bullying	Early stages of: • Gossiping • Teasing about possessions, clothes, looks • Calling minor names or making insulting remarks • Dirty looks • Excluding someone from a group • Ignoring • Mild pushing • Taking small items for a short period	• Verbal reprimand • Time owed • Timeout • Conference with teacher • Behavior Improvement Form • Behavior logged on teacher's behavior report form • Call home	Increased observation in problematic environments

Level 2 Bullying	• Level 1 behaviors that persist despite early-stage consequences and interventions
	• Mild and early stages of:
	  ○ Insulting someone's size, intelligence, race, ability, gender, disability, or sexual orientation
	  ○ Threatening physical harm
	  ○ Instigating fights
	  ○ Spitting
	  ○ Pushing or shoving
	  ○ Kicking
	  ○ Punching
	  ○ Defacing property
		One or more of the following:
		• Any Level 1 consequence
		• Notification to principal
		• Parent conference
		• Detention (during lunch or recess, before or after school)
		• Loss of privilege in environment
		• Structured seating and/or choice of activity
		• Response cost
		• Demerits
			One or more of the following:
			• Any Level 1 intervention
			• Lessons on respectful behavior or play
			• Small reinforcement system for respectful behavior or avoidance of bullying behaviors

Level 3 Bullying	• Level 1 and Level 2 behaviors that persist despite early-stage consequences and interventions • Prolonged harassment • Chronic gossip, exclusion, and public humiliation • Destroying personal property or theft • Repeated acts of violence or threats of violence • Major physical assault • Use of a weapon	One or more of the following: • Any Level 1 or Level 2 consequence • Office referral • Conference with principal, teacher, and parent • In-school suspension • Out-of-school suspension (while team creates an intervention plan)	One or more of the following: • Any Level 1 or Level 2 intervention • Referral to Student Study Team • Additional observation and data collection • Behavior Intervention Plan • Anger management training • Increased structure and supervision • Meaningful work • Connections check and connect system • Behavior contracting

 See Appendix C for printing directions.

Presentation 4: Analyzing Bullying Behavior, Policies, and School Needs

Figure 4f *Sample statement regarding a balanced approach to consequences and supports for bullying intervention (E-21)*

FOUNDATIONS SAMPLE

Statement Regarding a Balanced Approach to Consequences and Supports for Bullying Intervention

As part of our efforts to eliminate bullying at _____ school, we would like to educate and inform all members of our school community about the approaches we take to address bullying behavior and the rationale behind these approaches.

We believe that all students have the right to feel safe and respected in the school community. No student has the right to make others feel unsafe or disrespected. Therefore, we implement consequences for bullying behavior as outlined in our school policy.

We also recognize that purely punitive and consequence-driven approaches, such as zero-tolerance policies, have been shown to be ineffective in changing student behavior in the long term. In fact, some research indicates that zero-tolerance approaches may actually reinforce negative behavior. Zero-tolerance policies can result in suspension; students who are not in school lose opportunities for positive social engagement, and their connections with and engagement in school decreases. When students are not in school, school staff cannot intervene with meaningful solutions that can change the students' behavior. In addition, when suspension and expulsion are used as consequences for bullying, some students and staff members will be less likely to report bullying. These negative effects may increase the likelihood that a student will bully others at school.

We address bullying behaviors with a multifaceted approach. We provide:

1. Schoolwide training on responsible, respectful behavior and bullying prevention (for example, how to respond to bullying behavior and how to report bullying behavior).

2. A range of reasonable and consistent responses to bullying behavior that allows the school to match the severity of the consequence to the severity and frequency of the incident. This range includes minor corrections (such as discussion and an immediate timeout from activity), moderate corrections (such as lunchtime detention), and serious corrections (such as in-school suspension and out-of-school suspension).

3. Research-based interventions to increase positive and prosocial behaviors for students who engage in bullying behavior (for example, anger management training, mentoring, and increased supervision and structure).

4. Research-based interventions to provide supports for students who are frequent targets of bullying behavior (for example, increased engagement in school activities, social skills training, and mentoring).

If you are concerned that your student is being bullied or is engaging in bullying behavior, please contact _____ for support and assistance. We look forward to working together to eliminate bullying in our school and create a safe and positive learning environment for all of our children.

_____, Principal

 See Appendix C for printing directions.

The policy should also indicate supports and practices that may be initiated to improve outcomes for students who are victimized, including:

- Advising teachers and other staff to be aware of the bullying issue and provide increased vigilance.

- Increasing positive interactions with the student.

- Providing increased opportunities for friendship development and school engagement.

- Setting up structured check-ins with a supportive adult.

- Assessing mental health for depression and anxiety concerns.

- Referring to other supports and interventions as warranted.

12. **Does your policy call for the Foundations Team or bullying prevention task force to review schoolwide bullying data and update bullying policies and procedures at least annually?**

13. **Does your policy describe the school's plan for a comprehensive schoolwide approach to address bullying?**

    In other words, does your policy go beyond just stating the reporting and investigation procedures? Does it describe how the school will teach respectful behavior; teach staff, students, and families their responsibilities and ways to prevent bullying; and indicate appropriate responses to bullying and other schoolwide approaches? Specific methods for these tasks are discussed in the next presentation, so you may return to this question and update your policy after you've completed the tasks in Presentation 5.

14. **Does your policy indicate how the Foundations Team or bullying prevention task force will share and review policy information (at least quarterly) and reference the policies as occasions arise with staff, students, and families?**

    Again, you may wish to return to this question after completing Presentation 5, Tasks 1, 2, and 3, which are about training staff, students, and families about bullying issues and responsibilities.

Task 3 Action Steps & Evidence of Implementation

Action Steps	Evidence of Implementation
1. Answer each of the questions on School-Based Analysis of Bullying Policies (Form E-09). As you analyze your existing policy and make changes as necessary, follow any district requirements for making policy changes. Have appropriate personnel review and approve policies, if needed. 2. Decide whether some or all of these changes will go through the Improvement Cycle and be formally adopted by staff. By taking the time to make your policies a truly functional document that addresses the concerns and needs of your school, you will create a great resource to ensure that staff, students, and families have the information needed to prevent bullying and respond effectively when it occurs.	Foundations Process: Meeting Minutes, Presentations/ Communications With Staff, Communications With Parents Final policies will be placed in the Foundations Archive: Schoolwide Policies, Bullying Prevention

TASK 4

Analyze bullying data and determine priorities

In this task, you examine your schoolwide data in greater detail to determine priorities for universal prevention. To facilitate this analysis, we ask a series of questions about your schoolwide data and then ask you to identify which of the five STOIC variables or combination of STOIC variables will address problems and concerns revealed in the data. The form STOIC Analysis for Universal Prevention of Bullying (Form E-10) guides you through this task (the form appears in Figure 4g). You might wish to have a copy of this document to review and make notes on as you work through the task. You (the Foundations Team or bullying prevention task force) will answer each of the questions as the Action Steps for this task. Be prepared to spend sufficient time working through each question with the team.

The numbered items in this task correspond to items on Form E-10 (provided in the reproducibles).

Bullying prevention efforts will be most successful if your plan tackles bullying concerns from multiple angles, so to help you develop a comprehensive way to address your concerns, we suggest you analyze data using the STOIC acronym:

S   **Structure for success.**

T   **Teach expectations with clarity.**

O   **Observe and supervise.**

I   **Interact positively.**

C   **Correct fluently.**

Following is a detailed example of how the Foundations Team or bullying prevention task force can manipulate each of the STOIC variables to address a specific bullying concern.

Let's say that the team determines that bullying occurs most frequently in the hallways during transition time. They decide to gather additional information on behavior in the hallways, so they survey a randomly selected group of students. They also conduct a few formal observations of hallway transitions and have some informal discussions with students from different social groups about the hallways. From this information, they learn that most bullying situations occur in two of the hallways. These two hallways are where the oldest students in the school have most of their classes.

Figure 4g *STOIC Analysis for Universal Prevention of Bullying (E-10)*

STOIC Analysis of Universal Prevention of Bullying

Directions: Use the questions below to analyze which STOIC variables you might manipulate to address bullying problems and concerns. (Use Presentation 4, Task 4 as a guide while completing this form.)

1. Does the school have hot spots where more frequent bullying occurs?

2. Do cultural or social constructs contribute to bullying behavior?

3. Does bullying occur more often during specific times or activities?

4. What types of bullying are prevalent—physical, verbal, relational, or cyberbullying?

5. Are specific subgroups of students frequently targeted?

6. Which students most frequently bully? Which students are most frequently victimized?

7. How does each of the following groups respond when bullying occurs: a) students who are victimized, b) students who witness bullying, and c) staff members?

8. Do students report most bullying concerns? If not, can you determine why not?

 See Appendix C for printing directions.

The team discovers several issues that they identify as priorities for improvement:

- These hallways have little adult monitoring and supervision. Most of the teachers remain in their rooms during the transition, and other supervisors are assigned to areas of the school where there have been more overt problems, such as fights.

- The older students act as though they own these two hallways. They expect younger students to use alternate routes. If younger students do pass through these hallways, they're teased, pushed, and bullied. Most younger students are afraid to walk through the hallways, even if taking a longer route means they're late to their next class.

- Students in different grade levels do not mix in this school. Younger students who try to have older friends are accused of being poseurs, and older students are ridiculed when they're seen hanging out with the younger students.

To begin addressing the problem, the team considers the STOIC variables.

Structure: The team realizes that the clustering of students—scheduling most of the upper-grade classes in specific hallways—may contribute to the lack of age and grade mixing and the ownership problem in the hallways. Also, because many of the older students move to nearby classrooms during transitions, they don't need the allotted time to get to their next classes. Instead, they just mill around in the hallway.

The team decides that in the fall they may change the classroom schedule so that each grade has some classes in every hallway. However, this is a fairly major structural change that would be difficult to accomplish midyear, so they decide to try some other ideas for eliminating the bullying problem first.

Teach expectations: The team thinks about how they can teach students more appropriate behavior. They can teach expectations almost immediately, so they create lessons on how all parts of the school belong to everyone, and they plan to teach the lessons to all students.

The lessons explicitly teach that no students own any part of the school and the expectation is that all parts of the school are shared with everyone. They also teach that any students who spread or enforce the message that other students are not welcome in a part of the school will be subject to disciplinary action. Teachers of the older students agree to hold meaningful discussions with their classes about how the older students are the role models in the school and can improve the school climate for everyone.

Observe and monitor: The team decides to increase supervision in these two hallways immediately to ensure that older students are not overtly bullying younger students who attempt to pass through. However, it's difficult to determine whether the younger students are still using alternate routes, so increased supervision won't be enough. So the team creates several short assignments that teachers can give to students throughout the year. The assignments focus on interactions between older and younger students and how they're progressing. For example, when students are working on essays in language arts, they might write about their experiences mixing with students in other grades. Note that this activity fits in the Observe section of STOIC because the team is using an activity to find out more about the situation to help with decision making.

Interact positively: The team also realizes that emphasizing positive interactions is essential. Next fall, they plan to implement a program to increase the older students' accountability and connection to younger students and allow adults to positively reinforce students' efforts to break down the negative social climate. They will set up a peer mentoring system, in which older students will be partnered with younger students as peer buddies. When the school year begins, older students will be responsible for helping their peer buddies transition to classes. They will walk the younger students through the shortest routes, which should break down some of the hallway ownership problems. Adults will reinforce the older students who are mixing with and helping the younger students, and the team will plan peer-buddy activities throughout the school year.

Correct fluently: The team arranges for immediate training for adults on how to supervise carefully and watch for instances of bullying that target younger students in the school. If a student is sending messages of ownership in the hallways, one possible consequence is that he or she will not be allowed to transition in the hallways. Instead, the student must remain in the classroom until an adult can either escort or watch the student transition from one class to the next.

This example highlights how a team can use data to identify areas of concern, learn more about the factors that are contributing to the problem, and then use STOIC to develop a comprehensive plan for prevention and intervention.

There are eight questions on the form STOIC Analysis for Universal Prevention of Bullying (Form E-10). We expand on each question below.

1. **Does the school have hot spots where more frequent bullying occurs?**

    Think about whether you need to gather more specific information about why bullying occurs more frequently in these locations. Consider each STOIC variable, one by one, and whether there is a way to address the problem through the variables.

For example, let's say bullying happens most often in the locker banks. Is Structure a problem? If the locker banks are too close together, maybe spreading them out or moving some to different locations would create better traffic flow and increase the likelihood that you can provide good supervision. Then consider Teaching expectations—how can you teach appropriate behavior for the locker banks and have students practice the behavior? Then Observe. What additional supervision efforts might help? And so on.

2. **Do cultural or social constructs contribute to bullying behavior?**

   This question relates to the example we gave previously about the older students who acted as though they owned the hallways. This sort of social construct can also occur with race, for example, when there are Hispanic/Latino tables, Black/African American tables, and White tables in the cafeteria, and no one dares to sit at the "wrong" table. Social groups might take over certain locations or set social norms. For example, in some schools there is a jock hallway, a skater hallway, and a theater hallway, and students are told to stay out of each other's spaces.

   These kinds of social constructs can be difficult to identify because even with good supervision, students are pretty good at being covert and there may be little visible evidence. Because cultural and social constructs can be cryptic, follow-up focus groups, observations, interviews, and surveys about problem areas can help the team identify factors that may be contributing to the negative social climate.

   Address these kinds of constructs by breaking down each STOIC variable and implementing appropriate changes. For example, explicit teaching about inclusion and accepting diversity, along with activities to help students mix, might break down some of the social constructs.

3. **Does bullying occur more often during specific times or activities?**

   Let's say that bullying occurs most often on the playground, and some follow-up data indicate that a few specific playground games cause most of the problems. Explicit lessons for students on how to behave during these games can help, along with increased supervision and feedback from adults. If the problems with bullying arise because of too many students at recess at the same time, think about structure—can you alter the recess schedule so that only a few grades have recess at the same time?

   A great example of improved structure comes from Oak Grove Elementary School in Medford, Oregon. Oak Grove not only altered their lunch and recess schedules to reduce the number of students on the playground at one time, but they also began a structured recess program. A PE teacher and several classified staff taught students how to play a few whole-group games such as ultimate Frisbee.

Presentation 4: Analyzing Bullying Behavior, Policies, and School Needs

During recess, students are required to pick one of three structured games that the whole group will play. Students who have achieved self-monitor status, which is a reward program for good behavior, have the option to walk around the track or do something else, but all other students are expected to participate in one of the structured games.

What is so brilliant about this program is that all students participate. No one is left out. Because everyone participates, there are very few of the extraneous negative behaviors that you often see on playgrounds. What impressed us even more is that, on the day we observed, several of the classroom teachers came out to play with the students during their lunch periods, just for fun, creating an even better connection between students and staff.

4. **What types of bullying are prevalent? Physical, verbal, relational, or cyberbullying?**

To address this question, think especially about the Teach aspect of STOIC. Increase staff and family awareness about the type or types of bullying that are most prevalent in your school and ask for their help in watching for it, teaching alternate behaviors, and correcting the behavior. Staff and families should also be encouraged to watch for and acknowledge students who are doing the positive opposite of the bullying behavior—for example, they can praise students who keep their hands to themselves in line or recognize when a student makes an effort to include another student who is frequently excluded.

5. **Are specific subgroups of students frequently targeted?**

In general, the more you can create authentic opportunities for students to mix and get to know each another, the less likely students will be to cling to misguided stereotypes and discriminatory beliefs. One school we worked with came up with an authentic mixing strategy that varies the structure of the cafeteria. They created a random seating assignment by directing students to specific tables as they exited the lunch line. The first student was directed to Seat 1 at Table 1, the next student to Seat 1 at Table 2, the next to Seat 1 at Table 3, and so on. This pattern continued through all of the Seat 1s at every table. Then students were directed to the Seat 2s at each table. In this way, students were always randomly seated next to one another, and they got to know many more students outside of their usual social circles. This strategy broke down a lot of the cliquish behavior taking place in the school. This school also periodically provided structured questions and activities for students to engage in with their tablemates.

Another major consideration for addressing the targeting of specific subgroups is whether adults model respectful and positive interactions for the students.

6. **Which students most frequently bully? Which students are most frequently victimized?**

   Ensure that these students are linked with supports and intervention and that the support teams for these students consider STOIC variables when designing intervention plans.

7. **How do each of the following groups respond when they witness bullying?**
   - Students who are victimized
   - Students who witness bullying
   - Staff members

   The main structural consideration for this question is that reporting and investigation procedures are solidly in place. The Foundations Team should then consider providing additional teaching and practice on appropriate responses. Including families in this kind of training would be helpful. Think about training staff members to observe and intervene both positively and correctively for student responses, not just with the student who is perpetrating the bullying.

8. **Do students report most bullying concerns? If not, can you determine why not?**

   Have reporting and investigation procedures broken down? Do students feel that the school's responses to bullying problems are ineffective? If so, why? What STOIC variables can help you address students' perceptions and concerns?

Task 4 Action Steps & Evidence of Implementation

Action Steps	Evidence of Implementation
1. Analyze your school's collected data and answer each of the questions on the form STOIC Analysis for Universal Prevention of Bullying (Form E-10).	Foundations Process: Current Priorities
2. Collect additional follow-up data, if necessary—for example, to find out why a certain area is a hot spot for bullying. You may solicit suggestions from staff, students, and families about what factors the school needs to address.	Foundations Process: Data Summaries
3. Plan to conduct brief analyses and planning during each quarterly data review and apply STOIC analysis to any new areas of concern. Conduct in-depth analyses and planning annually to create a comprehensive plan for the school year.	Foundations Process: Planning Calendar

PRESENTATION FIVE

Schoolwide Bullying Prevention and Intervention

CONTENTS

Task 1: Train Staff to Respond to and Prevent Bullying
For the Foundations Team or bullying prevention task force

Task 2: Help Students Prevent Bullying
For the Foundations Team or bullying prevention task force

Task 3: Partner With Families to Prevent Bullying
For the Foundations Team or bullying prevention task force

Task 4: Actively Engage Students to Prevent Bullying
For the Foundations Team or bullying prevention task force

DOCUMENTS*

- Staff Training in Preventing and Responding to Bullying (E-11)
- Thought Exercise (E-23)
- Staff Training Activity (E-22)
- Student Training in Preventing and Responding to Bullying (E-12)
- Monthly Antibullying Themes and Activities (E-24)
- Lessons on Bullying Prevention
- Family Training in Preventing and Responding to Bullying (E-13)
- Dealing With Technology: Tips and Strategies for Parents (E-25)
- Summary of the Joint Impact Statement on the Impact of Entertainment Violence (E-17)
- Script for Talking With Families About a Student Who Was Victimized (E-26)
- Script for Talking With Families About a Student Who Bullied (E-27)
- Active Engagement for the Prevention of Bullying (E-14)

* See Appendix C for information on accessing these documents.

TASK 1

Train staff to respond to and prevent bullying

A major part of bullying prevention involves equipping staff members with the tools and strategies they need to respond effectively to bullying. In some schools, staff members are unaware that bullying is a problem in the school. They might also be unaware that bullying in general is a problem. This lack of awareness leads to ineffective supports and responses. In other schools, staff members are aware that bullying is a problem in the school, but they feel helpless to stop it because they don't know how to respond. This task helps the team determine how to increase staff awareness of bullying problems, train staff members in appropriate responses to bullying, and provide them with tools for building a positive and inclusive culture and climate that will prevent bullying.

> The numbered items in this task correspond to items on Form E-11 (provided in the reproducibles).

We present the task as a series of questions for the team to answer. These questions correspond to the form Staff Training in Preventing and Responding to Bullying (Form E-11 shown in Figure 5a). You might wish to have a copy of this document to review and annotate as you work through the task. You (the Foundations Team or bullying prevention task force) will answer each of the questions as the Action Steps for this task.

1. **When and how do you plan to get all staff members to commit to addressing bullying issues?**

   Research has shown that when adults respond quickly and consistently to bullying problems, students get the message that the behavior is not acceptable and not how you expect them to behave in school. Over time, quick and consistent responses can reduce or even stop bullying. Research has also shown that when adults think bullying is not a problem—they regard it as a normal part of growing up or they actively ignore incidents—bullying becomes more widespread. That's why it's essential for the team to work to get all staff members on board with addressing bullying within the school.

   Potential approaches to engaging all staff include:

   - Prepare a presentation on the schoolwide data you've collected on bullying. Be sure to highlight any discrepancies between staff and student perceptions of bullying problems.

   - Present research on the prevalence of and outcomes associated with bullying. You might develop a presentation using relevant information from

Figure 5a   *Staff Training in Preventing and Responding to Bullying (E-11)*

Staff Training in Preventing and Responding to Bullying

1. When and how do you plan to get all staff members to commit to addressing bullying issues?

2. When and how will you train staff on the definition of bullying and other major considerations?

3. When and how will you train staff in appropriate immediate responses to bullying incidents?

4. When and how will you train staff in following up after they witness or hear about an incident?

5. Will you provide lessons or training in teaching social-emotional skills that support students involved in bullying incidents? Will you provide lessons or training in addressing common behavioral and social skills deficits that may contribute to bullying issues?

6. When and how will you address positive adult modeling from all staff?

7. When and how will you provide ongoing communication and training about data related to bullying and improvement priorities that are identified throughout the year? When and how will you review bullying topics with staff?

 See Appendix C for printing directions.

Presentation 4, Task 1, which was about understanding bullying issues, or simply show part or all of the video of that task to your staff (or have them read it).

- Prepare activities to help staff members connect with the problem of bullying and identify their own experiences and biases around this issue. Following is a script of a sample scenario that you can share with staff to highlight the problems of bullying (see Sample E-23 in the reproducible materials).

Imagine that you walk into school tomorrow and every staff member you meet ignores you, even when you say hello or try to make small talk. You can see them rolling their eyes whenever you say something. Sometimes, when staff members get together in groups, you can hear them whispering about you in negative ways.

1. *How long could you persist in this environment? A few days? A few weeks? A whole year?*
2. *How would your work be affected?*
3. *What would this climate do to your motivation to come to work and do your best?*
4. *Would you eventually try to move to a different school or even a different career?*

We know of an actual example of a man who, after 20 years as a firefighter, switched careers to become a teacher because he wanted to enter a profession in which he could give even more back to his community. Because he was so passionate and excited about the idea of educating and molding young people, he was willing to take a drastic pay cut and loss of seniority. In his first year as a teacher, he made some decisions that all of the other staff members said they supported initially, but as time went on they gradually blackballed him. Eventually, no one even spoke to or looked at him unless forced to. This once idealistic man became so downhearted and defeated that he decided to quit the profession that he loved because he couldn't stand the negative climate and pervasive bullying that was going on in his school community.

Another activity that can help staff members identify with the issue of bullying is to have each staff member write (anonymously) a personal experience of being victimized, witnessing a bullying incident, or perpetrating a bullying incident. Ask them to include the emotions they felt during and after those experiences: anger, sadness, guilt, frustration, and so on.

Collect these written memories and create a single typed document. At the next staff meeting, use these statements to kindle a staff discussion about the effects of bullying on people who are targets of bullying, who bully, and who witness bullying. Discuss the effects of bullying on all members of the school community and why it's important for your school to work to address bullying. Discuss how even one person choosing to ignore bullying can be detrimental to schoolwide efforts to curb bullying behavior.

Select the strategy or strategies that the team thinks are most likely to reach most staff members. Be sure to connect your bullying prevention efforts with all of your other *Foundations* efforts to improve climate and safety, meet students' basic needs, and so on. All of these efforts are interrelated.

2. **When and how will you train staff on the definition of bullying and other major considerations?**

Ensure that all staff members can explain the key features of bullying, including imbalance of power and repetition. They should be able to describe the four different types of bullying and give some examples of each type. They should also understand how bullying is different from conflict and how methods for intervening with bullying and conflict differ. Conflict resolution and peer mediation may be used to solve conflicts, but they should *not* be used in bullying situations.

It's also useful to train staff members on the risk factors and warning signs of bullying. Staff members should watch for students who show signs of being bullied, such as:

- Students who are socially isolated or become increasingly withdrawn.
- Students who exhibit signs of depression, anxiety, or decreased self-esteem.
- Students who have frequent headaches or stomachaches, complain of feeling sick, or report changes in eating habits or difficulty sleeping.

Review the definition and forms of bullying. (See the box on the next page.)

3. **When and how will you train staff in appropriate immediate responses to bullying incidents?**

Perhaps the most important piece of your staff training involves empowering all staff members to intervene whenever they witness bullying, whether the incident is minor or severe. This is one of the most powerful actions your school can take to reduce bullying problems.

For minor misbehaviors, train staff members to deliver one-liners or short, minor consequences such as 1-minute stand-next-to-me timeouts. If the minor misbehaviors are pervasive and many students exhibit them, prepare a response that all staff members can deliver consistently whenever a student engages in the behavior.

Presentation 5: Schoolwide Bullying Prevention and Intervention

Definition and Forms of Bullying

Definition of Bullying

Bullying behavior is aggressive behavior that involves negative or unwanted actions by one or more people directed toward another person.

The actions involve a real or perceived imbalance of power between the student or students who bully and the student who is targeted.

The actions are repeated or are likely to repeated over time.

Forms of Bullying

Physical: Examples include pushing, hitting, kicking, physically intimidating, and taking or damaging another student's materials or items.

Verbal: Examples include threatening, name calling, teasing, and making inappropriate gestures.

Relational: Spreading rumors, excluding others, making friendship conditional, and staring in an intimidating way.

Cyberbullying: Using electronic means such as texting, emailing, social media, and online videos to tease, threaten, name-call, spread rumors, gossip, and embarrass others.

Here's an example of how correcting minor misbehavior with consistent, quick consequences can make a difference. An inappropriate phrase that used to be common in schools is, "That's so retarded," meaning that something is bad, wrong, or stupid. In many schools, staff members have become much more attuned to the insensitivity of this statement and how it can lead to bullying of students with developmental disabilities, so they've relentlessly corrected students with one-liners such as "That's inappropriate and disrespectful. Please use appropriate language." By delivering directions like this and requiring students to rephrase their language, staff have successfully reduced the use of this phrase in many schools.

However, a new inappropriate phrase has taken the place of "that's so retarded." In many schools, it is very common to hear "that's so gay" as a negative expression. The 2011 National School Climate Survey found that almost 90% of students heard the word *gay* used in a negative way frequently or often (Kosciw, et al., 2012). Many students simply don't realize that this expression is highly offensive, and many staff members don't intervene when they hear it. In fact, research indicates that teachers intervene far less often in response to homophobic remarks than to racist and sexist remarks.

One way to speak to students about this language is to ask, "When you say 'that's so gay,' are you using it in a positive way, like 'that's so great?' Or does it mean something bad, like 'that's so stupid?'" When students reflect on this question, they always indicate that they're saying something is stupid; thus, they are equating *gay* with *stupid*. Imagine if students regularly used expressions such as "that's so Black," "that's so White," "that's so Christian," or "that's so Muslim." These phrases sound ridiculous because in today's society, not many communities regard this kind of derogatory language as acceptable. "That's so gay" should not be acceptable language in school.

One-liners are quick, practiced responses you can use to correct students. One-liners can keep you from becoming sidetracked or emotional. You can say a one-liner quickly as you walk past a student using inappropriate language in the hallway (for example) and you don't have time to stop and discuss the behavior. Examples are: "That's not OK. The expectation is . . ." "That language is not acceptable here at school." "Take a timeout. When I come back, be ready to tell me what you need to do."

Words can hurt. Over 91% of students in the 2011 National School Climate Survey reported that they felt distressed because of derogatory language (Kosciw, et al., 2012). When staff members ignore such language, they send the message that it's OK to bully or discriminate against others. Because all students deserve to be respected and feel safe at school, it is the staff's job to eradicate this kind of discriminatory language.

Let's say your school has identified that a certain phrase, like "that's so gay," is pervasive. What can you do? We suggest that you teach a quick schoolwide lesson on why this language is not acceptable, using some of the information above. Provide alternative, appropriate words or language students can use, and tell students the possible consequences for using the inappropriate language. Then train staff members to intervene every time they hear the inappropriate language. They might say something like, "Remember our discussion about why that language is disrespectful. Stand silently with me for 30 seconds, and then you can tell me a more respectful message."

In addition, teach staff members to begin documenting incidents (they should be doing this with any behavior that occurs repeatedly). The documentation can

Presentation 5: Schoolwide Bullying Prevention and Intervention

consist of a simple tally or a brief bullying incident report. Even if staff don't turn in all of these reports during the early stages of a problem, it's important to keep a record of behaviors that happen repeatedly so that intervention is triggered when early-stage efforts don't stop the behavior.

Teach staff members that the key to improving any behavior, whether it's minor or severe, is to intervene immediately, even when the staff member is not sure how to respond appropriately. The only truly inappropriate response is to ignore the behavior. The response can be as simple as a one-liner or as involved as: "John, that was inappropriate. I'm going to escort you to your class, and I'll let you know by next period what consequences are necessary. I may have to talk to the principal to see what she thinks I should do."

The key to improving any behavior, whether it's minor or severe, is to intervene immediately, even when you are not sure how to respond appropriately. The only truly inappropriate response is to ignore the behavior.

For moderate or severe incidents with witnesses, staff should make a quick mental note of the witnesses' names, if they know them (and record the names later) and inform them that their responsibility is to move away from the incident as soon as possible. With any severe incident, especially one that poses a safety concern, emergency protocols as developed in Module E, Presentation 2, should be followed.

It's also important that staff know that they should not immediately try to sort out the facts of a bullying situation, question the students who are involved, or force an apology. They should escort the student who was perpetrating the incident to one location and tell the other student to go to another safe and private location. When the students are separated and the immediate threat is over, staff can follow established procedures for following up on and reporting the incident.

A sample training activity that can help staff members develop and practice their immediate responses to a variety of bullying situations appears in Figure 5b and is provided in the reproducible materials.

4. **When and how will you train staff in following up after they witness or hear about an incident?**

Train staff members on relevant areas of the school policy for bullying, such as when they are required to report incidents of bullying and the required documentation procedures. Staff members should know what information to gather and who to report to, the range of consequences they might implement, and when to refer an incident to an administrator. For example, you might want minor (Level

Figure 5b Staff training activity (E-22)

FOUNDATIONS SAMPLE

Staff Training Activity: Responding to Bullying

Preparation

Make one copy of the list of scenarios for each small group of four to six teachers. Cut the copies into strips (one scenario to a strip). Put one set of strips into an envelope for each group.

1. Introduce and review information on appropriate responses to bullying, including the following:

   - Deliver one-liner responses for mild and early-stage bullying behaviors (Level 1).
   - Deliver in-environment consequences for mild and moderate bullying behaviors (Levels 1 and 2). Explain the range of possible consequences and interventions that might be given for bullying behaviors at these levels.
   - Respond immediately to severe bullying behavior (Level 3). Explain that all Level 3 bullying behaviors must be referred to the office, review safety procedures, and describe the range of possible consequences and interventions that may be implemented by an administrator.
   - Follow school procedures for documenting chronic and serious bullying behaviors.

2. Have staff members form groups. Give each group an envelope that contains a set of scenario strips.

   a. Have each group sort the strips into Level 1, Level 2, and Level 3 categories.
   b. Have staff discuss and then role-play appropriate responses to the scenarios at each of the levels. For Level 1 and Level 2 scenarios, have them discuss and then role-play how their response would be different for a chronic problem.
   c. Select staff members from each group to role-play appropriate responses to scenarios at each of the levels in front of the whole staff.

Scenarios

- In the hallway, you overhear one student say to another student, "Why would you do that? That's so gay."
- As students are coming back from lunch, you see a student walking and holding his binder. You then see another student slap his hand down on the binder, causing it to fall and scatter papers across the floor.
- One student attempts to sit in a certain place in the cafeteria. Another student shoves her bag into the empty space and says, "You can't sit here. Only the popular kids sit at this table."
- You pass two students and overhear one say to the other, "Nobody likes you. We all wish you would just curl up and die."

 See Appendix C for printing directions.

Figure 5b (continued)   *Staff training activity (E-22)*

FOUNDATIONS SAMPLE

- Two students are passing notes in your class. When you approach the students and look at the note, you see that one student has written negative remarks about a student in another class. The student is telling her friend that she won't be friends with her anymore if she continues to hang out with the other student.
- You have repeatedly had to intervene with a student who calls another student "Miss Piggy." You have given multiple verbal reprimands and timeouts, but the student persists in calling the other student names.
- During lunch break, you are walking on the track and see a group of students behind the bleachers. As you approach, you see that a student in the middle of the group is being punched repeatedly by another student. The other students are cheering.
- You intercept a text message that was sent during your class. One student texted another that she is going to make life miserable for the other student if that student doesn't become her "slave" and do everything she orders her to do.
- A group of four students whisper racial epithets to another student whenever they pass him. You have caught them doing this twice, but other students have informed you that it happens multiple times each day. Today, you overhear two of them calling the student derogatory names.
- You frequently witness a group of students whispering and pointing at another student. When that student speaks, these students often roll their eyes or make audible sighing noises.
- A student is planning to try out for a sports team at school. You overhear a popular team member saying, "I can't believe you want to try out for the team. You are going to get laughed off the field. Don't waste your time or ours."
- While in the computer lab, you see that a student has posted a sexually explicit photo of another student on social media.
- Several students tell you that a student is pregnant. When you investigate, you find that the student is not pregnant and that the story was fabricated by another student to damage the student's reputation.
- You find out that a student has emailed his friends photographs of another student changing in the locker room. The email included a derogatory title.
- A student is sitting alone in the cafeteria. Another student walks by, tips her milk down the student's collar, and says sarcastically, "Oops, sorry."
- A student enters the classroom with an armful of books. Another student sticks out his foot and trips the student. Other students standing nearby laugh.
- Students are standing in the lunch line. A group of popular, older students bypass the line, shove their way into the front of the line, and laugh when other students complain.

 See Appendix C for printing directions.

1) and moderate (Level 2) incidents documented so that you can evaluate schoolwide data on these bullying behaviors. If so, staff members need to know those procedures as well as the criteria for chronic problems to refer to a counselor, administrator, or other interventionist for individual student concerns.

5. **Will you provide lessons or training in teaching social-emotional skills that support students involved in bullying incidents? Will you provide lessons or training in addressing common behavioral and social skills deficits that may contribute to bullying issues?**

   For example, would resiliency training for students improve their ability to cope with adversity, including bullying? Would anger management training increase students' abilities to cope with feelings of anger and find nonaggressive solutions to problems? Would lessons on friendship skills, empathy, understanding and appreciating diversity, and other efforts to improve peer interactions help increase student connectedness? If you identify any of these teaching efforts as priorities, you'll need to provide training and support for your teachers and other staff members in how to train students, reinforce them for using new skills, and correct behaviors that are incompatible with these skills.

   Several research-based social-emotional curricula and programs are available and might meet the needs of your school. One useful resource for choosing a social-emotional program is the Collaborative for Academic, Social and Emotional Learning (CASEL). The CASEL Guide to Effective Social and Emotional Learning Programs is available at www.casel.org.

6. **When and how will you address positive adult modeling from all staff?**

   The Office of Juvenile Justice, presenting research from the National Center for School Engagement, found that when schools provide a safe learning environment in which adults model positive behavior, they can mitigate the negative effects of bullying (Seeley, Tombari, Bennett, & Dunkle, 2011). Unfortunately, in some schools adults do not consistently model a culture of friendly, respectful, and inclusive interactions. Think back to the example of the staff members who blackballed the new teacher or the fact that 56.9% of lesbian, gay, bisexual, and transgender students have heard homophobic remarks from teachers or other staff (from the National School Climate Survey results we presented in Presentation 4). If the adults in the school do not model positive behaviors, it's unlikely that students will learn to exhibit positive behaviors.

   In light of this information, consider having staff members reflect on the following questions. You might decide to provide additional training or activities on these issues.

Presentation 5: Schoolwide Bullying Prevention and Intervention

- How do staff members talk to students?
- Are staff-student interactions respectful in their tone and message?
- Do all interactions convey respect for all students and all people?
- Do staff members use sarcasm or other negative messages to belittle or humiliate certain students?
- Do staff members coerce or threaten students to get them to behave or comply?

How staff members interact with students when students are behaving inappropriately or breaking the rules is very telling. It's very easy, especially with students who have chronic behavioral issues, to model a tone of anger, frustration, and even disrespect when those are the emotions and behavior that the students are projecting toward staff. But it is important that staff remember that they are the adults in the situation and must act like adults. It's their responsibility to teach students to rise above situations, and being treated badly is not an excuse to lower the standards.

Do adults in your school model this behavior of being the bigger person, being the adult? When a student is not respectful, do staff members maintain their composure and treat the student with respect, even when they must implement a consequence?

Another issue related to modeling is how staff members talk about students. It's natural for staff members to want to vent frustration at times, but venting can be highly unproductive and even damaging.

Example From the Field

I was visiting a school and happened to be standing near the front office. The entries to the nurse's office, the production room, and the front office were clustered fairly close together. I overheard the following conversation between two teachers in the production room:

Teacher 1: I can't believe Jordan hasn't been kicked out of school yet. He makes all of our lives miserable, and he hates it here. Let's just put us all out of our misery and expel him already. You know it's going to happen one day anyway.

Teacher 2: Yeah, I dread third period every day. I just cross my fingers each morning and hope that he's absent that day. Have you noticed that the kids you wish would just stay home are the ones who always come to school?

> As I walked toward the production room a few moments later, I noticed that the door to the nurse's office was open. Three students were seated inside, whispering excitedly to one another. I wondered whether they had overheard the teachers' conversation. I had been standing about 15 feet further away and heard every word the teachers said. Imagine that the three students heard the teachers and told others about the conversation. Not only would this gossip potentially damage Jordan and affect how other students treat him, it would also send a damaging message to students about what's acceptable to say about other people. We tell students as part of the antibullying message that gossip, especially negative gossip, isn't OK, but this overheard conversation completely contradicted our teaching.
> —J.S.

If venting is a problem in your school, remind staff members that although it's very natural to need to vent frustration, it's not appropriate to do so in school. People usually vent not to solve a problem, but rather to make themselves feel better by sharing a mutual dislike or frustration about a student. Collaborating with colleagues to brainstorm ways to solve a problem is great, but if the purpose is just to vent, it's not productive.

When staff members need to vent, they can talk with supportive family members at home or educators from different districts who have no connections to your students. Of course, student names should never be used. Staff need to keep in mind that it's OK to let frustrations out appropriately, but then they should quickly shift to working on solutions.

Here are some additional considerations about adult modeling to discuss with your staff at various times throughout the year:

- Do staff members model caring for all students?
- Do staff members make a conscious effort to express genuine care for the well-being of all students?
- Do staff members go beyond just showing interest in schoolwork—do they strive to learn more about who their students are and what's going on in their lives?
- Do staff members model inclusive and positive interactions with each other, including positive forms of conflict resolution, problem solving, and avoidance of bullying behaviors?
- Do staff members avoid gossip and talking behind each other's backs?
- Do staff members avoid cliquish behavior and exclusion? Do they try to welcome newcomers and get to know one other in positive ways?

All of these examples of positive vs. negative adult modeling can make a huge difference in setting a positive school climate and culture.

7. **When and how will you provide ongoing communication and training about data related to bullying and improvement priorities that are identified throughout the year? When and how will you review bullying topics with staff?**

Remember, addressing bullying is like vacuuming a carpet. You have to keep making vacuuming a priority if you want to keep the carpet clean. To keep bullying prevention near the top of your priority list, work to motivate all staff members. Regularly remind them of their commitment to creating an environment that discourages bullying and responding effectively when bullying behavior does occur.

Task 1 Action Steps & Evidence of Implementation

Action Steps	Evidence of Implementation
1. Complete each question on Staff Training in Preventing and Responding to Bullying (Form E-11).	Foundations Process: Current Priorities
2. Identify topics that your staff needs training on and develop informational presentations on those topics. Create a schedule for presenting them at staff meetings.	Foundations Process: Presentations/Communications With Staff, Planning Calendar

TASK 2

Help students prevent bullying

This task helps the team identify the information about bullying that should be communicated to students. It also covers a range of methods you can use to teach about bullying and infuse antibullying and positive expectations about peer behavior throughout the school year.

We present the task as a series of questions for the team to answer. These questions correspond to the form Student Training in Preventing and Responding to Bullying (Form E-12), which appears in Figure 5c. You might wish to have a copy of this document to review and annotate as you work through the task. You (the Foundations Team or bullying prevention task force) will answer each of the questions as the Action Steps for this task.

The numbered items in this task correspond to items on Form E-12 (provided in the reproducibles).

1. **Does your school use an antibullying curriculum? Does the curriculum address the specific concerns of your school?**

    If your school is using an antibullying curriculum that your school did not create and has not kept up to date, it's probably not as effective as it could be in preventing bullying in your school. Many antibullying implementations are not completely successful because the school purchases a curriculum without evaluating whether it meets the needs of the school and addresses the specific types of bullying taking place within the school community.

    Time is a valuable commodity. You need to spend time teaching students about expected behaviors and social and emotional skills, but that time needs to be used as efficiently as possible. If you have a curriculum but the lessons are too general or don't address the specific issues that occur in your school, work through the lessons to make them more applicable to your school or create lessons tailored to the needs of your students, staff, and families. Use the remaining questions in this task to evaluate your existing curriculum.

    If you don't have a curriculum, review the set of 11 sample lesson plans on bullying that we provide as part of this module. Outlines of the lessons appear at the end of this task (Figure 5e–v), and the outlines, student worksheets, and a sample scripted lesson are provided in the reproducible materials. We think these lessons include information about the important issues that most students need to know and understand. The lessons can serve as a starting point for developing a curriculum that will work for your school. You will likely need to adapt or expand the lessons to address other social-emotional skills that students need

Presentation 5: Schoolwide Bullying Prevention and Intervention

Figure 5c *Student Training in Preventing and Responding to Bullying (E-12)*

Student Training in Preventing and Responding to Bullying

1. Does your school use an antibullying curriculum? Does the curriculum address the specific concerns of your school?

2. How will your school teach students about the definition of bullying, types of bullying behaviors, and potential consequences for bullying?

3. What lessons will your school implement to teach students how to respond in bullying situations, both as a student who is targeted and as a witness or bystander?

4. Does your school have multiple methods for teaching and reminding students about bullying considerations throughout the year?

 See Appendix C for printing directions.

to be successful and the specific bullying concerns in your school. Use the questions in this task to evaluate the lessons and adapt them as needed or to guide the development of your own lessons and other activities.

Outlines of the Lessons on Bullying Prevention appear at the end of this task. The outlines, student worksheets, and one sample scripted lesson are provided in the reproducible materials.

---

2. **How will your school teach students about the definition of bullying, types of bullying behaviors, and potential consequences for bullying?**

   To begin discussing what appropriate and respectful behavior looks and sounds like compared with bullying behavior, use your Guidelines for Success and your school's policy on bullying. Define bullying (see our definition below) and give examples and nonexamples of each of the types of bullying: physical, verbal, relational, and cyberbullying. Provide examples that come from your school's data as well as examples that reflect the age of the students you're working with.

   Provide opportunities for students to discuss and give examples of bullying behaviors they've seen or experienced in the school, why those behaviors might be damaging, and how they can be avoided. Make it clear that bullying is not the same as back-and-forth fighting or back-and-forth teasing among peers. Bullying happens when someone in a position of power targets someone who is weaker. It's usually not a one-time event, but happens repeatedly over time.

   ### DEFINITION OF BULLYING

   Bullying behavior is aggressive behavior that involves negative or unwanted actions by one or more people directed toward another person.

   The actions involve a real or perceived imbalance of power between the student or students who bully and the student who is targeted.

   The actions are repeated or are likely to repeated over time.

   Because the concept of an imbalance of power is somewhat sophisticated, you will likely need to expand on "bullying involves an imbalance of power." Several of the *Foundations* lessons focus on personal power and control, as well as abuses of power. These lessons teach students that a person's position of power can shift depending on the activity and situation, and that a person in a position of power needs to handle the power responsibly.

Whatever method you use to teach students about bullying, be sure they understand that bullying behavior isn't limited to physical power or weakness. Bullying can involve emotion—targeted students might be troubled with depression or anxiety. It can be social—targeted students are socially isolated, shy, or have lower social status. Bullying can also be situational—it occurs just because the situation allows it.

An example of situational bullying comes from my (Jessica's) personal experience. I was pretty good at many things in school, except for activities in PE that involved throwing, kicking, catching, or spiking a ball. I had a tendency to just close my eyes when the ball was coming my way! In these PE and recess activities, I was in a significantly weaker position of power than my peers, so if peers teased or bullied me about my lack of skill, I had difficulty dealing with it. I was pretty competent, socially connected, and well adjusted in other areas of my life, so if someone relentlessly teased me about, say, music, I was able to just laugh because I was confident in my musical abilities. But because of my weaker abilities in PE, this same kind of teasing could have been very harmful.

Encourage your staff to think about similar examples to share. A key feature to keep in mind when teaching students is that they may not always recognize when someone is in a weaker position, so what they think is harmless teasing or a conflict between equals may actually be bullying. Again, this is a fairly sophisticated concept, so you may need to teach additional lessons on skills such as reading another person's social cues and evaluating relationships with others.

Throughout your discussions with students, keep referring back to your Guidelines for Success so you can emphasize that the key to avoiding bullying behaviors is treating all members of the school community with respect and kindness. And be sure students understand that although it is important to know what bullying behavior is, no aggressive or harmful behavior belongs in your school, whether the behavior fits the definition of bullying or not.

Also discuss how to inform students about the range of consequences and interventions that staff may assign based on the severity and frequency of bullying issues. Although you don't want to overstate the issue, students need to understand that bullying is serious and consequences can be serious, too. Be sure to cover possible legal ramifications and provide examples of recent bullying incidents that resulted in legal prosecution.

3. **What lessons will your school implement to teach students how to respond in bullying situations, both as a student who is targeted and as a witness or bystander?**

These lessons should provide explicit instruction and practice opportunities for how students should respond in the moment. What should their immediate response to the bullying situation be, and what should they do afterwards? What are the expectations and procedures for reporting, getting help, and so on?

Foundations Lessons on Bullying Prevention 9 and 10 provide specific information about the best kinds of responses students can give when they are targeted or when they witness a bullying incident. Following are some key points to teach students:

- A student who feels bothered or disrespected by another student's words or actions should look at that student and, in a clear, calm voice, tell him or her to stop. If the student doesn't express that the behavior is unwanted, the other student may not realize it is bothersome. Students should have the opportunity to practice saying confidently, "Please stop" (or another phrase). Stating this request meekly or in a frightened or anxious way may incite further inappropriate behavior from students who want to gain power over that student.

- A practice that may be beneficial in your school is to teach all students a signal phrase such as, "That's bothering me—you need to stop," or "I don't like that. Please stop." Then teach a corresponding lesson on how, when someone says that signal phrase, students need to stop what they're doing without making excuses. Teach students that saying things like "Lighten up" or "Jeez, can't you take a joke?" are not appropriate.

    Signal phrases are useful because they are clear and practiced cues that everyone knows. Students have been explicitly taught how to respond to them, and adults know to watch for them and intervene when necessary.

- Lessons should also include information about what to do if a student asks another student to stop, but the peer continues. Some options include:
    - Walk away and stay away.
    - Get an adult's assistance.
    - Move near or interact with other peers or adults so that the behavior stops.

Teach students explicitly that responses such as fighting back, either verbally or physically, or retaliating by gossiping or trying to get others on your side increase the likelihood that bullying problems will persist. These responses also make it more difficult for the school to sort out bullying situations. When students fight back by any means, staff can't tell whether the situation is conflict or bullying, and staff are legally required to follow up with consequences for all students who violate school rules, even when a student is responding to a bully.

Presentation 5: Schoolwide Bullying Prevention and Intervention

Many students and parents are unaware of these policies, and they get upset thinking that a student was unjustly assigned consequences when she was only defending herself from a bully. Ensure that these types of policies are clarified for staff, students, and parents at the beginning of the school year and are reviewed periodically during the year.

- The sample lessons include information on how to respond to cyberbullying and what students should do when they are bystanders to a bullying situation. For relational bullying and cyberbullying, for example, teach students that spreading gossip or rumors or sharing negative electronic messages, even if they didn't initiate them, is part of the bullying problem. Even if students don't agree with them, spreading negative gossip and messages and drawing attention to them makes the students part of the problem. Overtly teach about the damage that spreading negative gossip causes and teach alternate responses, such as ignoring the message or telling an adult.

- Students should also learn how to document and report cyberbullying issues and any bullying they witness as bystanders. They should know how to fill out a bullying incident report, who to see to report an incident, and any other relevant reporting procedures as determined by the team in Presentation 4, Task 3.

- Students need to understand that one responsibility that comes with being a member of the school community is to make the school a better, safer place by reporting incidents when they see or experience them.

- Include in your lessons the difference between *telling* and *tattling*. Overtly teach that students need to seek help when they observe dangerous or destructive acts; this is social responsibility, not tattling. *Tattling* is telling about other people's actions or words with the goal of getting them in trouble.

4. **Does your school have multiple methods for teaching and reminding students about bullying considerations throughout the year?**

Because your school will likely deliver numerous lessons on bullying and will need to review the concepts throughout the year, you should take multiple approaches to disseminating the information. For example, some lessons might present examples of schoolwide data on bullying and ask for students' help as partners to figure out how to address the concerns that are revealed in the data. Other lessons might include scenarios for discussion and analysis, or scripted and unscripted practice opportunities for students to role-play appropriate behavior and responses to bullying situations.

Also look for opportunities to embed bullying lessons in content-area curricula. An example of how to do this comes from *Bullying Prevention & Intervention: Realistic Strategies for Schools* (Swearer, Espelage, & Napolitano, 2009). In the chapter on using your own resources to combat bullying, there is a multiple-page list of books for students of different ages. These books can be used to increase awareness about bullying issues by embedding discussions within literacy activities. Students could also be assigned to write essays on various antibullying topics, design posters and slogans in art classes, do team-building activities and discussions in PE classes, and so on.

Teachers and other staff members should also be prepared to lead informal discussions about bullying issues, using situations that arise at school or in the media as teachable moments. The school might prepare schoolwide lessons for specific media events or historical anniversaries when it would be logical to discuss bullying.

Emphasize legal consequences. An increasing number of legal cases involve the prosecution of students who engage in bullying behavior, especially bullying behavior linked to a student's suicide or violence at school. For example, felony charges were pressed against a 12-year-old and a 14-year-old who posted abusive messages about a girl. The girl eventually committed suicide in 2013. One of the students even allegedly said, "I know I bullied her and she killed herself, but I don't care." The link to the *Los Angeles Times* article is http://articles.latimes.com/2013/oct/15/nation/la-na-nn-florida-bullying-two-girls-arrested-20131015. This and similar cases could be referenced by the school during discussions about the potentially huge consequences of engaging in bullying behavior. Not only did these girls engage in behavior that triggered a student's suicide, but they became part of a media firestorm. They became known throughout the nation as bullies, and they were arrested and detained. Regardless of the outcome of the case, these students will likely feel the negative effects of the bullying behavior for the rest of their lives.

In many of these cases, the behaviors that led to prosecution are not much different from the bullying behaviors common in the context of the day-to-day adolescent and preadolescent drama of many schools. Students need to realize that if they engage in these behaviors—name calling, abusive messages, or aggressive acts—and the behaviors trigger a catastrophic event such as suicide or school violence, they may even be prosecuted for creating the climate that contributed to the tragic event.

Discuss media concerns. Consider including lessons that explicitly discuss the media that students are exposed to and whether these entertainment forms should guide students' behavioral choices. Teachers might discuss with students the types of television shows, video games, and other entertainment they are viewing and whether these media portray the positive skills and behaviors that the school is advocating. Do they model positive conflict resolution, or is there unnecessary drama, fighting, and violence? Do these media emphasize gossip, rumors, social exclusion, and belittlement, or do they highlight positive, supportive relationships? Teachers can discuss this topic without judging students' viewing choices. They should help students understand that these entertainment forms are simply that—entertainment, not a model of the kind of behavior that will help them be successful in relationships and in life.

Schedule antibullying themes and activities. Throughout the year, schedule antibullying or positive peer relationship themes to keep up the energy and momentum of staff, students, and families. Figure 5d shows a sample list of monthly themes and activities (Sample E-24 in the reproducible materials). For example, during September you might focus on who you are as a community and provide activities that focus on building a strong and supportive school community. Activities might include initial lessons on bullying, exercises to build teams and help students develop a sense of group identity, and lessons on how to be inclusive, respectful, and caring. Choose or create themes that will help eliminate the specific bullying issues, behaviors, and attitudes that are problematic and at the same time help develop the traits, attitudes, and behaviors that you want your students to work on.

Students learn many skills in school. One of the most important is how to interact in social environments in productive and responsible ways. Schools have tremendous opportunities to provide guidance and explicit training to help students learn these important prosocial behaviors. Teaching students about bullying behavior, how to avoid it, and how to respond to it is one of those opportunities.

Task 2 Action Steps & Evidence of Implementation

Action Steps	Evidence of Implementation
1. Complete each of the questions on the form Student Training in Preventing and Responding to Bullying (Form E-12).	Foundations Process: Current Priorities
2. Modify your existing antibullying curriculum or develop a new curriculum based on the suggestions within this task. Develop lessons and plan when and how to teach them to students.	Foundations Archive: Lesson Plans for Bullying Prevention

Figure 5d *Monthly Antibullying Themes and Activities (E-24)*

> FOUNDATIONS SAMPLE
>
> **Monthly Antibullying Themes and Activities**   (p. 1 of 3)
>
> **THEME 1 (September): Who We Are as a Community**
>
> - Hold a Guidelines for Success assembly.
> - Teach lessons on appreciating individuals and the value of a cohesive school community. Lessons can present basic information on respectful social interactions and including others, as well as introductory material on preventing bullying and harassment.
> - Create activities for each class to:
>   - Build teamwork.
>   - Help students develop a sense of group identity.
>   - Celebrate and honor each student (one or two per day) for his or her talent, abilities, and uniqueness.
> - Introduce students to the range of available school activities and clubs.
>
> **Theme 2 (October): We Are Caring**
>
> - Adults award schoolwide reinforcement tickets to students who demonstrate acts of inclusion, empathy, or exceptional caring.
> - Teach lessons that focus on empathy, how acts of caring benefit the individual and the community, and bystander prevention in bullying situations.
> - Create classroom activities such as:
>   - Random Acts of Kindness campaign (each class has an RAK wall to list acts of kindness students witness among their peers).
>   - At the end of each day, have each student identify one caring act that someone did for him or her that day. Have each student identify two acts of caring or kindness he or she will do the following day.
>   - Show videos (from the news or Internet) of acts of kindness and caring to prompt discussion and action steps for students.
>
> **Theme 3 (November): We Can Work Together for Good**
>
> - Each class (or advisory group in secondary schools) identifies a service learning project and works to complete related activities throughout the month (for example, reading or mentoring younger students in the school, connecting with businesses to raise funds for a local charity, creating an activity night for senior citizens at a nearby nursing home, organizing a senior-citizen prom, setting up a community clothing or food drive).
> - Teach lessons on how group power and control can be used for positive *or* destructive purposes. Use examples from history and students' experiences.

 See Appendix C for printing directions.

Figure 5d (continued) *Monthly Antibullying Themes and Activities (E-24)*

FOUNDATIONS SAMPLE

(p. 2 of 3)

Theme 4 (December) We Are Digital Citizens

- Create activities to develop students' awareness of the responsible use of technology and to have them use technology to contribute to the growth and positive outcomes of the community and themselves.
- Possible activities include:
  - Find examples of people who have used technology to enable and empower their communities.
  - Have each class create a digital project to benefit the school or community.

THEME 5 (January): We Rise Above

- Teach lessons and conduct activities that focus on how to "be the bigger person." Provide concrete strategies for choosing the more difficult path of remaining calm and using peaceful means rather than resorting to violence or emotional reactions. Recognize those who choose to be the bigger person.
- Create lessons and activities that draw on historical figures, such as Martin Luther King, Jr., to prompt discussion and reflection.
- Incorporate the concept of resilience as a trait to foster for working through difficult times and rising above pettiness, violence, and deceit.

THEME 6 (February): We Build Each Other Up

- Teach lessons and conduct activities that focus on how members of a positive and productive community interact in ways that support each other rather than bring each other down.
- Classroom teachers deliver a short activity each day in which students compliment someone they do not typically interact with. These activities may require structure from the teacher to get students to talk to each other and learn more about one another.

THEME 7 (March): We Are Strong

- Teach lessons and conduct activities that focus on recognizing and acknowledging personal attributes and strengths. Students reflect on characteristics and behaviors they consider to be personal strengths.
- Include lessons that help students understand how positive self-talk relates to self-criticism. Extend this concept into the idea that the ratio of positive self-talk to critical self-talk should be at least three positive to one critical comment. This strategy can help solidify students' strengths and create a platform for further growth (next month's theme).

 See Appendix C for printing directions.

Figure 5d (continued)

FOUNDATIONS SAMPLE

(p. 3 of 3)

THEME 8 (April): We Grow

- Teach lessons and conduct activities that focus on helping students understand personal growth and how to achieve it in all aspects of their lives. This includes how to get and give feedback to others in ways that aid in growth and productive outcomes. Help students learn to accept things about themselves they cannot or should not have to change and develop a mindset for skills and traits that can benefit from growth.
- Create lessons on *strength-based* growth models as opposed to *deficit-based* efforts to improve. Incorporate concepts from the We Are Strong theme (March) to have students identify how they can capitalize on their strengths to become even stronger.

THEME 9 (May): We Celebrate Our Differences

- This theme honors the positive aspects that diversity and differences bring to our lives. Teach lessons and conduct activities to help students understand that our differences make the world a better place and on how to honor others for their unique characteristics, personalities, and contributions.
- Note that an Internet search on "diversity lessons" will guide you to a wealth of activities and lessons you can use to support this theme.

Figure 5e *Bullying Prevention, Lesson 1 Outline*

Module E, Presentation 5

Lesson Outline
Page 1 of 5

Bullying Prevention
Lesson 1

What Is Bullying?

OBJECTIVES

- Students will define bullying.
- Students will identify examples and non-examples of bullying.
- Students will explain why bullying behavior is unacceptable and should be avoided.

MATERIALS

- Document camera, whiteboard, or interactive whiteboard for recording student responses
- Copy of Bullying Prevention Lesson 1 Student Worksheet for each student

Introduction

1. Review or introduce the following concepts (see Lessons on Increasing Safety and Connectedness in Module E, Presentation 2 for more details):
   - Everyone has rights and responsibilities regarding physical safety at school.
   - Everyone has a right to feel emotionally safe and to feel a sense of purpose and belonging while at school.
   - No one has a right to interfere with anyone else's success in any way, including jeopardizing physical or emotional safety, sense of purpose, or sense of belonging.

2. Have students do a short 5-minute exercise reflecting on a bullying situation they witnessed or were part of sometime during their school years. Give students the option of writing a description or drawing a storyboard of the bullying situation.

3. Introduce the lesson and provide the rationale for why the school is addressing bullying behavior: Bullying disrupts the rights listed above. Everyone has a right to be free from bullying and harassment at school.

© 2014 Ancora Publishing • For use by purchasing school only   *Foundations: A Proactive and Positive Behavior Support System*

 See Appendix C for printing directions.

Figure 5e (continued)

Module E, Presentation 5

Lesson Outline

Page 2 of 5

Bullying Prevention
Lesson 1 • What Is Bullying?

Lesson Body

1. Introduce and display the definition of bullying. Bullying involves:

   - Negative or unwanted actions
   - One or more people directing such actions at another person
   - An imbalance of power
   - Repeated (or likely to be repeated) acts over time

   Have students fill in Item 1 on their worksheet with the bulleted portions of the definition above.

2. Clarify and discuss each part of the definition of bullying.

   a. Bullying involves negative or unwanted actions. Sometimes it is very clear when someone is doing something negative or unwanted to someone else, but sometimes it is not clear. The following lessons will help students learn how to identify when behavior might be considered bullying and how to deal with negative or unwanted actions from others.

   b. Bullying can be one person targeting another person, or it could be several people or a whole group targeting one person.

   c. There must be an imbalance of power. The person who is targeted is in a weaker position of power—physically, emotionally, socially, intellectually, or based on the situation.

   Provide an example for each kind of power imbalance, and have students provide examples of the different kinds of power imbalances. Students may work in pairs or groups to generate examples.

   Physical: One student is a champion martial artist. He threatens a student who is of similar size but has no training in fighting.

   Emotional: One student is confident and doesn't get bothered by anything, and the other student has a lot of anxiety and issues with depression.

   Social: One student is considered very popular and has lots of friends. She convinces other students not to talk to another student who has odd social skills and doesn't really fit in.

   Intellectual: A student who always gets good grades repeatedly makes fun of a student who tries really hard but doesn't do well in school.

   Situational: The stars of one of the sports teams pick on a student in PE who isn't athletically coordinated but is a very good musician.

© 2014 Ancora Publishing • For use by purchasing school only   *Foundations: A Proactive and Positive Behavior Support System*

Figure 5e (continued)   *Bullying Prevention, Lesson 1 Outline*

Module E, Presentation 5

Lesson Outline

Page 3 of 5

Bullying Prevention
Lesson 1 • What Is Bullying?

Explain that sometimes what seems like a back-and-forth interaction or drama is actually bullying because one student is in a significantly weaker position. Later lessons will deal with how to recognize and use personal power to avoid bullying situations.

    d. Actions must be repeated over time, or are likely to be repeated. A one-time event is not usually considered bullying, although serious incidents must still be reported and addressed.

4. Explain that bullying can be physical, verbal, relational, or cyber, emphasizing that it is not just physical bullying that is inappropriate. Provide examples and have students provide examples of bullying situations for each of the four kinds of bullying. Have students list at least three examples for each kind of bullying for Item 2 on their worksheet. For example:

   - **Physical:** pushing, stealing, spitting
   - **Verbal:** calling names, putting someone down, teasing
   - **Relational:** excluding someone, telling others not to be friends with someone, spreading rumors
   - **Cyber:** sharing embarrassing pictures of someone, sending threatening emails or texts, creating a fake account and pretending to be someone else

5. Discuss with students how any of these kinds of bullying can be direct—said or done to the person's face—or indirect—done behind the person's back or occurring around the person but not directly involving him or her. Have students discuss why and how direct and indirect forms are harmful. This is an important discussion because many students do not consider indirect forms as bullying or may not think they are harmful.

6. Explain that some situations are mistaken for bullying when they are actually conflicts or some other kind of aggressive behavior. If two people have equal power in a situation and engage in back-and-forth negative interactions, it is not bullying. It is conflict. Provide examples such as:

   > The leaders of two different popular groups in school dislike each other. They start insulting each other on social media, and each leader gets the students in her group to start insulting and doing mean things to the other leader. One student gets so tired of the situation that she reports to the office that she is being bullied.

   > Two students get into a physical fight during lunch. They have both been calling each other names and egging each other on for days.

© 2014 Ancora Publishing • For use by purchasing school only   *Foundations: A Proactive and Positive Behavior Support System*

 See Appendix C for printing directions.

Figure 5e (continued)

Module E, Presentation 5

Lesson Outline

Page 4 of 5

Bullying Prevention
Lesson 1 • What Is Bullying?

7. Have students share examples of aggressive interactions that may or may not be bullying with partners or small groups, then the whole class. Have students evaluate whether the situation is or is not an example of bullying based on the definition and information discussed in this lesson. Encourage students to consider whether the example they wrote about or drew at the beginning of the lesson truly was or was not an example of bullying.

8. Explain that both bullying and conflict are unacceptable behavior and interfere with students' rights to feel physically and emotionally safe at school. Discuss the following points with students:

   Note: If STP lessons have previously been taught (Module E, Presentation 3), connect the concepts below to these lessons.

   - Recognize that if you are in a situation that seems to be a conflict because there is some back-and-forth to the interaction, but the other person is significantly less powerful than you in one of these ways, it may actually be bullying.

   - If you are in a situation where you feel you are being bullied and you retaliate by fighting back (physically, verbally, or otherwise), it may appear to be a conflict, and you will likely be held accountable as well.

   - If someone does something aggressive one time and it is relatively minor, it is not considered bullying. Tell the person to stop, and then decide whether it is serious enough to report or whether you could wait to see if the person changes his behavior. If it is seriously aggressive (physically dangerous, racial, sexual, or other harassment, etc.), it should be reported immediately, even though it is not technically bullying.

9. Emphasize why it is important that all members of the school work to avoid and eliminate bullying behavior. In partners or small groups, have students discuss and list the harmful effects of bullying for all involved—those who bully, those who are bullied, and bystanders to bullying. Have students record the negative effects on Item 3 of their worksheets.

10. Have students share the effects they listed for Item 3 with the whole class. Provide the additional information that follows. Discuss why the research indicates that students involved in the different roles of bullying are more likely to experience these negative outcomes. Have students add the additional information to Item 3 on their worksheets.

© 2014 Ancora Publishing • For use by purchasing school only

Foundations: A Proactive and Positive Behavior Support System

Figure 5e (continued) Bullying Prevention, Lesson 1 Outline

Module E, Presentation 5

Lesson Outline
Page 5 of 5

Bullying Prevention
Lesson 1 • What Is Bullying?

Note: The following outcomes were taken from a variety of research-based sources, including stopbullying.gov, which is managed by the U.S. Department of Health and Human Services.

- Students who engage in bullying behavior are more likely to abuse alcohol and drugs, get into fights, drop out of school, have criminal convictions, and be abusive as adults.

- Students who are bullied are more likely to experience mental health symptoms such as depression, anxiety, and loss of interest in activities. They are more likely to have health complaints, including sleeping and eating problems. They are also more likely to miss school, have dropping and failing grades and test scores, and eventually drop out.

- Students who are bystanders to bullying are more likely to use tobacco, alcohol, and other drugs. They are more likely to miss or skip school and have mental health problems like depression and anxiety.

Conclusion
Review the key points of this lesson: the definition of bullying, how to distinguish behaviors that would be considered bullying from those that would not, and negative outcomes associated with bullying.

Preview the next lesson:

> The next lesson will help you understand the relationship between bullying and harassment as well as recognize when harassment is occurring.

© 2014 Ancora Publishing • For use by purchasing school only   *Foundations: A Proactive and Positive Behavior Support System*

 See Appendix C for printing directions.

Figure 5f Bullying Prevention, Lesson 1 Student Worksheet

Module E, Presentation 5

Student Worksheet
Page 1 of 1

Bullying Prevention
Lesson 1

Name _____ Class/Teacher _____ Period ____

What Is Bullying

Item 1
Copy the characteristics that define bullying behavior.

Bullying involves:

- _____

- _____

- _____
   This can be physical, emotional, social, intellectual, or based on the situation.

- _____

Item 2
Provide at least three examples of each kind of bullying:

- **Physical:** pushing _____
  _____

- **Verbal:** name calling, _____
  _____

- **Relational:** excluding someone on purpose, _____
  _____

- **Cyber:** sharing embarrassing pictures of someone, _____
  _____

Item 3
List negative school and life effects for individuals involved in bullying:

Students who engage in bullying behavior	Students who are targeted or victimized	Students who are bystanders to bullying

© 2014 Ancora Publishing • For use by purchasing school only   *Foundations: A Proactive and Positive Behavior Support System*

Figure 5g *Bullying Prevention, Lesson 2 Outline (page 1 only)*

Module E, Presentation 5

Lesson Outline
Page 1 of 5

Bullying Prevention
Lesson 2

What Is Harassment?

Note: This sample lesson outline focuses primarily on sexual harassment. Add additional information or use this lesson as a model to create lessons on other forms of harassment that occur in your school, such as harassment based on race, religion, national origin, color, age, or disability.

OBJECTIVES

- Students will describe what harassment and sexual harassment are.
- Students explain why school district personnel have a responsibility to help when harassment occurs.
- Students will identify examples of sexual harassment that might occur in their school.

MATERIALS

- Document camera, whiteboard, or interactive whiteboard for recording student responses
- Copy of Sexual Harassment Fact Sheet and Student Guide to Understanding Sexual Harrassment for each student

Introduction

1. Explain that sometimes bullying behavior also fits into the category of harassment, which is "unwelcome conduct based on a protected class (race, national origin, color, sex, age, disability, religion) that is severe, pervasive, or persistent and creates a hostile environment." (Definition from Stopbullying.gov)

    Students are protected from harassment by federal civil rights and other laws. People who are found to engage in harassment may be guilty of breaking the law.

2. Explain that because harassment can interfere with learning, school personnel have a responsibility to help stop it when it occurs.

Lesson Body

1. Explain the relationship between bullying and harassment. There is some crossover, but not all bullying incidents are harassment and vice versa.

    Sometimes incidents fit into both categories—bullying and harassment. All of the following examples are considered both bullying and harassment:

    - A group of students physically and verbally abuses another student. They use racial epithets and insult the physical characteristics related to the student's race.

© 2014 Ancora Publishing • For use by purchasing school only   *Foundations: A Proactive and Positive Behavior Support System*

 See Appendix C for printing directions.

Figure 5h   Bullying Prevention, Lesson 3 Outline (page 1 only)

Module E, Presentation 5

Lesson Outline

Page 1 of 3

Bullying Prevention
Lesson 3

Personal Power and Control, Part 1

OBJECTIVES

- Students will explain the concept that in different situations or conditions, different people have a disproportionate degree of power. Students will identify types of situations in which power can be disproportionate.

- Students will explain how, if power is abused, it can reduce other people's sense of power and thus reduce their potential for success.

MATERIALS
Document camera, whiteboard, or interactive whiteboard for recording student responses

---

Introduction

1. Provide interactive review of concepts from previous lessons:

   - Everyone has rights and responsibilities regarding physical safety at school.

   - Everyone has a right to be free from bullying and harassment at school.

   - Everyone has a right to feel emotionally safe and have a sense of purpose and belonging while at school.

   - No one has a right to interfere with anyone else's success in any way, including jeopardizing that person's physical or emotional safety, or sense of purpose and belonging.

2. Introduce the lesson and provide the rationale:

   It is important to know how to use personal power and control in responsible ways so as not to reduce other people's sense of power and potential for success. This lesson will help students recognize when they are in a situation with a disproportionate amount of power so they can make decisions to use their power in responsible ways.

© 2014 Ancora Publishing • For use by purchasing school only   *Foundations: A Proactive and Positive Behavior Support System*

Figure 5i   Bullying Prevention, Lesson 4 Outline (page 1 only)

Module E, Presentation 5

Lesson Outline

Page 1 of 3

Bullying Prevention
Lesson 4

Personal Power and Control, Part 2

OBJECTIVES

- Students will describe how power (or superiority or advantage) shifts from one situation to the next.
- Students will give examples of abusing and not abusing power in a variety of situations.

MATERIALS

- Document camera, whiteboard, or interactive whiteboard for recording student responses
- Student Exit Tickets generated at the end of Lesson 3

Introduction

1. Provide interactive review of the following concepts:

   - Bullying behavior involves an imbalance of power. One person is in a stronger position of power than the other person, so negative actions and behaviors carry more serious and negative effects.

   - Power can be disproportionate between people based on physical or emotional strength, social standing, intellectual ability, or the situation. Someone may have more knowledge, skill, experience, or ability in a situation, or a more advantageous or fortunate position (e.g., family income). For simplicity's sake, we refer to all these circumstances as being in a position of power.

   - Power can be abused through violence or harassment, and there can be legal consequences for these kinds of abuses of power.

   - Power can be abused in subtler but still destructive ways, such as insulting, using exclusive vocabulary, bragging, excluding someone, patronizing, or using sarcasm.

   - No one has a right to interfere with anyone else's success in any way, including jeopardizing the person's physical or emotional safety, sense of purpose, or sense of belonging.

2. Introduce the lesson and provide a rationale: Power can and does shift from one situation to the next, so this lesson will help students understand how to avoid abusing power based on their relative position.

© 2014 Ancora Publishing • For use by purchasing school only   *Foundations: A Proactive and Positive Behavior Support System*

 See Appendix C for printing directions.

Figure 5j Bullying Prevention, Lesson 5 Outline (page 1 only)

Module E, Presentation 5

Lesson Outline
Page 1 of 5

Bullying Prevention
Lesson 5

Group Power and Control:
Everyone Shares Responsibility

OBJECTIVES

- Students will identify how being part of a group places one in a position of power.
- Students will explain how group power can be used in positive or negative ways.
- Students will identify ways to responsibly handle group power and control.

MATERIALS

- Document camera, whiteboard, or interactive whiteboard for recording student responses
- Copy of Bullying Prevention Lesson 5 Student Worksheet for each student
- Video or true story of a group of students using a position of power to do something positive (recommended: video from CBS titled "On the Road: Middle School Football Players Execute Life-Changing Play" about the Olivet Eagles football team)
- Chart paper and markers for groups of students

Introduction

1. Review previous concepts about personal power and control:
    - People have disproportionate amounts of power in different situations.
    - Bullying behavior occurs when a person in a stronger position of power exhibits negative or unwanted behavior toward a person in a weaker or subordinate position.
    - Power can be abused through violence or harassment, or it can be abused in subtler ways, such as by spreading rumors, excluding someone, or using sarcasm.

2. Introduce the lesson and provide rationale:

    > In this lesson, we will talk about how being part of a group puts you in a position of power, and with that power comes responsibility. Group power and control can be used for good or bad, and we are going to learn ways to use group power for positive outcomes and avoid being part of negative group behavior.

© 2014 Ancora Publishing • For use by purchasing school only   *Foundations: A Proactive and Positive Behavior Support System*

Figure 5k *Bullying Prevention, Lesson 5 Student Worksheet*

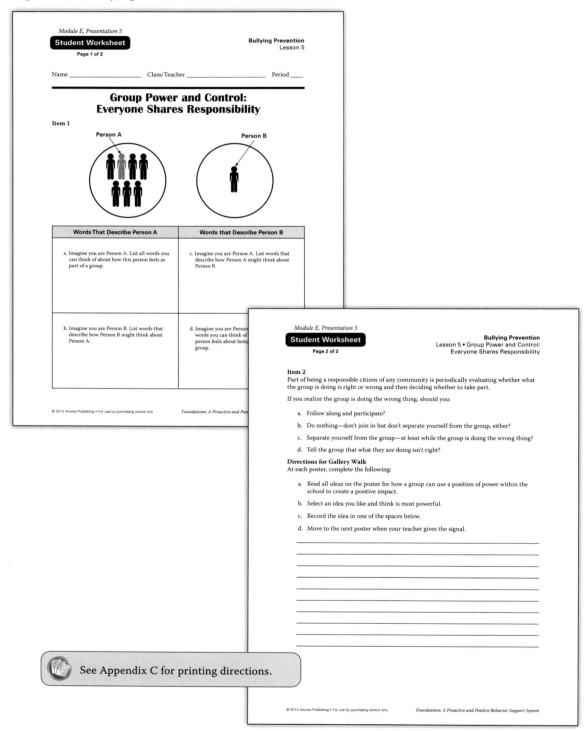

Figure 5l Bullying Prevention, Lesson 6 Outline (page 1 only)

Module E, Presentation 5

Lesson Outline

Page 1 of 4

Bullying Prevention
Lesson 6

Teasing and Destructive Humor Can Be an Abuse of Power

OBJECTIVES

- Students will explain how destructive humor and teasing can be an abuse of power.
- Students will describe and give examples of productive and destructive uses of humor.

MATERIALS

- Document camera, whiteboard, or interactive whiteboard for recording student responses
- (Optional) Video clips from movies or TV that show sarcastic or potentially destructive humor

---

Introduction

1. Provide interactive review of the following concepts:

   - Bullying is distinguished by an imbalance of power. Have students identify different kinds of power imbalances (e.g., physical, emotional. social, intellectual, situational, being a part of a group).

   - People in positions of power must carefully consider how they treat others so as not to abuse their power.

   - When someone is in a position of power, that person has a responsibility to use the power skillfully. That means, among other things, avoiding bragging, showing off, and insulting others. Ask students how else they might use a position of power skillfully—what should they do and what should they avoid?

   - No one has a right to interfere with anyone else's success in any way, including jeopardizing physical safety, emotional safety, sense of purpose, or sense of belonging.

2. Introduce the lesson and provide a rationale: Humor can be a wonderful thing. It can connect us, make us happy, and make us laugh. It can be fun, enjoyable, and respectful. But when humor is not used skillfully, it can be incredibly hurtful and mean spirited.

   Give students a moment to reflect on a time when they or someone else was trying to be funny but what was said or done just came across as hurtful or mean. (You may or may not decide to have students share, without naming names, depending on the

© 2014 Ancora Publishing • For use by purchasing school only   *Foundations: A Proactive and Positive Behavior Support System*

Figure 5m *Bullying Prevention, Lesson 6 Student Worksheet*

Module E, Presentation 5
Student Worksheet
Page 1 of 4

Bullying Prevention
Lesson 6

Name _____ Class/Teacher _____ Period ____

Teasing and Destructive Humor Can Be an Abuse of Power

Item 1

- Productive humor is _____ , enjoyable for all, and _____.
  It brings people closer together.

- Destructive humor is _____ and _____.
  It separates and divides people.

Item 2

Things I don't mind being teased about: _____
_____
_____
_____
_____
_____

Things I prefer not to be teased about: _____
_____
_____
_____
_____
_____

© 2014 Ancora Publishing • For use by purchasing school only   *Foundations: A Proactive and Positive...*

Module E, Presentation 5
Student Worksheet
Page 2 of 4

Bullying Prevention
Lesson 6 • Teasing and Destructive Humor
Can Be an Abuse of Power

Item 3

PRODUCTIVE HUMOR	DESTRUCTIVE HUMOR

Exit Ticket

1. Identify one thing you usually do not mind being teased about.
   _____
   _____
   _____

   a) Why don't you mind? _____
   _____
   _____
   _____
   _____

© 2014 Ancora Publishing • For use by purchasing school only   *Foundations: A Proactive and Positive Behavior Support System*

See Appendix C for printing directions.

Figure 5m (continued)

Module E, Presentation 5
Student Worksheet
Page 3 of 4

Bullying Prevention
Lesson 6 • Teasing and Destructive Humor
Can Be an Abuse of Power

b) Have there been times when you did mind being teased about this thing? Briefly describe the situation.

_____
_____
_____
_____
_____
_____

c) Why did you mind at that time? _____
_____
_____
_____
_____
_____
_____

2. Identify one thing you don't like being teased about.

_____
_____
_____

a) Why do you mind? _____
_____
_____
_____
_____
_____

© 2014 Ancora Publishing • For use by purchasing school only   *Foundations: A Proactive and Pos...*

Module E, Presentation 5
Student Worksheet
Page 4 of 4

Bullying Prevention
Lesson 6 • Teasing and Destructive Humor
Can Be an Abuse of Power

b) Is there anyone who can tease you about this thing and you don't mind? What is your relationship with that person?

_____
_____
_____
_____
_____
_____

c) Why don't you mind being teased by that person? _____
_____
_____
_____
_____
_____
_____

© 2014 Ancora Publishing • For use by purchasing school only   *Foundations: A Proactive and Positive Behavior Support System*

Figure 5n *Bullying Prevention, Lesson 7 Outline (page 1 only)*

Module E, Presentation 5

Lesson Outline

Page 1 of 3

Bullying Prevention
Lesson 7

When You Are on the Receiving Side of an Abuse of Power

OBJECTIVES

- Students will explain how harassment, bullying, and destructive humor can make someone feel inferior only when he or she lets it.
- Students will explain when it is appropriate to get help from an adult for handling an abuse-of-power situation and when to handle such a situation on their own.
- Students will describe strategies for handling abuse-of-power situations on their own.

MATERIALS
Document camera, whiteboard, or interactive whiteboard for recording student responses

---

Introduction

1. Provide interactive review of the following concepts with students:

   - Power can be disproportionate depending on the situation or context.
   - When you are in a position of power, you should handle it skillfully.
   - Teasing and destructive humor can be abuses of power.
   - In this school, no one has the right to interfere with anyone else's feelings of physical or emotional safety.

2. Introduce the lesson and provide the rationale:

   > It can be difficult to know how to handle a situation in which someone else is abusing power. Should you ignore the problem? Should you tell the person to stop? Should you report it? This lesson will help you analyze the situation and make decisions about what to do when you feel you are on the receiving side of someone who is abusing power.

© 2014 Ancora Publishing • For use by purchasing school only   *Foundations: A Proactive and Positive Behavior Support System*

 See Appendix C for printing directions.

Figure 50 Bullying Prevention, Lesson 8 Outline (page 1 only)

Module E, Presentation 5

Lesson Outline
Page 1 of 4

Bullying Prevention
Lesson 8

Giving and Getting Feedback

Note: If this lesson is implemented schoolwide, predetermine a schoolwide signal phrase for students to use when they want someone to stop. For example, select one of the following:

- Please stop doing _____. It is not respectful.
- I don't appreciate it when you _____. Please stop.
- That is not OK with me. Please do not do that again.

If this lesson is not being implemented schoolwide, select a signal phrase for your class and modify the steps below accordingly.

OBJECTIVES

- Students will explain the importance of telling someone to stop when that person is doing something that they don't like.
- Students will explain the importance of listening to and following someone's request to stop.
- Students will demonstrate asking someone to stop and skillful ways of stopping when asked to do so.

MATERIALS
Document camera, whiteboard, or interactive whiteboard for recording student responses

---

Introduction

1. Review concepts from the previous lesson:
   - Skillful ways to respond to an abuse of power when handling it on your own
   - When to report an abuse of power
   - Recognizing that, even though abuses of power may occur, they do not have to make you feel inferior

© 2014 Ancora Publishing • For use by purchasing school only   *Foundations: A Proactive and Positive Behavior Support System*

Figure 5p *Bullying Prevention, Lesson 9a Outline (page 1 only)*

Module E, Presentation 5

Lesson Outline
Page 1 of 3

Bullying Prevention
Lesson 9a

How to Respond if You Are Targeted, Part 1: Responding in the Moment

OBJECTIVES
Students will explain and demonstrate appropriate ways of responding in the moment if they experience a bullying situation.

MATERIALS

- Document camera, whiteboard, or interactive whiteboard for recording student responses
- Chart paper and pens for small groups
- Small exit ticket sheets for each student

Introduction

1. Provide interactive review of concepts from previous lessons:
   - If someone is doing something that bothers you, it is essential that you tell that person, in a safe and respectful way, to stop.
   - If you experience minor or early-stage abuses of power, there are numerous strategies you can use to handle the situation on your own.
   - If there is a major abuse of power, or minor abuse continues after you have tried various strategies, it may be necessary to seek help.
   - Everyone has the right to physical and emotional safety at school.

2. Introduce the lesson and provide the rationale:

   This lesson will prepare you to respond to bullying in the moment in ways that will reduce the likelihood it continues and minimize the harm it could cause you.

Lesson Body

1. Explain that it may be bullying when someone uses the schoolwide signal phrase to tell someone else to stop and that person doesn't stop. When this happens, it is important to continue responding in skillful ways in the moment, and then to report the continued inappropriate behavior.

© 2014 Ancora Publishing • For use by purchasing school only   *Foundations: A Proactive and Positive Behavior Support System*

 See Appendix C for printing directions.

Figure 5q Bullying Prevention, Lesson 9b Outline (page 1 only)

Module E, Presentation 5

Lesson Outline
Page 1 of 4

Bullying Prevention
Lesson 9b

How to Respond if You Are Targeted, Part 2: Document, Get Assistance, and Report

OBJECTIVES

- Students will explain the importance of reporting ongoing abuses of power that may be considered bullying or harassment.
- Students will identify how to document incidents and get assistance in dealing with potential bullying or harassment.
- Students will learn how to make a report.

MATERIALS

Note: In advance of this lesson, get the following information from an administrator:

- Your current schoolwide policies regarding bullying and harassment. Modify steps below as needed.
- Your school's standard documentation forms for bullying and harassment
- Who receives reports on bullying and harassment
- How students request an appointment to report bullying or harassment, and what to do in an emergency situation or severe incident

OTHER MATERIALS

Document camera, whiteboard, or interactive whiteboard for recording student responses

---

Introduction

1. Provide interactive review of the following concepts:

    - In some situations, it may be most effective to skillfully handle an abuse of power on your own.
    - If an abuse of power is serious or ongoing, it is important to use the school's signal phrase to tell the person to stop.

© 2014 Ancora Publishing • For use by purchasing school only   *Foundations: A Proactive and Positive Behavior Support System*

Figure 5r *Bullying Prevention, Lesson 9c Outline (page 1 only)*

Module E, Presentation 5

Lesson Outline
Page 1 of 7

Bullying Prevention
Lesson 9c

How to Respond if You Are Targeted, Part 3: Responding to Cyberbullying

Note: Because of the complexity of this issue, this lesson has more content than other lessons in this module. It may be worth dividing the lesson across two or even three sessions in order to cover the material in enough depth for students to process the information.

OBJECTIVES

- Students will explain why cyberbullying is harmful and unacceptable, and identify behaviors and actions that qualify as cyberbullying.
- Students will explain actions they can take to protect themselves from certain kinds of cyberbullying.
- Students will determine appropriate and inappropriate responses to cyberbullying, both as someone who is targeted and as a bystander.
- Students will explain the steps to document and report cyberbullying when necessary.

MATERIALS

- Document camera, whiteboard, or interactive whiteboard for recording student responses
- In advance of this lesson, find out from your administration if incidents of cyberbullying that occur off school grounds will be addressed through school intervention and consequences. In some states and districts, schools are required to address any incidents that have the effect of creating a hostile educational environment, which includes communication and incidents that take place off school grounds and outside school hours. Even if the school is unable to address such incidents per state or district policy, this lesson should still be taught, but with increased emphasis on the self-protective measures students can take.

Introduction

1. Provide interactive review of the following:

   - The definition of bullying: Bullying involves negative or unwanted actions by one or more people directed at another person. There is an imbalance of power, and acts are repeated over time.
   - Bullying can be physical, verbal, relational, or cyber. All of these forms are equally unacceptable.
   - No one has a right to interfere with anyone else's success in any way, including jeopardizing physical safety, emotional safety, sense of purpose, or sense of belonging.

© 2014 Ancora Publishing • For use by purchasing school only   *Foundations: A Proactive and Positive Behavior Support System*

 See Appendix C for printing directions.

Figure 5s Bullying Prevention, Lesson 9d Outline (page 1 only)

Module E, Presentation 5

Lesson Outline

Page 1 of 5

Bullying Prevention
Lesson 9d

How to Respond if You Are Targeted, Part 4: Ways to Empower Yourself

OBJECTIVES

- Students will identify how their mindset, attitude, and decisions can play a part in whether bullying leads to a positive or a negative outcome.
- Students will identify positive ways of empowering themselves if and when bullying situations occur.

MATERIALS

- Document camera, whiteboard, or interactive whiteboard for recording student responses
- Copy of each outcome scenario (pp. 4–5) for each group.

Introduction

1. Provide the following warm-up activity. Have students identify and write answers to the following on their own:

    a. List two people at school you enjoy being around (staff or students)

    b. List two people outside of school you enjoy being around (family or friends)

    c. List two things at school you enjoy doing

    d. List two things outside of school you enjoy doing

    Note: Try to find time to meet with any students who are unable to think of something for one or more of these categories. For example, if a student indicates that she does not enjoy anything at school, sit down with her to see if there is a way you can help find something she enjoys, like a school job, participation in a school club, etc. If the problem seems significant, discuss with a school counselor or other intervention specialist.

2. Introduce the lesson and provide the rationale:

    > Research indicates that one of the best things you can do when faced with a bullying situation is empower yourself so that the other person doesn't have power over you. The best way to do this is to surround yourself with people you enjoy being around and by doing things you enjoy doing. This lesson will help you identify people and things that will keep you strong and happy, even if you are faced with a bullying situation. It will help you stay out of the victim category, even if you are targeted.

© 2014 Ancora Publishing • For use by purchasing school only   *Foundations: A Proactive and Positive Behavior Support System*

Figure 5t *Bullying Prevention, Lesson 10 Outline (page 1 only)*

Module E, Presentation 5

Lesson Outline
Page 1 of 6

Bullying Prevention
Lesson 10

How to Respond if You Are a Bystander

OBJECTIVES

- Students will identify pros and cons of responses bystanders can make to bullying situations.
- Students will determine which responses contribute to and which can stop or lessen the impact of bullying.
- Students will explain how groups have immense power to make a difference in eliminating bullying.
- Students will identify how they can respond in positive ways if they are bystanders to a variety of bullying situations.

MATERIALS

- Document camera, whiteboard, or interactive whiteboard for recording student responses
- Copy of Bullying Prevention Lesson 10 Student Worksheet for each student

---

Introduction

1. Provide interactive review of the following concepts:
   - Everyone has a right to be a part of the school and to be successful at school.
   - Teasing, harassment, and other abuses of power interfere with a person's ability to be successful at school (i.e., students can't thrive in a place where they do not feel emotionally or physically safe).
   - Everyone in the school has a responsibility to contribute to the safety (physical and emotional) of all others in the school.

2. Introduce the lesson and provide the rationale:

    > Most of the time when bullying occurs, at least one person witnesses the situation. These witnesses, or bystanders, can have great power to either prompt bullying to continue or help stop it. This lesson will help you understand your options for responding if you witness a bullying situation as a bystander. It will help you be socially responsible and do the right thing so that you aren't part of the bullying problem.

© 2014 Ancora Publishing • For use by purchasing school only   *Foundations: A Proactive and Positive Behavior Support System*

 See Appendix C for printing directions.

Figure 5u Bullying Prevention, Lesson 10 Student Worksheet

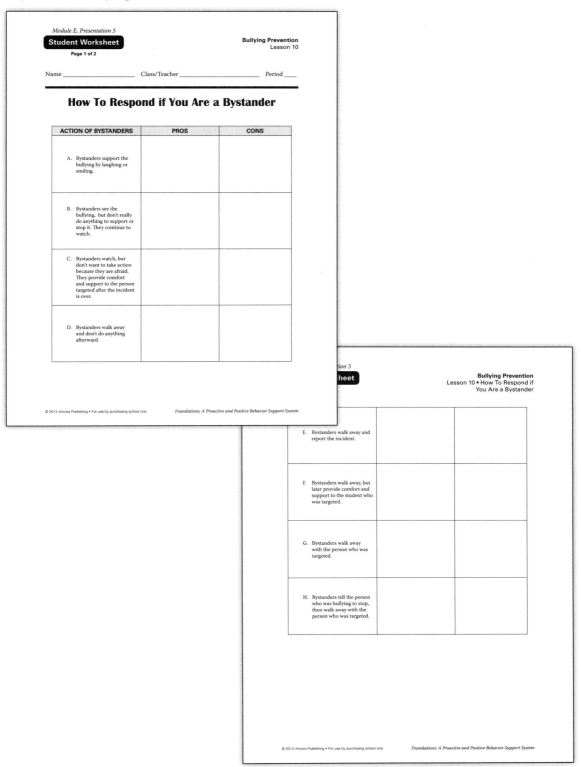

Presentation 5: Schoolwide Bullying Prevention and Intervention

Figure 5v *Bullying Prevention, Lesson 11 Outline (page 1 only)*

Module E, Presentation 5

Lesson Outline
Page 1 of 2

Bullying Prevention
Lesson 11

Potential Long-Term Ramifications— What You Need to Know

Prior to delivering this lesson, review the laws regarding bullying in your state. Some states have laws that directly pertain to bullying and/or cyberbullying, and others do not. See Stopbullying.gov's section on Policies and Laws to learn more about laws in your state.

OBJECTIVES

- Students will identify potential long-term consequences for students who perpetrate bullying or harassment.

- Students will describe the laws that pertain to bullying and harassment and possible legal consequences for participation in illegal acts.

MATERIALS
Document camera, whiteboard, or interactive whiteboard for recording student responses

---

Introduction
Introduce the lesson and provide the rationale:

> Bullying can have serious and long-lasting consequences. In this lesson, you will learn about the laws that relate to bullying in our state, but we will also consider the consequences of participating in acts of bullying.

Lesson Body

1. Explain that in recent years, it has become more and more common for bullying to be considered a criminal act. Explain the following points:

   - Although there are no federal laws that relate to bullying, an increasing number of states have implemented laws about bullying in schools and cyberbullying. If your state has anti-bullying laws, explain them to students and have them take notes.

   - When bullying and harassment overlap—the bullying is based on race, national origin, sex, disability, or religion—the school has an obligation to resolve the harassment. If it is not adequately resolved, the U.S. Department of Education's Office for Civil Rights and the U.S. Department of Justice's Civil Rights Division can help.

   - If bullying takes the form of serious assault, theft, stalking, or hacking, or involves pornographic images of a minor, students may face criminal charges.

© 2014 Ancora Publishing • For use by purchasing school only   *Foundations: A Proactive and Positive Behavior Support System*

 See Appendix C for printing directions.

TASK 3

Partner with families to prevent bullying

In this task, the team answers a series of questions to solidify processes and procedures for training all families about bullying issues and for forming partnerships with families to prevent bullying problems. This task also helps you determine ways of communicating with families to increase the likelihood that adequate support and partnership will occur when bullying situations arise.

The questions correspond to the form Family Training in Preventing and Responding to Bullying (Form E-13), which appears in Figure 5w. You might wish to have a copy of this document to review and annotate as you work through the task. You (the Foundations Team or bullying prevention task force) will answer each of the questions as the Action Steps for this task.

> The numbered items in this task correspond to items on Form E-13 (provided in the reproducibles).

1. **What initial information will you provide to families about bullying policies, processes and procedures for handling bullying incidents, and student responsibilities?**

   At the start of the school year, give all parents written information about the following topics:

   - The definition of bullying, including examples of each type (physical, verbal, relational, and cyberbullying)
   - School policies related to bullying
   - Methods of reporting bullying incidents
   - Student responsibilities related to avoiding bullying behavior and responding appropriately when bullying occurs, as either a student who is targeted or a bystander (provide specific examples of appropriate and inappropriate responses)
   - Student responsibilities to report incidents
   - Names, job titles, and contact information for staff who are responsible for investigating and following up on bullying incidents
   - Possible consequences and intervention procedures that may be implemented to help a student who engaged in bullying behavior learn to behave more responsibly and to help support a student who was victimized

   Because dealing with bullying situations can become emotional and heated, be sure that all parents know and understand the following key points:

   The school must follow due process. Consequences will not be implemented until the investigation into an incident is complete.

Figure 5w Family Training in Preventing and Responding to Bullying (E-13)

Family Training in Preventing and Responding to Bullying

1. What initial information will you provide to families about bullying policies, processes and procedures for handling bullying incidents, and student responsibilities?

2. What information about schoolwide data and specific bulllying concerns will you provide regularly throughout the year?

3. Can the school provide parents with general tips and tools that may prevent bullying—for example, positive parenting methods, ways to provide supervision and structure, and suggestions for training students in social-emotional skills?

4. What information will you provide to family members about how they should respond when their child is reportedly victimized?

5. What information will you provide to family members about how they should respond when their child reportedly engages in bullying behavior?

6. Are methods of communication with individual families about bullying concerns productive for both students who are victimized and students who bully?

 See Appendix C for printing directions.

Zero-tolerance policies are ineffective in changing behavior. The school typically uses a mixed approach to address students who bully that combines appropriate consequences with interventions to change the students' bullying behaviors. (Module D, Presentation 1, Task 2 provides more information about zero-tolerance policies.)

The school may implement interventions to help students who are chronically targeted. These interventions will teach behaviors that can protect such students against victimization. Interventions might include, for example, social skills training to help students establish meaningful friendships, coping skills for anxiety, and meaningful school jobs to increase the students' feelings of worth and value. The interventions do not imply that students who are targeted have done something wrong and deserve to be bullied. Rather, school staff want to provide students with tools or skills that can reduce the likelihood that they will be targeted again and increase the likelihood that they can handle any bullying that does occur.

The school must follow regulations and policies about what can and cannot be shared with students and families about incidents and their outcomes. This topic is governed by the Family Educational Rights and Privacy Act (FERPA) and your district's procedural and legal requirements. Parents might wonder, for example, whether you can disclose information to a student who is targeted about the consequences that were assigned to the student who bullied.

Unproductive communications between schools and families can significantly escalate bullying problems. If you teach families the concepts above at the beginning of every school year, you might reduce the likelihood of misunderstandings or conflicts with families. You might have parents and guardians sign a pledge or other document stating that they have received information about school policies, then keep those documents on file in case a misunderstanding occurs.

2. **What information about schoolwide data and specific bullying concerns will you provide regularly throughout the year?**

Partnering with parents may be one of the best ways to reduce bullying issues in your school. Though some parents lack the interest, tools, or skills to help their children develop the appropriate behaviors, many of them would do more to help if the school provided additional guidance. Information that can benefit parents and help them help their children includes schoolwide data related to bullying in your school and actions parents can take to help reduce problems.

For example, provide talking points that parents can use to discuss bullying problems specific to the school and their children's responsibilities to avoid these behaviors. If the school discovers major problems with gossip and spreading rumors on social media that are leading to bullying issues at school, share this information with families. You might provide lessons and activities that parents can conduct at home about why gossip and rumors are harmful and how to avoid becoming involved. Provide tips for talking with children about responsible social media behavior and how parents can provide additional supervision and oversight of social media use. When messages like this are taught at home as well as at school, they're much more likely to be effective.

Here's another example of actions parents can take: If data show that bullying is occurring in specific locations at the school, provide parents with some questions to ask their children about what's going on in that area and what the children can do to improve the situation. Helping families start a dialogue with their children about bullying can go a long way toward stopping their children's participation in the problem.

3. **Can the school provide parents with general tips and tools that may prevent bullying—for example, positive parenting methods, ways to provide supervision and structure, and suggestions for training students in social-emotional skills?**

    Consider sending tips and tools through various media to equip families with knowledge and skills to reduce bullying behavior. This should be done regularly throughout the year. Although many parents and families are well intentioned, they may be unaware of some of the issues that contribute to bullying and that the school deals with, and they can benefit from additional information on actions they can take to help.

    For example, many parents know that part of their job is to help their children learn how to use technology in responsible ways. However, because the parents didn't grow up with these technologies, they may not even be aware of some of the risks, and they may be completely at a loss as to how to help their children learn to use technology responsibly. The school can be a huge help in this area.

    Dealing With Technology: Tips and Strategies for Parents is shown in Figure 5x (Form E-25). Consider handing this out to all parents, perhaps at your fall back-to-school night, or make it available through the school website.

    Dealing with technology is just one issue you might provide tips and strategies for. Consider developing tips and strategies for parents for other subjects, such as:

    - Authoritative vs. authoritarian parenting methods
    - Addressing bullying situations among siblings
    - Fostering social-emotional skills such as resilience, anger management, and friendship

Figure 5x   *Dealing With Technology: Tips and Strategies for Parents (E-25)*

FOUNDATIONS SAMPLE

Dealing With Technology: (p. 1 of 3)
Tips and Strategies for Parents

In today's world, technology is everywhere. Children are exposed to technology in a multitude of forms throughout each day: They text, email, use social media, surf the Internet, watch television and movies, and the list goes on and on. In fact, for many children, technology is one of the main ways they interact with and learn about the world. Thus, it is important that they have some guidance as they negotiate this increasingly technological world.

We have created this tip sheet to help you consider what you can do to help your children remain safe, act responsibly with technology, and learn how to be good digital citizens.

Talk early and often with your children about safety when dealing with technology. Inform children that:

- They should never share passwords with anyone other than parents or guardians (even a best friend).
- They should never give out personally identifiable information.
- They should never agree to meet in person anyone they met online or give anyone their location.

Discuss identity theft, sexual and monetary predators, and other risks in age-appropriate terms.

Frequently discuss and review what appropriate and respectful behavior looks and sounds like when communicating through technology. Use the following guidelines:

- If you wouldn't do it or say it in front of a trusted and respected adult, don't do it online or by text.
- Participating in cyberbullying by sharing, reposting, or commenting about negative remarks about someone else makes the problem worse. The only appropriate response is to not respond and tell a parent or another adult about the cyberbullying immediately.
- If you wouldn't want a comment shared or said about you, don't share or say it.
- Think before you post or text, especially if you are upset or angry. Once a photo or message is in the electronic world, it never really goes away and can seriously affect your reputation, success, and future.
- NEVER send photos or images that contain nudity or messages with sexually explicit content.

> *Note:* Sexting—sending sexually explicit photos or messages by phone or other technology—is a phenomenon that has become increasingly common, especially among teenage girls. It carries serious risks, such as messages being forwarded to others. In addition, those who send or possess sexually explicit photos of a minor can face felony child pornography charges.

 See Appendix C for printing directions.

Presentation 5: Schoolwide Bullying Prevention and Intervention

Figure 5x (continued) Dealing With Technology: Tips and Strategies for Parents (E-25)

FOUNDATIONS SAMPLE

(p. 2 of 3)

Establish procedures and rules regarding technology in your household. For example:

- Set appropriate limits on how long and where technology can be used. Consider procedures and rules such as the following:
    - No more than 2 hours of nonacademic technology use each day on weekends, and less on weekdays.
    - Some cell phones and computers can be set to have time limits or to prevent access during specified hours. Create a password for your child and set the device with the specified features.
    - All electronic devices are turned off 1 hour before the child's bedtime. Studies have shown that bright lights (such as those on computers, cell phones, and TVs) can interrupt human sleep cycles and delay sleep.
    - During dinner, place all cell phones (including parents' phones!) in a box away from the dinner table.
    - Create the expectation that electronic devices are not allowed in children's bedrooms. This includes cell phones, computers, TVs, gaming devices, and so on. One possible way to set this expectation is to establish a charging station in the parents' bedroom; all charging cords stay at this station. At bedtime, place all technological devices in the parents' room to charge.

> *Note:* Technology should not be allowed in children's bedrooms for several reasons:
> - Electronic devices in bedrooms have been linked to sleep problems in children and teens. Lack of sleep contributes to attention problems, difficulty concentrating and learning, aggressive behavior, increased risk of depression, and a host of other health, behavioral, and emotional issues.
> - Access to technology in the privacy of the bedroom can lead to increased risk for sexting, involvement in cyberbullying and conflict, and engaging in behaviors that can put a child at risk for predatory behavior.
> - For children who have unsupervised access to technology, night is a prime time for cyberbullying. When a child is victimized through cyberbullying, it is important to limit and monitor the child's access to technology so that he or she is not bombarded with negative messages 24 hours a day.

- Create a Technology Contract that outlines specific rules and expectations for your children's use of technology. Include expectations for time, location, respectful and appropriate behavior, responsible use of personal information, appropriate sites and inappropriate sites, and how use will be monitored and supervised.

 See Appendix C for printing directions.

Figure 5x (continued)

FOUNDATIONS SAMPLE

(p. 3 of 3)

You may wish to include responsibility clauses that allow children additional technology privileges for exceptional behavior, as well as penalty clauses that outline potential consequences for violating aspects of the contract.

Supervise and teach your child about technology use.

- Although filters and parental control features are available and can be a useful starting place, be aware that many children know how to bypass these controls. In addition, your child will likely visit places where there are with no filters and no supervision. Therefore, the best supervisor and teacher is YOU!
- Talk with your children about the websites they visit, what they do there, and who they communicate with.
- When your children are first exploring technology, explore it with them and give guidance about good vs. bad sites, how to evaluate the information they are viewing, and how to make responsible and safe decisions.
- Periodically review your children's cell phone and computer histories. Set the expectation that only a designated adult can erase cell phone, browser, and email histories. If a history is erased by the child, the adult should assume that something inappropriate has occurred and consequences should be put in place.
- Over time, as your children demonstrate increased maturity, responsibility, and appropriate use of technology, you may decide to gradually release responsibility to them. However, always remain involved by talking with your children, providing periodic spot checks, and reminding them about the essentials of safety and responsibility as a digital citizen.

Additional Resources

- Common Sense Media: www.commonsensemedia.org
- Family Online Safety Institute: http://www.fosi.org
- Internet Safety Tips for Parents, U.S. Department of Justice: http://www.justice.gov/usao/ian/psc/Elementary%20Safety%20Tips%20for%20Parents.pdf
- *Kids and technology: Tips for parents in a high-tech world,* Centers for Disease Control and Prevention: http://www.cdc.gov/media/subtopic/matte/pdf/cdcelectronicregression.pdf
- *NetSmartz Workshop,* National Center for Missing and Exploited Children: http://www.netsmartz.org/Parents
- *10 Ways to Keep Kids Safe Online,* Tech Savvy: http://techsavvymag.com/2014/04/07/online-safety-kids-parents/
- *Tips for Parents,* National Crime Prevention Council: http://www.ncpc.org/topics/internet-safety/tips-for-parents

Some ways to disseminate this information include:

- Informative articles in newsletters and emails
- Pamphlets
- Robocalls
- Talking points for open-house evenings, parent-teacher conferences, and PTA meetings
- Public-service announcements for local radio and TV
- Special training sessions for parents

4. **What information will you provide to family members about how they should respond when their child is reportedly victimized?**

Provide information and training on the best ways that family members can respond when their children report they've been bullied or when someone else suggests that bullying is occurring. Parents should also be aware of the warning signs of bullying, such as social withdrawal, increased physical complaints, and signs of depression and anxiety, and be on the alert for these signs in their children.

Some key points family members should know about responding when their children are victimized include the following:

- Listen and offer support by sympathizing, but don't get overly emotional or imply that the bullying is the student's fault. Families need to know that dismissing bullying concerns and engaging in heightened emotional responses are both unproductive and can worsen the situation for their child.

- Don't contact the child who bullied or the child's family. These contacts often turn out badly. The accused child or family may become defensive, and both sides may become oppositional and overly emotional. Instead, families should work with school staff, who can contact the other family and serve as liaisons.

- Schools will keep a record of all incidents, and families should keep records as well. Families should use the Bullying Incident Report form (Form E-07) to document each incident in as much detail as possible, even if they choose not to turn in every incident report to the school.

- Help children evaluate whether a situation fits the definition of bullying. Consider whether an incident is serious enough to be reported and addressed or whether it is minor enough to ignore for the time being and address only if the situation continues or escalates.

- Talk to children about ways to be assertive and to communicate that behavior is unwanted, without fighting back. Then talk to children about how to engage an advocate in authority, if needed.

- Help children develop competence and independence, make friends, and get involved in positive activities. Research suggests that these actions are the best defenses against bullying. Students who are isolated are more likely to be bullied. Having strong and supportive friendships is a great buffer—when bullying situations occur, students with friends are not affected as much as those without friends.

Students who are involved in activities that they like and that promote confidence are also less likely to be adversely affected by bullying problems. There are many examples of students who, despite persistent bullying, became involved in a club, sport, or other activity that bolstered their self-esteem and friendships. When they subsequently experienced bullying, they didn't dwell on it and instead focused on all of the positive things in their lives.

5. **What information will you provide to family members about how they should respond when their child reportedly engages in bullying behavior?**

Families should know that if their children are reported to be engaging in bullying behavior, it's important to talk to them about why the behavior is occurring and to do so in a calm but serious manner. Children need to know that bullying is unacceptable. Consequences are probably necessary, but yelling, overly harsh consequences, extreme emotion, and violence are not appropriate responses and may increase aggressive behaviors.

Another unproductive response is blaming the other student. Families should clarify that no excuse is OK in this situation. Even if the child maintains that the other student started the problem, parents need to talk to the child about whether she knew that her behavior was inappropriate, aggressive, or disrespectful and clarify that the behavior is not acceptable and needs to stop immediately.

The school can also provide guidance to families about logical consequences they might implement at home for bullying behavior. Provide a sample home-based consequences list similar to your list of school-based consequences (as discussed in Module E, Presentation 4, Task 3). If school staff contact the family to discuss bullying problems, review these possible consequences with parents.

Perhaps the most logical consequence is one we introduced in Presentation 4, Task 1: Students who show aggressive behaviors lose access to violent forms of entertainment, such as violent video and computer games and violent television and movies. In Presentation 4, Task 1, we discussed the Joint Statement on the Impact of Entertainment Violence, a landmark report signed by six leading medical and psychological associations. The statement indicates that entertainment violence leads to an increase in aggressive attitudes, values, and behavior in some people, particularly children.

Provide all parents with a copy of this statement. Suggest that a logical consequence for children who display aggressive behaviors is loss of access to violent media until they demonstrate they are responsible enough to handle the content by not engaging in violent and aggressive acts. A condensed version of the statement that you can include in a school newspaper, email blast, or other communication with families is shown in Figure 5y on the next page and available as Form E-17 in the reproducible materials.

You can find the complete Joint Statement on the Impact of Entertainment Violence on Children online (www2.aap.org/advocacy/releases/jstmtevc.htm).

Consider establishing that, as standard practice when they telephone parents about aggressive acts, staff discuss the student's television and entertainment consumption and recommend that the student's access to violent forms be temporarily removed. If parents are willing to participate in this plan, work with them to develop a contract for how and when the student can earn back these privileges based on the absence of aggressive behavior at school and at home.

6. **Are methods of communication with individual families about bullying concerns productive for both students who are victimized and students who bully?**

Because bullying is such an emotional and heated topic, it is worth analyzing how staff members communicate with families when bullying incidents occur and consider whether staff can do anything to reduce the likelihood that conversations break down and become emotional or defensive. The more productive and collaborative the relationship between the school and the families of students who are victimized and students who engage in bullying, the more likely bullying situations will be resolved.

When relationships with these families become contentious, the situation can escalate significantly. Parents of students who were victimized might initiate legal action because they think the school is not addressing their concerns. Parents of students who were bullying might defend their children's actions and say things to the children that undermine the school's message.

Contacting families of students who have been victimized. We suggest you create a script of talking points to guide conversations when staff call families about students who are victimized. A sample script appears in Figure 5z on pp. 200–201 (Sample E-26). A conversation about a student who was victimized should begin by reassuring the parent that the student is currently OK physically and emotionally:

Figure 5y *Summary of the Joint Statement on the Impact of Entertainment Violence (E-17)*

Summary of the Joint Statement on the Impact of Entertainment Violence

"Viewing entertainment violence can lead to increases in aggressive attitudes, values and behavior, particularly in children."

—Joint Statement on the Impact of Entertainment Violence on Children

In 2000, six of the leading mental health and medical associations signed a joint statement to clarify the strong consensus among the public health community that entertainment violence has a negative effect on children. This statement, based on over 1,000 reputable research studies, dispels the common perception that viewing violent entertainment does not lead to increases in violent or aggressive behavior.

Key points for parents to know and discuss are:

- Some children are more negatively affected than others by entertainment violence.
- Children who see a lot of violence are more likely to view violence as an effective and acceptable way of settling conflicts.
- Viewing violence can lead to:
    - Emotional desensitization toward violence in real life.
    - Increased fear and mistrust of others.
    - May lead to a higher tendency for violent and aggressive behavior later in life.
- Preliminary research indicates that these negative effects may be significantly worsened when students use "violent interactive entertainment" such as violent video or computer games.
- Effects of entertainment violence are measurable and long lasting.

Note from Principal _____: If your child exhibits violent or aggressive tendencies, consider the above information as you make decisions about helping your child learn appropriate behavior. Contact _____ if you would like assistance and support in creating a plan at home for addressing aggressive behaviors.

The full statement is available at http://www2.aap.org/advocacy/releases/jstmtevc.htm.

 See Appendix C for printing directions.

Figure 5z *Script for Talking With Families About a Student Who Was Victimized (E-26)*

> FOUNDATIONS SAMPLE
>
> **Script for Talking With Families About a Student Who Was Victimized** (p. 1 of 2)
>
> 1. **Introduce yourself and provide an appropriate greeting:**
>
>   Hello, Mr. Monson? This is Principal Evans at Highline. How are you today? I hope I didn't interrupt—may I take a moment of your time?
>
> 2. **Inform the family that you are calling about an incident. Indicate the student's present physical and emotional condition:**
>
>   I am calling to inform you about an incident at school today that involved Janelle and some other students. Janelle is pretty upset at the moment, but I want to start by assuring you that she is physically safe and uninjured. She is in the office right now talking with one of our counselors.
>
> 3. **Describe the incident objectively:**
>
>   According to Janelle and other students who witnessed the event, Janelle was walking alone in the hallway when a group of five girls blocked her and began calling her names and making unkind comments about her appearance. Some of the girls also pushed her repeatedly and knocked her books to the floor. They continued taunting her until an adult intervened. Janelle told me this is not the first time this has happened to her.
>
> 4. **Describe what the school intends to do to investigate the incident further and potential consequences for the perpetrators (follow FERPA laws and school regulations about disclosure):**
>
>   I want to assure you that we are taking this incident very seriously and are investigating further to get more information. Our counselor is working with Janelle right now to find out more, and we will talk to as many other students as necessary to understand what is going on.
>
>   Because of privacy laws, I can't inform you about the specific consequences and interventions that will be given to other students, but we will absolutely address the negative behaviors of the other students through consequences and interventions.
>
>   We have a wide range of consequences and interventions for the kind of behavior that occurred. They are listed in our antibullying policy. We will work to create a plan to prevent similar incidents in the future. If you have any questions about the range of measures that could be put in place, please feel free to ask.
>
> 5. **Describe what the school intends to do to support the student who was victimized. Consider using questions to segue into supports:**
>
>   In addition to our efforts to deal with this particular incident, we want to make sure we are doing everything we can to support Janelle and reduce the likelihood that she has to go through anything like this again. We also want to make sure that she has the adult and peer support she

 See Appendix C for printing directions.

Module E: Improving Safety, Managing Conflict, and Reducing Bullying

Figure 5z (continued)

FOUNDATIONS SAMPLE

(p. 2 of 2)

needs to feel strong, safe, and connected at school. I know this incident was very distressing for her. May I ask you some questions to help us design a support plan for Janelle?

Do you know if Janelle has any adults she trusts and feels connected with at school?

We want to ensure that she has at least one adult here whom she really likes and feels she can talk to about any problems—academic, social, or otherwise. We will work to try and find a mentor who she will get along with. Can you tell me the kind of personality you think Janelle might connect with?

Do you know if Janelle has any peers at school she likes and enjoys being around?

I've noticed that Janelle often seems to be alone between classes and during lunchtime. I would love to see if we can create some opportunities for her to connect with some peers here at Highline. Having some friends may increase her general positive feeling about school, and it can also be a major deterrent to incidents like the one that occurred today. I'm going to have the counselor talk with her about some school activities that can help her connect with other students with similar interests. Would you like the counselor to call you to talk through some of these options?

6. **Make suggestions about how the family might help the child:**

   I encourage you to talk to Janelle tonight about the incident. Please call me if you discover any additional information the school should know. When these kinds of incidents occur, it is helpful when family members not only listen with a caring ear, but also help the student think about or do something that takes their mind off the incident, makes them feel good and happy about themselves, and helps create a connection with other students and adults. If Janelle has something that she really loves doing or is interested in, I encourage you to foster that interest to help her self-esteem.

7. **Indicate follow-up measures if any are necessary:**

   I would like to follow up with you and Janelle in 2 weeks to see how she is doing and whether these incidents have stopped. In the meantime, I'll tell Janelle that if anything else occurs, she should tell her mentor, you, or come directly to me. I hope this was a one-time incident, but it is possible that we will need to take additional measures, and the only way we know whether we need to do that is if we know what is going on. I'll plan to call you in 2 weeks to check in, but if Janelle reports any other issues to you in the meantime, please contact me.

   Date of Contact: October 25

   Notes on the Contact: Meet with Janelle and call Mr. Monson on Nov. 8 to follow up.

I am calling to inform you about an incident that occurred at school today. First, I want to assure you that Sanjay is safe and uninjured. He's in the office right now talking with one of our counselors.

The conversation should describe what happened in specific, objective terms; don't just say that the student was a target of bullying. Within the bounds of FERPA laws and your school's regulations on disclosure, describe the investigation that will take place and the potential consequences that might be assigned. Even if you cannot disclose the specific consequence that will be assigned, reference the range of consequences included in your school policy. Explain that the school will provide interventions and consequences to address concerns with the student who is bullying as well as provide supports for the student who was victimized, as necessary. Describe what these supports might look like.

Something as simple as asking if family members would like to visit the school to talk about these or other concerns in person can go a long way toward creating a partnership that will be productive if bullying concerns persist.

Another topic to think through carefully and script before calling or meeting with family members is how to discuss the behaviors or skills you would like to help the student with to reduce the likelihood of bullying. For example, the student might need to work on social skills or developing friendships. You don't want the parents to think that you are saying it's their child's fault that he was bullied. This misunderstanding could easily break down a collaborative relationship. So be diplomatic. Ask questions such as, "Does John have many close friends outside of school?" "Do you know whether John has many peers at school that he likes and enjoys being around?" Then segue into something like, "We've noticed that John spends a lot of time on his own at school, and we're trying to brainstorm ways to help him connect with others. We have a small group that gets together during lunchtime, and we'd like to see if John might enjoy getting to know some of the other kids in a smaller setting."

That suggestion sounds very different from saying, "John has a really hard time engaging other students appropriately, so the other students are bullying him because he bothers them. We'd like to put him in a social skills group." Parents are more likely to collaborate with you if you use more tactful language.

Contacting families of students who have bullied. When contacting the families of students who perpetrate bullying behavior, we recommend you prepare a list of talking points or a worksheet that staff members can complete to guide the conversation. A sample script appears in Figure 5aa (Sample E-27 in the reproducible materials).

Figure 5aa *Script for Talking With Families About a Student Who Bullied (E-27)*

FOUNDATIONS SAMPLE

Script for Talking With Families About a Student Who Bullied

(p. 1 of 2)

1. **Introduce yourself and provide an appropriate greeting:**

   Hello, Mrs. Santos? This is Principal Evans at Highline. How are you today? How did the move go? I know that moving can be such a struggle. May I take a moment of your time? I'll try to make this call quick because I know you are busy.

2. **Inform the family that you are calling about an incident:**

   I am calling because I want to speak with you about an incident that occurred this week.

3. **Describe the problem (use an objective description of events, and avoid labeling or passing judgment on the child):**

   Monika was involved in an incident. She and four other girls blocked another student from walking down the hallway. Then they spent several minutes calling the student names and insulting her appearance. Several of the girls pushed the student and knocked her books to the floor. While Monika does not appear to have physically touched the student, she was involved in the name calling, taunting, and blocking her from getting away.

4. **Describe why the behavior is a problem. Emphasize that you know the student can be successful:**

   We are concerned about this kind of behavior because all students in this school have the right to feel physically and emotionally safe. We also know that these kinds of actions can have long-term negative effects on the students who are involved, whether they are the students who are victimized, perpetrate, or witness. We are concerned that if Monika continues to be involved in these kinds of interactions, it will interfere with her success at school and cause other difficulties for her.

   I know Monika can be very kind and compassionate and is a good friend to many of our students. I'm confident that she can make better choices.

5. **If appropriate, ask whether the family has any insight into why the behavior may be occurring. If they share with you, adjust the remainder of the call based on what you learn.**

   One of the reasons I am calling is to find out if you know of anything that might be bothering Monika and contributing to this kind of aggression toward a peer at school.

6. **Describe what the school intends to do to investigate the incident further, the consequences that were assigned and consequences that may be assigned in the future, and the interventions or supports that may be put in place for the student:**

   We are currently investigating reports that this is not the first time Monika and some of her peers have demonstrated this kind of behavior. We will let you know as soon as we have more information about the results of the investigation.

 See Appendix C for printing directions.

Figure 5aa (continued)   *Script for Talking With Families About a Student Who Bullied (E-27)*

FOUNDATIONS SAMPLE

(p. 2 of 2)

As a consequence for this particular incident, we have assigned Monika 1 week of lunch detention. During detention, she will be getting instruction and practice on respectful behavior toward peers. If we find that Monika has been or continues to be involved in incidents of aggression toward her peers, we will put together a plan with additional consequences as well as interventions to deter this kind of behavior. We will also likely want to meet with you and Monika at that time to talk about how we can work together to solve this problem.

7. **Make suggestions about how the family might help the child:**

   I am *not* calling to tell you to punish Monika or what measures you should take at home. I am concerned about the choices she is making, and I hope you will talk to her about the problem.

   Although how you address this issue at home is entirely up to you, one possible consequence is to limit Monika's access to television and other media that depicts aggression, "girl drama," or violence for a week for the first incident and for a longer time if the problem continues. We think this consequence is logical to use with students involved in the kinds of incidents that Monika was involved in. Parents who use this approach explain to their child that these media are entertainment, not guides for behavior, and until the child can demonstrate respectful behavior toward others, they will be off limits.

   As I said, I know that Monika is very capable of avoiding involvement in these kinds of situations and of doing the right thing. Please let her know that I look forward to seeing her tomorrow. I will call in a few days to let you know how things have been going at school and the results of our investigation. Feel free to call me as well.

   Date of Contact: October 25

   Notes on the Contact:

   - Investigate reports of additional incidents.
   - Provide a follow-up call to Mrs. Santos on October 27 to report on Monika's behavior and the results of the investigation.

 See Appendix C for printing directions.

Rather than emphasizing what the student is doing wrong that's harming others, try to couch the tone and message of the conversation in terms of safety—the goal of the school is to keep all students physically and emotionally safe and help all students be successful. You might say something like:

> *We're concerned that these behaviors are getting in the way of Susie's success, so we'd like to work with you and her to try and get her the help and support she needs to make good choices and be successful.*

Prepare responses for any anticipated roadblocks, such as the family member becoming defensive and focusing on what the other student was doing wrong. Say something like:

> *Thank you for sharing that information with me. I'll definitely look into your concerns, and I can assure you that we'll be working with the other student as well to prevent any future problems. With that in mind, we'd like to talk to you more about how we can work with your child so that she responds in a more productive way if something happens again.*

You might even role-play a potentially difficult conversation with another staff member. He or she can give you feedback on any areas of the conversation that might trigger emotional responses from the family member or lead to escalation.

Families can be some of your biggest allies in preventing bullying. On a schoolwide level, you can do a great deal to equip families with skills and knowledge to empower them to help their children make good choices and be responsible. Many parents are hungry for this kind of knowledge and empowerment. On an individual level, you can create meaningful partnerships when bullying incidents occur as you work to find productive solutions and develop supports and interventions that students need to eliminate the bullying problem.

Task 3 Action Steps & Evidence of Implementation

Action Steps	Evidence of Implementation
1. Complete each of the questions on the form Family Training in Preventing and Responding to Bullying (Form E-13).	Foundations Process: Current Priorities
2. Develop written information for families on: • Bullying policies, procedures, and student responsibilities • Data and specific bullying concerns in the school (as needed) • Tips and tools on positive parenting methods, providing supervision and structure, and training students in social-emotional skills • Recommendations for how families respond when their children are targeted by bullying • Recommendations for how families respond when their children are engaging in bullying behavior	Foundations Process: Communications With Parents Foundations Archive: Bullying Prevention
3. Develop scripts to facilitate conversations with families of students who were targeted and students who bullied.	Foundations Process: Communications With Parents Foundations Archive: Bullying Prevention

TASK 4

Actively engage students to prevent bullying

One of the best things schools can do to prevent bullying is to get all students meaningfully engaged at school. This is also one of the most effective things a school can do to support students who are targeted. Increasing engagement for students who perpetrate bullying can also go a long way toward reducing other aggressive and problematic behaviors.

Consider the following questions about student engagement from the perspective of both the school and an individual student. In general, the questions ask whether your school connects students who are struggling with bullying with supports and interventions to improve engagement. These questions correspond to the form Active Engagement for the Prevention of Bullying (Form E-14), which appears in Figure 5ab. You might wish to have a copy of this document to review and annotate as you work through the task. You (the Foundations Team or bullying prevention task force) will answer each of the questions as the Action Steps for this task.

> The numbered items in this task correspond to items on Form E-14 (provided in the reproducibles).

1. **Are students meaningfully engaged in academic tasks?**

    When students are bored, do not participate in their classes, or have difficulty understanding the content because of academic deficits or ineffective teaching practices, they are more likely to disengage from school and engage in risky behavior, including bullying. When students are engaged and participate in academic and other school tasks, there will likely be fewer bullying problems. Although it is beyond the scope of this task to discuss how to increase academic engagement, we do encourage you to ensure that all students can access the content in their classes, are challenged while still demonstrating success, and feel confident in their abilities at school.

    To attain that goal, make sure that all staff members are equipped with the tools and training they need to explicitly teach their content, foster active student participation throughout their classes, frequently assess student understanding, and provide modification and remediation as necessary. Your efforts to improve engagement will have much stronger results if you also effectively address academic engagement.

Figure 5ab *Active Engagement for the Prevention of Bullying (E-14)*

Active Engagement for the Prevention of Bullying

1. Are students meaningfully engaged in academic tasks?

2. Does your school provide activities that include all students?

3. Does your school make frequent overt efforts to promote respect for all individual students?

4. Does your school provide training on the responsible use of power for student groups that are in positions of power?

5. Does your school use methods to ensure that all students have at least one adult who knows them well and who they feel cares about them?

6. Does your school comprehensively address the transition from elementary to middle school or from middle school to high school?

7. Does your school identify students who are at risk because of either externalizing or internalizing issues and link them with small group and individual interventions?

 See Appendix C for printing directions.

2. **Does your school provide activities that include all students?**

Consider the wide range of strategies available to promote inclusion and mixing of all students, from informal classroom activities to highly structured after-school programs and whole-school activities. A few of the following ideas have been mentioned in other presentations in *Foundations*, but most are new examples.

Grouping. Encourage teachers to frequently have students form random groups and partnerships rather than allow students to always choose their groups or seating arrangements. Train teachers in several methods to create these groupings, such as:

- *3-6-9.* Students are directed to touch three walls, then six tables, then nine chairs. Whoever is closest to them when they finish is their partner or their group.

- *Use playing cards.* Each student has a playing card taped to his or her desk. Students are grouped according to their cards; different grouping methods can be used on different days. For example, students might form groups according to the suits or numbers on the cards. To split the suit groups even more, the teacher could divide the groups in half, with numbers below 7 in one and 7s and above in the other.

Weekly ballot. This next example was developed by an elementary teacher to identify students who are lonely, disconnected, or struggling to connect. It can be easily adapted for middle and high school students. Each week, the teacher has her students fill out a simple ballot with the names of four students they would like to sit beside during the next week, as well as one student who has been an exceptional classroom citizen that week. She then looks for patterns, such as:

- Who is not requested by anyone else?
- Who doesn't know who to request?
- Who never gets noticed enough to be nominated?
- Who had lots of requests last week and none this week?

Although the teacher sometimes uses the ballots to honor student requests for seating partners or to acknowledge exceptional class citizens, her main goal is to uncover trends in student interactions. When asked how long she had been using the system, the teacher said, "Ever since Columbine. Every single Friday afternoon since Columbine."

Figure 5ac shows an example of how teachers can formalize this system using a spreadsheet with a student name assigned to each row and Week 1, Week 2, Week

Figure 5ac   Sample spreadsheet of student nominations

	Who nominated the student?					
	Week 1	Week 2	Week 3	Week 4	Week 5	Week 6
Andy	David Enrique	David Enrique	David Enrique Horace			
Ann	Farrah Zac Siri	Farrah Siri				
Beatrice	Ann					
Ben	Juan	Juan	Juan Zac			
David						
Deidre	Randi Michelle	Zac	Randi			
Enrique	David	David	David			
Farrah	Ann Siri	Ann Siri	Ann Siri			
Horace	Andy		Andy			
Juan	Ben Tomas Noah	Ben Noah	Ben Tomas Noah			

3, and so on in the columns. Each week, simply enter the names of the students who nominated each child. The patterns of who has many nominations and who has none will emerge pretty quickly. Students with no nominations might be good candidates for activities to help them connect with peers and get engaged in activities, as well as possibly some social skills instruction. Students with many nominations may be classroom leaders and might be good candidates for some additional emphasis on responsible use of power. They might also be partnered with some of the students who are more socially isolated.

Staff support survey. The staff as a whole might want to assess which students need additional support to get involved in school activities. Post or hand out a list of all student names during a staff meeting and have staff members initial next to the names of students they mentor, coach, tutor, supervise in a Meaningful Work job, or work with in student council, a club, and so on. Have the staff members list the activities next to the student names. Students with no initials next to their names should be identified for additional efforts to connect them with an activity. A detailed method for conducting this exercise is included in Module D, Presentation 5, Task 2.

Random cafeteria seating. Create random seating at cafeteria tables. As students exit the lunch line, direct them to specific tables. The first student is directed to Seat 1 at Table 1, the next student to Seat 1 at Table 2, the next to Seat 1 at Table 3, and so on. This pattern continues through all of the Seat 1s at every table.

Then students are directed to the Seat 2s at each table. In this way, students are always randomly seated next to one another, and so they get to know many more students outside of their usual social circles. Consider using a strategy like this periodically, perhaps 1 week per month.

Structured recess program. A PE teacher and several classified staff teach students how to play a few whole-group games such as Ultimate Frisbee. During recess, students are required to pick one of three structured games that the whole group will play. Students who have achieved self-monitor status, which is a reward program for good behavior, have the option to walk around the track or do something else, but all other students are expected to participate in the selected game. All students are included and engaged, and the self-monitor component allows more autonomy and choice for students who have proven to be responsible. (Thanks to Oak Grove Elementary School in Medford, Oregon, for this idea.)

Student activities. Ensure that your school is providing a range of clubs, after-school activities, and other events that interest your students. Also make sure that students know what is available in your school. Many schools offer great opportunities, but the students don't know about them or aren't sure how to join or participate. Here are a few ideas for ensuring that students know what activities are available and how to join:

- Create a mini-magazine that highlights all clubs and other opportunities. Have each club create an advertisement for the magazine and posters to display around the school.

- Host a Club Day before or shortly after the start of the school year for existing clubs and any student or staff member who is interested in forming a club. Each club can present information to the student body during an assembly or during a dedicated period during the school day.

- Create opportunities for club representatives to speak to classes. They can explain what the club does and how it operates, and solicit new members.

- Have clubs set up and staff information booths during lunch periods.

- Create a mini-worksheet for students. Students indicate the activities they are interested in, and then staff provide the students' names to the club leaders. The clubs can seek out those students and issue a personal invitation to join the club. Students can also write ideas for new clubs and activities on the form. A staff member follows up with the student and, if possible, looks into developing the activity or connecting the student with an existing activity that might interest him or her.

Presentation 5: Schoolwide Bullying Prevention and Intervention

- To advertise activities in elementary schools, you might devote a little bit of time every few months to demonstrate after-school activities during school hours. For example, have activity coordinators run the games and activities during lunchtime or recess to spark students' interest in what the school offers. Have students sign up to try the various activities.

When thinking about clubs, pay special attention to groups of students who have been historically discriminated against or who experience increased victimization (according to your school's collected data). Culture clubs and student organizations for these groups and other students who identify with or support the groups can provide strong positive identity and self-esteem for those students. They can also increase understanding and respect both within the group and among the student body and staff. For example, compared with students in schools without Gay-Straight Alliances (GSAs), students in schools with GSAs who identify as lesbian, gay, bisexual, transgender, or questioning (LGBTQ) are less likely to experience depression or to drop out. They have higher self-esteem and are more likely to succeed in higher education. They are more likely to feel safe and feel they belong at school, and less likely to miss school (National Association of School Psychologists, 2011).

We recommend that every middle school and high school have a GSA that includes a faculty advisor who is an ally for sexual orientation issues. The National Association of School Psychologists (NASP) indicates that GSAs have a positive impact on school climate. NASP cites numerous benefits of GSAs, and recommends that school psychologists support GSAs (National Association of School Psychologists, 2011). Numerous organizations provide recommendations and assistance to students and schools interested in starting a Gay-Straight Alliance, including the Gay, Lesbian, and Straight Education Network, the American Civil Liberties Union, and the National Association of GSA Networks.

> ## ತಿ FOUNDATIONS RECOMMENDATION ಞ
>
> *Every middle school and high school should support a Gay-Straight Alliance that includes a faculty advisor who is an ally for sexual orientation issues.*

In 2011, the U.S. Department of Education issued a guidance letter to public schools indicating that not only does the department and administration back GSAs because they promote safe schools and foster affirming learning environments, but schools are legally required to afford all student groups the same opportunities to form, convene on school grounds, and have access to the same resources, according to the Equal Access Act of 1984. If schools prohibit GSAs from forming on campus, they could face legal action.

3. **Does your school make frequent overt efforts to promote respect for all individual students?**

Your school is probably already making an effort to infuse messages of tolerance and acceptance of others. Consider whether your school can commit to additional efforts because there is tremendous potential for schools to promote respect for all students. These strategies can be as simple as staff members asking questions, showing interest, and learning more about each student in the school, and as comprehensive as districtwide diversity initiatives to inform and represent students from all schools, races, cultures, and so on.

The Fort Bend ISD in Texas promotes respect for all students by holding an annual Diversity Conference for the entire district. Student leaders from each campus meet each month to plan their presentations for the daylong event. The conference is attended by more than 500 students, and it sets the tone for honoring and celebrating diversity throughout the year. This action-packed event provides students with the opportunity to discover new ideas, recognize the importance of shared leadership, and develop an energized approach for promoting diversity.

At the classroom level, teachers can instill messages of understanding, respect, and appreciation for diversity in curricula. For example, they can teach lessons about cultural leaders who represent a variety of races and ethnicities, provide information on LGBTQ leaders, and teach lessons about successful and inspirational people with disabilities. Black History Month is a great platform, but appreciation of diversity shouldn't be just a once-a-year message. Infuse the message throughout the school year in small and large ways. On the schoolwide level, your school might select a different culture or diversity topic each month and design activities for each content area around the diversity theme.

Staff understanding of diversity issues and commitment to teaching them is, of course, essential to making this initiative work. Create activities to help staff self-reflect about their interactions with students and whether they hold or display any personal biases that may be interfering with efforts to include and respect all students. Provide training to help staff members understand the history and experiences of diverse groups of people, including the cultures, races, and ethnicities of their students. Knowledge of their students' lives—their cultural customs and beliefs, and the discrimination they may experience, for example—may increase staff members' abilities to empathize and respond in culturally appropriate ways.

Following is a thought exercise for staff to help them reflect on personal biases that might affect how they interact with students.

Presentation 5: Schoolwide Bullying Prevention and Intervention

Identify one male and one female student who are very easy to like, get along with, and interact with frequently. Label these students Student A and Student B. Then identify one male student and one female student who are difficult to like, tough to get along with, and difficult to interact with. Label these students Student C and Student D. (Each staff member should identify these students privately and silently.)

	Student			
	A	**B**	**C**	**D**
Male	X		X	
Female		X		X
Easy to get along with	X	X		
Tough to get along with			X	X

Now imagine giving a direction to Student B, the easy-to-get-along-with female. For some reason, she snaps at you, "I'm not going to do that. Forget it." How would you respond? What would you say or do to change the student's behavior or connect with her?

Now imagine giving the same direction to Student C, the tough-to-get-along-with male. You receive the same response: "I'm not going to do that. Forget it." How would you respond? Would your response be the same or different from your response to Student B?

If your response was different, can you justify the difference? Was your response based on a behavior improvement plan or some other planned decision to help the student improve behavior? Does the student have a chronic problem that has been addressed by a plan that includes responding to misbehavior as you responded?

If Student C does not have any kind of behavior improvement plan, ask yourself why your response to Student C was different from your response to Student B. Is it simply because you don't like the student? Although it might be a natural response to treat these students differently because your relationships with them are different, how well you like a student should not dictate differences in your management plan. Physicians don't provide patients with different quality of care based on whether they personally like the patients. Also reflect on whether your response might be different because Student B is female and Student C is male and whether other biases such as race, family background, sexual orientation, religious views, weight, and so on are affecting your behavior.

Conduct the same exercise with different combinations of imaginary students: A and D, A and B, and C and D, for example.

Another area you should carefully evaluate is your library. Does it provide materials that are of interest and relevance to a wide variety of students, including books and videos on different belief systems, various cultural and racial groups, LGBTQ issues, and so on?

4. **Does your school provide training on the responsible use of power for student groups that are in positions of power?**

You've probably heard many anecdotes and examples of football teams, cheerleaders, and other strong groups in schools abusing their powers by using their social status to belittle or harm others. They sometimes seem to be energized by a mob mentality. We would like to present a phenomenal example of the opposite student behavior. In 2013, the *CBS Evening News* ran a story about a group of middle school football players in Olivet, Michigan, who hatched a plan to do something special for a classmate, a boy with a learning disability and social skills deficits. The team secretly conspired for weeks. They didn't tell their coaches or parents about the plan.

During one of their home games, the team purposely stopped the ball at the 1-yard line. Then they brought the student with special needs onto the field. As the next play began, the quarterback quickly handed the football to the boy, and the other players surrounded him so that he could carry the ball over the goal line for the touchdown.

"We wanted to prove that he was part of the team and one of us," explained one team member. Another team member admitted, "Nothing could wipe that smile off my face. I went from being someone who cared only about myself and my friends to someone who cared about everyone and making everyone's day." The parents of the student with special needs said, "Somebody's always going to have his back from now until the time he graduates." The reporter pointed out that "when the football team decides you're cool, pretty much everyone follows suit."

You can find the whole story at http://www.cbsnews.com/news/mich-middle-school-football-team-conspires-for-touching-touchdown/.

Imagine if students in positions of power were shown examples like this. Imagine they received explicit training and participated in discussions about ways they could use power responsibly and for the good of the school, as well as ways they should *not* use power. Imagine the difference this new way of thinking might make in your school.

5. **Does your school use methods to ensure that each student has at least one adult who knows them well and who they feel cares about them?**

   Identify ways to assess whether each student has a trusted adult in the building; for students who do not, try to improve their connections to the school. A simple way to assess is to create a questionnaire and have each student write the names of one or two staff members he or she would feel comfortable talking to about difficulties at school and one or two staff members he or she would feel comfortable talking to about difficulties outside of school. Students who think that no staff members fit these roles should still complete the questionnaire and indicate that they have no one. For confidentiality reasons, the principal should compile the data. For students who do not identify any staff members, inform the students' teachers and provide general advice and encouragement for connecting with the student. You might also connect the student more formally with a staff support person or mentor.

   If the administrator has time to put all the data into a spreadsheet, without staff names, he could share the data with staff to show that some staff members have many connections with students and some have few or none. If the administrator does not have time to create a spreadsheet, a simple scan of the data can reveal whether some staff names are mentioned frequently. The administrator can acknowledge those staff members and inform them that they are making a difference. He might want to speak privately with staff members whose names never or rarely appear to encourage them to make efforts to connect.

   Another assessment method is to post or hand out a list of all student names during a staff meeting and have staff initial next to the students they feel they can converse with in more detail than they would with a stranger—they can discuss more than the student's classwork, for example. Encourage staff members to try to connect with those students with zero, one, or two initials next to their names. Ask each staff member to identify two or three students they will especially target. Conduct this activity every year, once during the fall and once during winter, so that as staff members develop deeper connections with the students they identify, fewer and fewer students have no staff connections. A detailed method for conducting this exercise is included in Module D, Presentation 5, Task 2.

6. **Does your school comprehensively address the transition from elementary to middle school or from middle school to high school?**

   The frequency of bullying situations tends to increase during these transition periods, especially the transition from elementary to middle school. So part of your work on reducing bullying should involve identifying how to smooth the transition, minimize students' sense that they need to jockey for position within the student body, and provide the supports necessary to reduce students' anxiety and feelings of being lost or alone in the school.

Here's a practice that might be especially beneficial for identifying problems and formulating actions you can take to ease the transition for students. Toward the end of the school year, create a task force of students who were new to the school at the beginning of the year—for example, ninth graders who will begin tenth grade in the fall. These students should represent all different social groups. Through focused discussions, have students describe what went well about their transitions, what was problematic, and how the transition might be improved. Be sure to include a range of students, from very successful ones to those who have had significant difficulties, whether academic, social, or emotional. Use their recommendations to plan the transition for the next cohort that will enter the school.

Following are additional strategies for easing transitions and reducing the likelihood that students will engage in bullying behavior or experience victimization.

- Set up a peer mentoring system that links new students with responsible older students who can show them the ropes.

- During the spring, set up several tours and activities for students who will be transitioning to your school in the fall. For at-risk students and those who experienced significant difficulties in the old school, intensify your efforts to familiarize them with their new environment. For example, arrange for an adult mentor in middle school for a student who experienced frequent victimization in elementary school, and provide several opportunities before the new school year for the student and adult to get to know each other and develop rapport.

- If multiple schools feed into your school, offer structured activities for students from the feeder schools to meet and develop friendships with older students before the start of the new school year or even during the previous year.

- If your school has strong systems defined for classroom and common area management, assist the feeder schools in conducting activities to familiarize students with the expectations they will need to know in the fall. Also distribute information about clubs and activities, such as the magazine we suggested above in Question 2 of this task. Provide families with this information so they can help their children review the expectations and available activities over the summer.

Presentation 5: Schoolwide Bullying Prevention and Intervention

- Establish a Freshman Academy or something similar—a summer program to familiarize students with their new school. Students spend time in their new school, learn the expectations, and get advice on how to be successful.

7. **Does your school identify students who are at risk because of either externalizing or internalizing issues and link them with small group and individual interventions?**

Part of your effort to increase engagement should be to identify students who are at risk for bullying others or being bullied. Indicators include depression and anxiety, lack of anger management skills, hostile attribution bias, and academic, social skill, or coping deficits. Then link these students with appropriate supports.

Module F provides more information about developing Multi-Tiered Systems of Support, including universal screening and red-flag criteria, and identifying adults to advocate for students by linking them with interventions. It is worth noting that students who are identified as at risk because of externalizing issues may be more prone to bullying behavior, whereas students with internalizing issues may be at high risk for being targeted. This general guideline might help inform early interventions for students. So, as part of your tasks for this module, make note of how and when you will apply the information in Module F to bullying situations.

Staff members should try to connect at-risk students with suitable activities and clubs, engage the students, and connect them with appropriate skill groups, interventions, and supports.

Task 4 Action Steps & Evidence of Implementation

Action Steps	Evidence of Implementation
1. Complete each of the questions on the form Active Engagement for the Prevention of Bullying (Form E-14).	Foundations Process: Current Priorities
2. Develop activities, clubs, organizations, written information, policies, and procedures based on the suggestions in this task to improve student engagement, respect, and inclusiveness.	Foundations Archive: Students' Basic Needs, Bullying Prevention

BIBLIOGRAPHY

Adams, C. (2011). Recess makes kids smarter. *Instructor, 120*(5), 55–59. Retrieved from http://www.scholastic.com/teachers/article/recess-makes-kids-smarter

Allensworth, E. M., & Easton, J. Q. (2007). *What matters for staying on track and graduating in Chicago public schools: A close look at course grades, failures, and attendance in the freshman year.* Retrieved from http://ccsr.uchicago.edu/sites/default/files/publications/07%20What%20Matters%20Final.pdf

American Academy of Pediatrics, American Academy of Child and Adolescent Psychiatry, American Psychological Association, American Medical Assocation, American Association of Family Physicians, & American Psychiatric Association. (2000). *Joint statement on the impact of entertainment violence on children: Congressional Public Health Summit.* Retrieved from www2.aap.org/advocacy/releases/jstmtevc.htm

American Lung Association, Epidemiology and Statistics Unit, Research and Health Education Division (2012). *Trends in asthma morbidity and mortality.* Retrieved from http://www.lung.org/finding-cures/our-research/trend-reports/asthma-trend-report.pdf

Ameircan Psychological Association (2010). *Bullying: What parents, teachers can do to stop it.* Retrieved from http://www.apa.org/news/press/releases/2010/04/bullying.aspx

Applied Survey Research and Attendance Works (2011). *Attendance in early elementary grades: Associations with student characteristics, school readiness and third grade outcomes* (mini-report). Retrieved from http://www.attendanceworks.org/wordpress/wp-content/uploads/2010/04/ASR-Mini-Report-Attendance-Readiness-and-Third-Grade-Outcomes-7-8-11.pdf

Archer, A., & Gleason, M. (1990). *Skills for school success.* North Billerica, MA: Curriculum Associates.

Baker, M. L., Sigmon, N., & Nugent, M. E. (2001). *Truancy reduction: Keeping students in school* (Juvenile Justice Bulletin). Retrieved from U.S. Department of Justice, National Criminal Justice Reference Service website: http://www.ncjrs.gov/pdffiles1/ojjdp/188947.pdf

Balfanz, R., Bridgeland, J. M., Fox, J. H., DePaoli, J. L., Ingram, E. S., & Maushard, M. (2014). *Building a grad nation: Progress and challenge in ending the high school dropout epidemic.* Retrieved from http://diplomasnow.org/wp-content/uploads/2014/04/BGN-Report-2014_Full.pdf

Balfanz, R., & Byrnes, V. (2012). *Chronic absenteeism: Summarizing what we know from nationally available data.* Retrieved from Johns Hopkins University Center for Social Organization of Schools website: http://new.every1graduates.org/wp-content/uploads/2012/05/FINALChronicAbsenteeismReport_May16.pdf

Balfanz, R., & Byrnes, V. (2013). *Meeting the challenge of combating chronic absenteeism: Impact of the NYC mayor's interagency task force on chronic absenteeism and school attendance and its implications for other cities.* Retrieved from Johns Hopkins School of Education website: http://new.every1graduates.org/wp-content/uploads/2013/11/NYM-Chronic-Absenteeism-Impact-Report.pdf

Bazelon, E. (2013). *Sticks and stones: Defeating the culture of bullying and rediscovering the power of character and empathy.* New York, NY: Random House.

Becker, W. C., & Engelmann, S. (1971). *Teaching: A course in applied psychology.* Columbus, OH: Science Research Associates.

Boyse, K. (2010). *Television and children.* Retrieved from http://www.med.umich.edu/yourchild/topics/tv.htm

Brophy, J. E. (1980). *Teacher praise: A functional analysis.* East Lansing, MI: Institute for Research on Teaching.

Brophy, J. E. (1986). Teacher influences on student achievement. *American Psychologist, 4*(10), 1069–1077.

Brophy, J. (1987). Synthesis of research on strategies for motivating students to learn. *Educational Leadership, 45*(2), 40–48.

Bruner, C., Discher, A., & Chang, H. (2011). *Chronic elementary absenteeism: A problem hidden in plain sight.* Retrieved from http://www.attendanceworks.org/wordpress/wp-content/uploads/2010/04/ChronicAbsence.pdf

Cameron, J., & Pierce, W. D. (1994). Reinforcement, reward, and intrinsic motivation: A meta-analysis. *Review of Educational Research, 64*(3), 363–423.

Centers for Disease Control and Prevention (n.d.). *Kids and technology: Tips for parents in a high-tech world.* Retrieved from http://www.cdc.gov/media/subtopic/matte/pdf/cdcelectronicregression.pdf

Centers for Disease Control and Prevention. (2012). Youth risk behavior surveillance—United States, 2011. *MMWR 2012, 61*(4). Retrieved from http://www.cdc.gov/mmwr/pdf/ss/ss6104.pdf

Chang, H., & Romero, M. (2008). *Present, engaged, and accounted for: The critical importance of addressing chronic absence in the early grades.* New York, NY: National Center for Children in Poverty.

Collins, J. (2001). *Good to great: Why some companies make the leap . . . and others don't*. New York, NY: HarperCollins Publishers.

Colvin, G. (Writer/Producer). (1992). *Managing acting-out behavior: A staff development program* [video]. Longmont, CO: Sopris West.

Colvin, G., & Scott, T. M. (2015). *Managing the cycle of acting-out behavior in the classroom* (2nd ed.). Thousand Oaks, CA: Corwin.

Cook, C. R., Williams, K. R., Guerra, N. G., Kim, T. E., & Sadek, S. (2010). Predictors of bullying and victimization in childhood and adolescence: A meta-analytic investigation. *School Psychology Quarterly, 25*, 65–83.

Cooper, J. O., Heron, T. E., & Heward, W. L. (2007). *Applied behavior analysis* (2nd ed.). Upper Saddle River, NJ: Pearson.

Cotton, K. (1990). *Schoolwide and classroom discipline* (Close-Up #9). Portland, OR: Northwest Regional Educational Laboratory.

Council for Exceptional Children. (2009). *CEC's policy on physical restraint and seclusion procedures in school settings*. Retrieved from http://www.cec.sped.org/~/media/Files/Policy/Restraint%20and%20Seclusion/policy%20on%20r%20and%20s.pdf

Craig, W.M., & Pepler, D. (1997). Observations of bullying and victimization in the schoolyard. *Canadian Journal of School Psychology, 2*, 41–60.

Devoe, J. F., & Bauer, L. (2011). *Student victimization in U.S. schools: Results from the 2009 school crime supplement to the national crime victimization survey* (NCES 2012-314). Washington, DC: U.S. Department of Education, National Center for Education Statistics.

Dishion, T., & Dodge, K.A. (2005). Peer contagion in interventions for children and adolescents: Moving towards an understanding of the ecology and dynamics of change. *Journal of Abnormal Child Psychology, 33*(3), 395–400.

Donovan, M. S., & Cross, C. T. (Eds.) (2002). *Minority students in special education and gifted education*. Washington, DC: National Academy Press.

Duncan, A. (2011, June 14). *Key policy letters from the education secretary and deputy secretary* [Dear Colleague letter]. Retrieved from http://www2.ed.gov/policy/elsec/guid/secletter/110607.html

Emmer, E. T., & Evertson, C. M. (2012). *Classroom management for middle and high school teachers* (9th ed.). Upper Saddle River, NJ: Pearson.

Esler, A., Godber, Y., & Christenson, S. (2008). Best practices in supporting school-family partnerships. In A. Thomas & J. Grimes (Eds.), *Best practices in school psychology V* (pp. 917–936). Bethesda, MD: National Association of School Psychologists.

Espelage, D. (2002). *Bullying in early adolescence: The role of the peer group.* ERIC Digest. (ED471912) Retrieved from http://files.eric.ed.gov/fulltext/ED471912.pdf

Espelage, D. L, & Swearer, S. M. (Eds.). (2010). *Bullying in North American schools: A social-ecological perspective on prevention and intervention* (2nd ed.). London: Routledge.

Evertson, C. M., & Emmer, E. T. (2012). *Classroom management for elementary teachers* (9th ed.). Upper Saddle River, NJ: Pearson.

Fabelo, T., Thompson, M. D., Plotkin, M., Carmichael, D., Marchbanks, M. P. III, & Booth, E. A. (2011). *Breaking schools' rules: A statewide study of how school discipline relates to students' success and juvenile justice involvement.* Retrieved from http://csgjusticecenter.org/wp-content/uploads/2012/08/Breaking_Schools_Rules_Report_Final.pdf

Farmer, T. W., Petrin, R. A., Robertson, D. L., Faser, M. W., Hall, C. M., Day, S. H., & Dadisman, K. (2010). Peer relations of bullies, bully-victims, and victims: The two social worlds of bullying in second-grade classrooms. *Elementary School Journal, 110,* 364–392.

Farrington, D. P., & Ttofi, M. M. (2009). School-based programs to reduce bullying and victimization: A systematic review. *Campbell Systematic Reviews, 5*(6).

Feather, N. T. (1982). Expectancy-value approaches: Present status and future directions. In N. T. Feather (Ed.), *Expectations and actions: Expectancy-value models in psychology.* Hillsdale NJ: Erlbaum.

Ferguson, C. J., Miguel, C. S., Kilburn, J. C., & Sanchez, P. (2007). The effectiveness of school-based anti-bullying programs: A meta-analytic review. *Criminal Justice Review, 32*(4), 401–414.

Furlong, M., Felix, E. D., Sharkey, J. D., & Larson, J. (2005). Preventing school violence: A plan for safe and engaging schools. *Principal Leadership, 6*(1), 11–15. Retrieved from http://www.nasponline.org/resources/principals/Student%20Counseling%20Violence%20Prevention.pdf

Get Schooled and Hart Research (2012). *Skipping to nowhere: Students share their views about missing school.* Retrieved from https://getschooled.com/system/assets/assets/203/original/Hart_Research_report_final.pdf

Glossary of education reform for journalists, parents, and community members. (n.d.) Retrieved from http://edglossary.org/school-culture/

Goodenow, C., Szalacha, L., & Westheimer, K. (2006). School support groups, other school factors, and the safety of sexual minority adolescents. *Psychology in the Schools, 43*, 573–589. doi: 10.1002/pits.20173

Gottfredson, D. C., Gottfredson, G. D., & Hybl, L. G. (1993). Managing adolescent behavior: A multiyear, multischool study. *American Educational Research Journal, 30*(1), 179–215.

Graham, S. (2014). *Bullying: A module for teachers.* Retrieved from http://www.apa.org/education/k12/bullying.aspx?item=1

Hartman, S. (October 26, 2013). Mich. middle school football team conspires for touching touchdown [video]. *CBS Evening News.* Retrieved from http://www.cbsnews.com/news/mich-middle-school-football-team-conspires-for-touching-touchdown/

Jensen, E. (2009). *Teaching with poverty in mind: What being poor does to kids' brains and what schools can do about it.* Alexandria, VA: Association for Supervision and Curriculum Development.

Jenson, W., Rhode, G., & Reavis, H. K. (2009). *The Tough Kid tool box.* Eugene, OR: Ancora Publishing.

Kerr, J., & Nelson, C. (2002). *Strategies for addressing behavior problems in the classroom* (4th ed.). Englewood Cliffs, NJ: Merrill/Prentice Hall.

Kerr, J., Price, M., Kotch, J., Willis, S., Fisher, M., & Silva, S. (2012). Does contact by a family nurse practitioner decrease early school absence? *Journal of School Nursing, 28*, 38–46.

Kim, C. Y., Losen, D. J., and Hewitt, D. T. (2010). *The school-to-prison pipeline: Structuring legal reform.* New York, NY: New York University Press.

Klem, A. M., & Connell, J. P. (2004). Relationships matter: Linking teacher support to student engagement and achievement. *Journal of School Health, 74*(7), 262–273.

Kosciw, J. G., Greytak, E. A., Bartkiewicz, M. J., Boesen, M. J., & Palmer, N. A. (2012). *The 2011 national school climate survey: The experiences of lesbian, gay, bisexual, and transgender youth in our nation's school.* New York, NY: GLSEN. Retrieved from http://www.glsen.org/sites/default/files/2011%20National%20School%20Climate%20Survey%20Full%20Report.pdf

Kounin, J. S. (1977). *Discipline and group management in classrooms.* Huntington, NY: Krieger Publishing.

Kowalkski, R. M., & Limber, S. P. (2007). Electronic bullying among middle school students. *Journal of Adolescent Health, 41*, 22–30.

Losen, D. J. (2011). *Discipline policies, successful schools, and racial justice.* Boulder, CO: National Education Policy Center. Retrieved from http://nepc.colorado.edu/publication/discipline-policies

Losen, D. J., & Martinez, T. E. (2013). *Out of school & off track: The overuse of suspension in American middle and high schools.* Retrieved from http://civilrightsproject.ucla.edu/resources/projects/center-for-civil-rights-remedies/school-to-prison-folder/federal-reports/out-of-school-and-off-track-the-overuse-of-suspensions-in-american-middle-and-high-schools/OutofSchool-OffTrack_UCLA_4-8.pdf

Maag, J. (2001). *Powerful struggles: Managing resistance, building rapport.* Longmont, CO: Sopris West.

Marzano, R. J. (2003). *Classroom management that works: Research-based strategies for every teacher.* Alexandria, VA: Association for Supervision and Curriculum Development.

Maslow, A. H. (1962). Some basic propositions of a growth and self-actualization psychology. In A. W. Combs (Ed.), *Perceiving, behaving, becoming: A new focus for education* (pp. 34–49). Washington, D.C: Association for Supervision and Curriculum Development.

McNeely, C. A., Nonnemaker, J. A., & Blum, R. W. (2002). Promoting school connectedness: Evidence from the National Longitudinal Study of Adolescent Health. *Journal of School Health, 72*(4), 138–146.

Melton, G. D. (2014, January 30). Share this with all the schools, please [Web log post]. Retrieved from http://momastery.com/blog/2014/01/30/share-schools/

Merrell, K. W., Gueldner, B. A., Ross, S. W., & Isava, D. M. (2008). How effective are school bullying intervention programs? *School Psychology Quarterly, 23,* 26–42.

Musgrove, M., & Yudin, M. K. (2013). *Dear Colleague letter.* Washington, DC: U.S. Department of Education, Office of Special Education and Rehabilitative Services. Retrieved from https://www2.ed.gov/policy/speced/guid/idea/memosdcltrs/bullyingdcl-8-20-13.pdf

Nader, K. (2012). *Violence prevention and school climate reform* (School Climate Brief No. 5). New York, NY: National School Climate Center. Retrieved from http://www.schoolclimate.org/climate/schoolclimatebriefs.php

Nansel, T.R., Overpeck, M., Pilla, R.S., Ruan, W.J., Simons-Morton, B., & Scheidt, P. (2001). Bullying behavior among U.S. youth: Prevalence and association with psychosocial adjustment. *Journal of the American Medical Association, 285,* 2094–2100.

National Association for Sport and Physical Education (2006). *Recess for elementary school children* (Position Statement). Retrieved from http://www.eric.ed.gov/PDFS/ED541609.pdf

National Association of School Psychologists (2001). *Zero tolerance and alternative strategies: A fact sheet for educators and policymakers.* Retrieved from http://www.nasponline.org/resources/factsheets/zt_fs.aspx

National Association of School Psychologists. (2011). *Lesbian, gay, bisexual, transgender, and questioning (LGBTQ) youth* (Position Statement). Bethesda, MD: Author. http://www.nasponline.org/about_nasp/positionpapers/LGBTQ_Youth.pdf

National Center for Education Statistics (2012). *Digest of Education Statistics* (NCES 2014-015). Retrieved from http://nces.ed.gov/programs/digest/d12/ and http://nces.ed.gov/programs/digest/d12/tables/dt12_122.asp

O'Leary, K. D., & O'Leary, S. G. (1977). *Classroom management: The successful use of behavior modification* (2nd ed.). New York, NY: Pergamon Press.

Olweus, D., Limber, S., & Mihalic, S. F. (1999). *Bullying prevention program: Blueprints for violence prevention.* Boulder, CO: Center for the Study and Prevention of Violence, Institute of Behavioral Science, University of Colorado.

O'Neill, R. E., Horner, R. H., Albin, R. W., Storey, K., & Sprague, J. R. (1996). *Functional assessment and program development for problem behavior: A practical handbook* (2nd ed.). Belmont, CA: Cengage.

Payne, C. (2008). *So much reform, so little change: The persistence of failure in urban schools.* Boston, MA: Harvard Education Press.

Pearce, M. (October 15, 2013). Two Florida girls charged with bullying 12-yearold to death. *Los Angeles Times.* Retrieved from http://articles.latimes.com/2013/oct/15/nation/la-na-nn-florida-bullying-two-girls-arrested-20131015

Pellegrini, A. D. (2002). Bullying, victimization, and sexual harassment during the transition to middle school. *Educational Psychologist, 37*(3), 151–164.

Pellegrini, A. D., Bartini, M., & Brooks, F. (1999). School bullies, victims, and aggressive victims: Factors relating to group affiliation and victimization in early adolescence. *Journal of Educational Psychology, 91*(2), 216–224.

Polanin, J. R., Espelage, D. L., & Pigott, T. D. (2012). A meta-analysis of school-based bullying prevention programs' effects on bystander intervention behavior. *School Psychology Review, 41*(1), 47–65.

Purkey, W. W., & Novak, J. M. (2005). *Inviting school success: A self-concept approach to teaching, learning, and democratic practice in a connected world* (4th ed.). New York, NY: Wadsworth Publishing.

Ready, D. (2010). Socioeconomic disadvantage, school attendance, and early cognitive development: The differential effects of school exposure. *Sociology of Education, 83*(4), 271–289.

Rhode, G. R., Jenson, W. R., & Reavis, H. K. (2010). *The Tough Kid book: Practical classroom management strategies* (2nd ed.). Eugene, OR: Ancora Publishing.

Rideout, V. J., Foehr, U. G., & Roberts, D. F. (2010). Generation M2: Media in the lives of 8- to 18-year-olds. Menlo Park, CA: Henry J. Kaiser Family Foundation. Retrieved from http://www.kff.org/entmedia/upload/8010.pdf

Robers, S., Kemp, J., and Truman, J. (2013). *Indicators of school crime and safety: 2012* (NCES 2013-036/NCJ 241446). Washington, DC: U.S. Department of Education, National Center for Education Statistics, and U.S. Department of Justice, Bureau of Justice Statistics, Office of Justice Programs.

Rodkin, P. C. (2011). White house report/Bullying—and the power of peers. *Educational Leadership, 69*(1), 10–16.

Rodkin, P. C. (2012). Bullying and children's peer relationships. *Colleagues, 8*(2).

Ross, S. W., & Horner, R. H. (2009). Bully prevention in positive behavior support. *Journal of Applied Behavior Analysis, 42*, 747–759.

Rossen, E., & Cowen, K. C. (2012). *A framework for schoolwide bullying prevention and safety* [Brief]. Bethesda, MD: National Association of School Psychologists. Retrieved from http://www.nasponline.org/resources/bullying/bullying_brief_12.pdf

Salmivalli, C. (2009). Bullying and the peer group: A review. *Aggression and Violent Behavior, 15*, 112–120.

Seeley, K., Tombari, M. L., Bennett, L. J., & Dunkle, J. B. (2011). *Bullying in schools: An overview.* Juvenile Justice Bulletin. U.S. Department of Justice, Office of Juvenile Justice and Delinquency Prevention. Retrieved from http://www.ojjdp.gov/pubs/234205.pdf

Senate Committee on the Judiciary. (1999). *Children, violence, and the media: A report for parents and policy makers.* Retrieved from http://www.indiana.edu/~cspc/ressenate.htm

Sheets, R. H., & Gay, G. (1996). Student perceptions of disciplinary conflicts in ethnically diverse classrooms. *NASSP Bulletin, 80*(580), 84–94.

Skiba, R. J., Horner, R. H., Chung, C.-G., Rausch, M. K., May, S. L., & Tobin, T. (2011). Race is not neutral: A national investigation of African American and Latino disproportionality in school discipline. *School Psychology Review, 40*(1), 85–107.

Skiba, R. J., Michael, R. S., Nardo, A. C., & Peterson, R. L. (2002). The color of discipline: Sources of racial and gender disproportionality in school punishment. *Urban Review, 34*(4), 317–342.

Skiba, R., & Peterson, R. (2003). Teaching the social curriculum: School discipline as instruction. *Preventing School Failure, 47,* 66–73.

Smith, J. D., Schneider, B. H., Smith, P. K., & Ananiadou, K. (2004). The effectiveness of whole-school antibullying programs: A synthesis of evaluation research. *School Psychology Review, 33,* 548–561.

Smith, P. K., & Brain, P. (2000). Bullying in schools: Lessons from two decades of research. *Aggressive Behavior, 26,* 1–9.

Snakenborg, J., Van Acker, R., & Gable, R. (2011). Cyberbullying: Prevention and intervention to protect our children and youth, *Preventing School Failure: Alternative Education for Children and Youth, 55*(2), 88–95, doi: 10. 1080/1045988X.2011.539454

Sparks, S. D. (2010). Districts begin looking harder at absenteeism. *Education Week, 30*(6), 1, 12–13.

Spinks, S. (n.d.). Adolescent brains are works in progress. *Frontline.* Retrieved from http://www.pbs.org/wgbh/pages/frontline/shows/teenbrain/work/adolescent.html

Sprague, J. R., & Walker, H. M. (2005). *Safe and healthy schools: Practical prevention strategies.* New York, NY: Guilford Press.

Sprague, J. R., & Walker, H. M. (2010). Building safe and healthy schools to promote school success: Critical issues, current challenges, and promising approaches. In M. R. Shinn, H. M. Walker, & G. Stoner (Eds.), *Interventions for achievement and behavior problems in a three-tier model including RTI* (pp. 225–258). Bethesda, MD: National Association of School Psychologists.

Sprick, R. S. (1995). School-wide discipline and policies: An instructional classroom management approach. In E. Kame'enui & C. B. Darch (Eds.), *Instructional classroom management: A proactive approach to managing behavior* (pp. 234–267). White Plains, NY: Longman Press.

Sprick, R. S. (2009a). *CHAMPS: A proactive and positive approach to classroom management* (2nd ed.). Eugene, OR: Ancora Publishing.

Sprick, R. S. (2009b). *Stepping in: A substitute's guide to managing classroom behavior.* Eugene, OR: Ancora Publishing.

Sprick, R. S. (2009c). *Structuring success for substitutes.* Eugene, OR: Ancora Publishing.

Sprick, R. S. (2012). *Teacher's encyclopedia of behavior management: 100+ problems/500+ plans* (2nd ed.). Eugene, OR: Ancora Publishing.

Sprick, R. S. (2014). *Discipline in the secondary classroom: A positive approach to behavior management* (3rd ed.). San Francisco: Jossey-Bass.

Sprick, R. S., & Garrison, M. (2000). *ParaPro: Supporting the instructional process.* Eugene, OR: Ancora Publishing.

Sprick, R. S., & Garrison, M. (2008). *Interventions: Evidence-based behavior strategies for individual students* (2nd ed.). Eugene, OR: Ancora Publishing.

Sprick, R. S., Wise, B. J., Marcum, K., Haykin, M., McLaughlin, B., & Hays, S. (2016). *Leadership in behavior support: Administrator's guide* (2nd ed.). Eugene, OR: Ancora Publishing.

Sprick, R. S., Swartz, L., & Glang, A. (2005). *On the playground: A guide to playground management* [CD program]. Eugene, OR: Ancora Publishing and Oregon Center for Applied Sciences.

Sprick, R. S., Swartz, L., & Schroeder, S. (2006). *In the driver's seat: A roadmap to managing student behavior on the bus* [CD and DVD program]. Eugene, OR: Ancora Publishing and Oregon Center for Applied Sciences.

Stiller, B. C., Rhonda, N. T., Tomlanovich, A. K., Horner, R. H., & Ross, S. W. (2013). *Bullying and harassment prevention in positive behavior support: Expect respect.* Eugene, OR: University of Oregon. Retrieved from http://www.pbis.org/common/cms/files/pbisresources/2013_02_18_final_covr_manual_123x.pdf

StopBullying.gov. (n.d.). Misdirections in bullying prevention and intervention. Retrieved from http://www.stopbullying.gov/prevention/at-school/educate/misdirections-in-prevention.pdf

Sugai, G., Horner, R. H., Dunlap, G., Hieneman, M., Lewis, T., Nelson, C. M., & Wilcox, B. (2000). Applying positive behavior support and functional behavioral assessment in schools. *Journal of Positive Behavioral Interventions, 2,* 131–143.

Swearer, S. M., Espelage, D. L., & Napolitano, S. A. (2009). *Bullying prevention and intervention: Realistic strategies for schools.* New York, NY: Guilford Press.

Szalacha, L. A. (2003). Safer sexual diversity climates: Lessons learned from an evaluation of Massachusetts' safe schools program for gay and lesbian students. *American Journal of Education, 110*(1), 58–88.

U.S. Department of Education. (n.d.). *Misdirections in bullying prevention and intervention.* Retrieved from http://www.stopbullying.gov/prevention/at-school/educate/misdirections-in-prevention.pdf

U.S. Department of Education. (1998). *Preventing bullying: A manual for schools and communities.* Washington, DC: Author. (ED 453 592). Retrieved from http://files.eric.ed.gov/fulltext/ED453592.pdf

U.S. Department of Education. (2000). *Safeguarding our children: An action guide.* Retrieved from http://www2.ed.gov/admins/lead/safety/actguide/action_guide.pdf

U.S. Department of Education. (2012). *Restraint and seclusion: Resource document.* Retrieved from http://www2.ed.gov/policy/seclusion/restraints-and-seclusion-resources.pdf

U.S. Department of Education, Office Of Special Education And Rehabilitative Services. (2013). *Effective evidence-based practices for preventing and addressing bullying* [Dear Colleague letter]. Retrieved from https://www2.ed.gov/policy/speced/guid/idea/memosdcltrs/bullyingdcl-enclosure-8-20-13.pdf

U.S. Department of Education, U.S. Department of Health and Human Services, and U.S. Department of Justice (n.d.). StopBullying.gov [Web site]. Retrieved from http://www.stopbullying.gov

U.S. Department of Health and Human Services, Centers for Disease Control and Prevention (2009). *Fostering school connectedness: Improving student health and academic achievement.* Retrieved from http://www.cdc.gov/healthyyouth/protective/pdf/connectedness_administrators.pdf

U.S. Department of Health and Human Services, Centers for Disease Control and Prevention. (2012). *Youth violence: Facts at a glance.* Retrieved from http://www.cdc.gov/violenceprevention/pdf/yv_datasheet_2012-a.pdf

U.S. Department of Health and Human Services, Centers for Disease Control and Prevention. (2013a). *Asthma and schools.* Retrieved from http://www.cdc.gov/healthyyouth/asthma/index.htm

U.S. Department of Health and Human Services, Centers for Disease Control and Prevention. (2013b). *State and program examples: Healthy youth.* Retrieved from http://www.cdc.gov/chronicdisease/states/examples/pdfs/healthy-youth.pdf

U.S. Department of Justice, Office of Justice Programs, Office of Juvenile Justice and Delinquency Prevention. (2006). *Statistical briefing book.* Retrieved from http://www.ojjdp.gov/ojstatbb/offenders/qa03301.asp

University of Utah, Utah Education Policy Center. (2012). *Research brief: Chronic absenteeism.* Retrieved from Utah Data Alliance website: http://www.utahdataalliance.org/downloads/ChronicAbsenteeismResearchBrief.pdf

Wald, J., & Losen, D. J. (2003). Defining and redirecting a school-to-prison pipeline. *New Directions for Youth Development, 99,* 9–15. doi:10.1002/yd.51

Walker, H. (1995). *The acting-out child: Coping with classroom disruption.* Longmont, CO: Sopris West.

Walker, H. M., Colvin, G., & Ramsey, E. (1995). *Antisocial behavior in school: Strategies and best practices.* Pacific Grove, CA: Brooks/Cole.

Walker, H., Ramsey, E., & Gresham, F. M. (2003–2004a). Heading off disruptive behavior: How early intervention can reduce defiant behavior—and win back teaching time. *American Educator, Winter,* 6–21, 45–46.

Walker, H., Ramsey, E., & Gresham, F. M. (2003–2004b). How disruptive students escalate hostility and disorder—and how teachers can avoid it. *American Educator, Winter,* 22–27, 47–48.

Walker, H. M., Ramsey, E., & Gresham, F. M. (2004). *Antisocial behavior in school: Evidence-based practices* (2nd ed.). Belmont, CA: Cengage Learning.

Walker, H. M., Severson, H. H., & Feil, E. F. (2014). *Systematic screening for behavior disorders* (2nd ed.). Eugene, OR: Ancora Publishing.

Walker, H., & Walker, J. (1991). *Coping with noncompliance in the classroom: A positive approach for teachers.* Austin, TX: Pro-Ed.

Wentzel, K. R., & Brophy, J. E. (2013). *Motivating students to learn* (4th ed.). New York, NY: Taylor & Francis.

Wise, B. J., Marcum, K., Haykin, M., Sprick, R. S., & Sprick, M. (2011). *Meaningful work: Changing student behavior with school jobs.* Eugene, OR: Ancora Publishing.

Wiseman, R (2009). *Queen bees and wannabes.* New York, NY: Three Rivers Press.

Wright, A. (n.d.). Limbic system: Amgdala. In J. H. Byrne (Ed.). *Neuroscience online.* Retrieved from http://neuroscience.uth.tmc.edu/s4/chapter06.html

APPENDIX A
Foundations Implementation Rubric and Summary

The rubric is a relatively quick way for the Foundations Team to self-reflect on the implementation status of each of the modules. If you are just beginning *Foundations*, you might use this rubric toward the end of your first year of implementation. Thereafter, work through the rubric each year in the spring and consider using it in mid- to late fall to guide your work during the winter.

Each column—Preparing, Getting Started, Moving Along, and In Place—represents a different implementation status. The text in each row describes what that status looks like for each *Foundations* presentation. For each presentation, read the four descriptions from left to right. If the statements in the description are true, check the box. Each description assumes that the activities preceding it in the row have been attained. Stop working through the row when you reach a description that you cannot check off because you haven't implemented those tasks.

Notice that the descriptions for the In Place status include a section about evidence, which suggests where to find objective evidence that the described work is truly in place. If no documentation exists, think about whether the work has really been thoroughly completed. Throughout *Foundations*, we recommend archiving all your work so that policies and procedures are not forgotten or lost when staff changes occur.

When you've worked through every row, summarize your assessment on the Rubric Summary. If any items are rated as less than In Place, or if it has been more than 3 years since you have done so, work through the Implementation Checklist for that module. Of course, if you know that you need to begin work on a module or presentation, you can go directly to the corresponding content.

> For directions to print the rubric and summary, see Appendix C.

For Module B, evaluate (separately) the common areas and schoolwide policies that you have implemented—that is, you've structured them for success and taught students the behavioral expectations. Use the rows labeled Other for your school's common areas and schoolwide policies that do not appear on the rubric by default.

Figure A-1 shows a summary form completed by an imaginary school in the spring of their second year of *Foundations* implementation. They have highlighted the checkboxes to create a horizontal bar graph, giving the evaluation an effective visual component. They've done a great job on most of Module A, the common areas they've prioritized so far (hallways and cafeteria), and Welcoming New Staff, Students, and Families (C7). They need to work a bit more on staff engagement and unity (A5) and most of Module C, which they began in Year 2. Modules D, E, and F are blank because they plan to work on them in future years.

Figure A-1 Sample Foundations Rubric Summary

	Preparing (1)	Getting Started (2)	Moving Along (3)	In Place (4)
Module A Presentations				
A1. Foundations: A Multi-Tiered System of Behavior Support	X	X	X	X
A2. Team Processes	X	X	X	X
A3. The Improvement Cycle	X	X	X	X
A4. Data-Driven Processes	X	X	X	X
A5. Developing Staff Engagement and Unity	X	X		
Module B Presentations				
Hallways	X	X	X	X
Restrooms				
Cafeteria	X	X	X	X
Playground, Courtyard, or Commons				
Arrival				
Dismissal				
Dress Code				
Other:				
Other:				
Other:				
Other:				
Module C Presentations				
C2. Guidelines for Success	X	X	X	
C3. Ratios of Positive Interactions	X	X		
C4. Improving Attendance	X	X	X	
C5 & C6. School Connectedness and Programs and Strategies for Meeting Needs	X	X		
C7. Welcoming New Staff, Students, and Families	X	X	X	X
Module D Presentations				
D1. Proactive Procedures, Corrective Procedures, and Individual Interventions				
D2. Developing Three Levels of Misbehavior				
D3. Staff Responsibilities for Responding to Misbehavior				
D4. Administrator Responsibilities for Responding to Misbehavior				
D5. Preventing the Misbehavior That Leads to Referrals and Suspensions				
Module E Presentations				
E1. Ensuring a Safe Environment for Students				
E2. Attributes of Safe and Unsafe Schools				
E3. Teaching Conflict Resolution				
E4. Analyzing Bullying Behaviors, Policies, and School Needs				
E5. Schoolwide Bullying Prevention and Intervention				
Module F Presentations				
F2. Supporting Classroom Behavior: The Three-Legged Stool				
F3. Articulating Staff Beliefs and Solidifying Universal Procedures				
F4. Early-Stage Interventions for General Education Classrooms				
F5. Matching the Intensity of Your Resources to the Intensity of Your Needs				
F6. Problem-Solving Processes and Intervention Design				
F7. Sustainability and District Support				

Additional information about the rubric appears in Module F, Presentation 7, Task 1.

Thanks to Carolyn Novelly and Kathleen Bowles of Duval County Public Schools in Florida. We modeled the Foundations Implementation Rubric on a wonderful document they developed called the School Climate/Conditions for Learning Checklist. Thanks also to Pete Davis of Long Beach, California, for sharing samples of rubrics and innovation configuration scales.

School Name _____ Date _____ **Module A**

Foundations Implementation Rubric and Summary (p. 1 of 8)

Directions: In each row, check off each description that is true for your *Foundations* implementation. Then summarize your assessment on the Rubric Summary form. For Module B, evaluate each common area and schoolwide policy separately, and use the rows labeled Other for common areas and schoolwide policies that do not appear on the rubric by default. *Note:* Each block assumes that the activities in previous blocks in the row have been attained.

Presentation	Preparing (1) ☐	Getting Started (2) ☐	Moving Along (3) ☐	In Place (4) ☐
A1 Foundations: A Multi-Tiered System of Behavior Support	Staff are aware of the *Foundations* approach and basic beliefs, including that *Foundations* is a process for guiding the entire staff in the construction and implementation of a comprehensive approach to behavior support.	*Foundations* multi-tiered system of support (MTSS) processes are coordinated with academic MTSS (RTI) processes, and team organization has been determined (e.g., one MTSS Team with a behavior task force and an academic task force).	Staff have been introduced to the STOIC acronym and understand that student behavior and motivation can be continuously improved by manipulating the STOIC variables: Structure, Teach, Observe, Interact positively, and Correct fluently.	A preliminary plan has been developed for using the *Foundations* modules. For a school just beginning the process, the plan includes working through all the modules sequentially. For a school that has implemented aspects of positive behavior support, the team has self-assessed strengths, weaknesses, and needs using this rubric. **Evidence:** Foundations Implementation Rubric
A2 Team Processes	Foundations Team members have been identified. They directly represent specific faculty and staff groups, and they have assigned roles and responsibilities.	Foundations Team attends trainings, meets at school, and has established and maintains a Foundations Process Notebook and Foundations Archive.	Foundations Team members present regularly to faculty and communicate with the entire staff. They draft proposals and engage staff in the decision-making process regarding school climate, behavior, and discipline.	Foundations Team is known by all staff and is highly involved in all aspects of climate, safety, behavior, motivation, and student connectedness. **Evidence:** Staff members represented by Foundations Team members and presentations to staff are documented in the Foundations Process Notebook.
A3 The Improvement Cycle	Foundations Team is aware of the Improvement Cycle and keeps staff informed of team activities.	Foundations Team involves staff in setting priorities and in implementing improvements.	Foundations Team involves staff in using multiple data sources to establish a hierarchical list of priorities and adopt new policies. Team members seek input from staff regarding their satisfaction with the efficacy of recently adopted policies and procedures.	All staff actively participate in all aspects of the Improvement Cycle, such as setting priorities, developing revisions, adopting new policies and procedures, and implementation. Foundation Team presents to staff at least monthly. **Evidence:** Memos to staff and PowerPoint presentation files are documented in the Foundations Process Notebook.
A4 Data-Driven Processes	Administrators and Foundations Team review discipline data and establish baselines.	Common area observations and student, staff, and parent climate surveys are conducted yearly.	Discipline, climate survey, and common area observation data are reviewed and analyzed regularly.	Based on the data, school policies, procedures, and guidelines are reviewed and modified as needed (maintaining the Improvement Cycle).
A5 Developing Staff Engagement and Unity	Foundations Team regularly communicates with staff through staff meetings, scheduled professional development, memos, and so on.	Foundations Team members understand that they play a key role in staff unity. They periodically assess whether any factions of staff are disengaged and how they can develop greater staff engagement in the *Foundations* process.	A building-based administrator attends most *Foundations* trainings and plays an active role in team meetings and in assisting the team in unifying staff.	For districts with more than five or six schools, a district-based team meets at least once per quarter to keep the *Foundations* continuous improvement processes active in all schools. **Evidence:** Meeting minutes and staff presentations are documented in the Foundations Process Notebook.

If any items are rated as less than In Place or if it has been more than 3 years since you have done so, work through the Module A Implementation Checklist.

Foundations Implementation Rubric and Summary (p. 2 of 8)

School Name _____ Date _____ *Module B*

Common Area	Preparing (1)	Getting Started (2)	Moving Along (3)	In Place (4)
Hallways	☐ Common area observations are conducted and data from multiple sources are collected and analyzed.	☐ Current structures and procedures have been evaluated and protected, modified, or eliminated.	☐ Lesson plans have been developed, taught, practiced, and re-taught, when necessary.	☐ Common area supervisory procedures are communicated to staff and monitored for implementation. **Evidence:** Policies, procedures, and lessons are documented in the Foundations Archive and, as appropriate, in the Staff Handbook.
Restrooms	☐ Common area observations are conducted and data from multiple sources are collected and analyzed.	☐ Current structures and procedures have been evaluated and protected, modified, or eliminated.	☐ Lesson plans have been developed, taught, practiced, and re-taught, when necessary.	☐ Common area supervisory procedures are communicated to staff and monitored for implementation. **Evidence:** Policies, procedures, and lessons are documented in the Foundations Archive and, as appropriate, in the Staff Handbook.
Cafeteria	☐ Common area observations are conducted and data from multiple sources are collected and analyzed.	☐ Current structures and procedures have been evaluated and protected, modified, or eliminated.	☐ Lesson plans have been developed, taught, practiced, and re-taught, when necessary.	☐ Common area supervisory procedures are communicated to staff and monitored for implementation. **Evidence:** Policies, procedures, and lessons are documented in the Foundations Archive and, as appropriate, in the Staff Handbook.
Playground, Courtyard, or Commons	☐ Common area observations are conducted and data from multiple sources are collected and analyzed.	☐ Current structures and procedures have been evaluated and protected, modified, or eliminated.	☐ Lesson plans have been developed, taught, practiced, and re-taught, when necessary.	☐ Common area supervisory procedures are communicated to staff and monitored for implementation. **Evidence:** Policies, procedures, and lessons are documented in the Foundations Archive and, as appropriate, in the Staff Handbook.
Arrival	☐ Common area observations are conducted and data from multiple sources are collected and analyzed.	☐ Current structures and procedures have been evaluated and protected, modified, or eliminated.	☐ Lesson plans have been developed, taught, practiced, and re-taught, when necessary.	☐ Common area supervisory procedures are communicated to staff and monitored for implementation. **Evidence:** Policies, procedures, and lessons are documented in the Foundations Archive and, as appropriate, in the Staff Handbook.
Dismissal	☐ Common area observations are conducted and data from multiple sources are collected and analyzed.	☐ Current structures and procedures have been evaluated and protected, modified, or eliminated.	☐ Lesson plans have been developed, taught, practiced, and re-taught, when necessary.	☐ Common area supervisory procedures are communicated to staff and monitored for implementation. **Evidence:** Policies, procedures, and lessons are documented in the Foundations Archive and, as appropriate, in the Staff Handbook.
Other: _____	☐ Common area observations are conducted and data from multiple sources are collected and analyzed.	☐ Current structures and procedures have been evaluated and protected, modified, or eliminated.	☐ Lesson plans have been developed, taught, practiced, and re-taught, when necessary.	☐ Common area supervisory procedures are communicated to staff and monitored for implementation. **Evidence:** Policies, procedures, and lessons are documented in the Foundations Archive and, as appropriate, in the Staff Handbook.
Other: _____	☐ Common area observations are conducted and data from multiple sources are collected and analyzed.	☐ Current structures and procedures have been evaluated and protected, modified, or eliminated.	☐ Lesson plans have been developed, taught, practiced, and re-taught, when necessary.	☐ Common area supervisory procedures are communicated to staff and monitored for implementation. **Evidence:** Policies, procedures, and lessons are documented in the Foundations Archive and, as appropriate, in the Staff Handbook.

If any items are rated as less than In Place or if it has been more than 3 years since you have done so, work through the Module B Implementation Checklist.

Foundations Implementation Rubric and Summary (p. 3 of 8) — Module B

School Name _____ Date _____

Schoolwide Policy	Preparing (1)	Getting Started (2)	Moving Along (3)	In Place (4)
Dress Code	☐ Foundations Team has discussed the clarity and consistency of the current schoolwide policy.	☐ Data from multiple sources about the efficacy of the policy have been gathered and analyzed.	☐ The policy has been analyzed for clarity, efficacy, and consistency of enforcement.	☐ Schoolwide policies, lessons, and procedures have been written and are reviewed as needed with staff, students, and parents. **Evidence:** Policies, lessons, and procedures are documented in the Foundations Archive and, as appropriate, in the Staff Handbook.
Other: _____	☐ Foundations Team has discussed the clarity and consistency of the current schoolwide policy.	☐ Data from multiple sources about the efficacy of the policy have been gathered and analyzed.	☐ The policy has been analyzed for clarity, efficacy, and consistency of enforcement.	☐ Schoolwide policies, lessons, and procedures have been written and are reviewed as needed with staff, students, and parents. **Evidence:** Policies, lessons, and procedures are documented in the Foundations Archive and, as appropriate, in the Staff Handbook.
Other: _____	☐ Foundations Team has discussed the clarity and consistency of the current schoolwide policy.	☐ Data from multiple sources about the efficacy of the policy have been gathered and analyzed.	☐ The policy has been analyzed for clarity, efficacy, and consistency of enforcement.	☐ Schoolwide policies, lessons, and procedures have been written and are reviewed as needed with staff, students, and parents. **Evidence:** Policies, lessons, and procedures are documented in the Foundations Archive and, as appropriate, in the Staff Handbook.
Other: _____	☐ Foundations Team has discussed the clarity and consistency of the current schoolwide policy.	☐ Data from multiple sources about the efficacy of the policy have been gathered and analyzed.	☐ The policy has been analyzed for clarity, efficacy, and consistency of enforcement.	☐ Schoolwide policies, lessons, and procedures have been written and are reviewed as needed with staff, students, and parents. **Evidence:** Policies, lessons, and procedures are documented in the Foundations Archive and, as appropriate, in the Staff Handbook.
Other: _____	☐ Foundations Team has discussed the clarity and consistency of the current schoolwide policy.	☐ Data from multiple sources about the efficacy of the policy have been gathered and analyzed.	☐ The policy has been analyzed for clarity, efficacy, and consistency of enforcement.	☐ Schoolwide policies, lessons, and procedures have been written and are reviewed as needed with staff, students, and parents. **Evidence:** Policies, lessons, and procedures are documented in the Foundations Archive and, as appropriate, in the Staff Handbook.
Other: _____	☐ Foundations Team has discussed the clarity and consistency of the current schoolwide policy.	☐ Data from multiple sources about the efficacy of the policy have been gathered and analyzed.	☐ The policy has been analyzed for clarity, efficacy, and consistency of enforcement.	☐ Schoolwide policies, lessons, and procedures have been written and are reviewed as needed with staff, students, and parents. **Evidence:** Policies, lessons, and procedures are documented in the Foundations Archive and, as appropriate, in the Staff Handbook.
Other: _____	☐ Foundations Team has discussed the clarity and consistency of the current schoolwide policy.	☐ Data from multiple sources about the efficacy of the policy have been gathered and analyzed.	☐ The policy has been analyzed for clarity, efficacy, and consistency of enforcement.	☐ Schoolwide policies, lessons, and procedures have been written and are reviewed as needed with staff, students, and parents. **Evidence:** Policies, lessons, and procedures are documented in the Foundations Archive and, as appropriate, in the Staff Handbook.
Other: _____	☐ Foundations Team has discussed the clarity and consistency of the current schoolwide policy.	☐ Data from multiple sources about the efficacy of the policy have been gathered and analyzed.	☐ The policy has been analyzed for clarity, efficacy, and consistency of enforcement.	☐ Schoolwide policies, lessons, and procedures have been written and are reviewed as needed with staff, students, and parents. **Evidence:** Policies, lessons, and procedures are documented in the Foundations Archive and, as appropriate, in the Staff Handbook.

If any items are rated as less than In Place or if it has been more than 3 years since you have done so, work through the Module B Implementation Checklist.

School Name _____ Date _____

Foundations Implementation Rubric and Summary (p. 4 of 8)

Module C

Presentation	Preparing (1)	Getting Started (2)	Moving Along (3)	In Place (4)
C2 Guidelines for Success (GFS)	☐ All staff understand what Guidelines for Success (GFS) are and why they are important.	☐ Foundations Team has drafted proposals and engaged all stakeholders in the decision-making process of developing GFS.	☐ GFS have been finalized and posted and are reviewed regularly.	☐ GFS are embedded into the culture and are part of the common language of the school. **Evidence:** Procedures for teaching and motivating students about GFS are documented in the Foundations Archive, Staff Handbook, and Student and Parent Handbook.
C3 Ratios of Positive Interactions	☐ Staff have been taught the concept of 3:1 ratios of positive interactions and the importance of creating a positive climate and improving student behavior.	☐ Staff have been taught how to monitor ratios of positive interactions and are encouraged to evaluate their interactions with students.	☐ Administrator plans for teachers to observe and calculate other teachers' classroom ratios of interactions; the teachers involved meet to discuss outcomes.	☐ Observation data show that most staff at most times strive to interact with students at least three times more often when students are behaving responsibly than when they are misbehaving. **Evidence:** Procedures for teaching and motivating staff are documented in the Foundations Archive and Staff Handbook.
C4 Improving Attendance	☐ Average daily attendance is monitored to view long-term trends and patterns. Faculty and staff have been made aware of the importance of encouraging regular attendance by all students.	☐ All students with chronic absenteeism (absent 10% or more of school days) are identified at least quarterly; Foundations Team determines whether universal intervention is warranted.	☐ Each student with chronic absenteeism is identified and assigned one school-based support person who monitors whether additional support is needed. Foundations Team has analyzed attendance data and analyzed policies for clarity and efficacy.	☐ Every student with chronic absenteeism that has been resistant to universal and Tier 2 supports becomes the focus of a multidisciplinary team effort. **Evidence:** Data on average daily attendance and chronic absenteeism as well as efforts to improve attendance (e.g., parent newsletters) are documented in the Foundations Process Notebook.
C5 & C6 School Connectedness and Programs and Strategies for Meeting Needs	☐ Foundations Team has analyzed the degree to which current programs and practices meet the needs of all students (outstanding, average, and at risk).	☐ Foundations Team has developed proposals for programs and practices that might help meet unmet needs of students (e.g., the average student's need for purpose and belonging).	☐ Faculty and staff have implemented programs and practices designed to meet basic needs of all students (e.g., Mentorship, Student of the Week, Meaningful Work).	☐ Programs to meet students' basic needs are in place and analyzed at least once per year to determine their effectiveness and assess whether the needs of any student groups are not being met. **Evidence:** Analysis is documented in the Foundations Process Notebook, and programs and practices for meeting needs are documented in the Foundations Archive.
C7 Welcoming New Staff, Students, and Families	☐ Foundations Team has reviewed the welcoming aspects of the school, such as signage, website, and phone and front office procedures, and has suggested improvements.	☐ Foundations Team has analyzed and suggested improvements for welcoming and orienting new students and families at the beginning of the school year. (New students include those in a new grade-level cohort [e.g., ninth graders in high school] and students who are not part of that cohort.)	☐ Foundations Team has analyzed procedures and suggested improvements for welcoming new students and families who arrive during the school year. Improvements might include written information about rules, procedures, GFS, and so on.	☐ Foundations Team has analyzed procedures and suggested improvements for welcoming new staff members, both professional and nonprofessional, at the beginning of the year. New staff members are oriented to essential procedures and the culture and climate defined by the school's behavior support procedures. **Evidence:** All policies and procedures for welcoming and orienting staff, students, and families are documented in the Foundations Archive.

If any items are rated as less than In Place or if it has been more than 3 years since you have done so, work through the Module C Implementation Checklist.

School Name _____ Date _____ *Module D*

Foundations Implementation Rubric and Summary (p. 5 of 8)

Presentation	Preparing (1) ☐	Getting Started (2) ☐	Moving Along (3) ☐	In Place (4) ☐
D1 Proactive Procedures, Corrective Procedures, and Individual Interventions	Foundations Team is aware of data and staff opinions about consistency in correcting misbehavior, including clarity of staff roles in discipline compared with administrative roles.	Staff understand the potential limitations of office referral as a corrective procedure and avoid using it whenever possible.	Staff have been made aware of the limited benefits and potential drawbacks (including disparate impact) of out-of-school suspension (OSS) as a corrective consequence.	Staff avoid pressuring administrators to use OSS. Staff perceptions of consistency and administrative support for disciplinary actions are documented in staff survey results. **Evidence:** Discussions on these topics are documented in the Foundations Process Notebook.
D2 Developing Three Levels of Misbehavior	Staff are aware of the concept of three levels of misbehavior: Level 1 (mild), Level 2 (moderate), and Level 3 (severe) misbehavior.	Annually, staff discuss and agree on what behavior *must* be sent to the administrator, what can be sent to the administrator, and what should be handled in the setting in which the infraction occurred (3-level system for responding to misbehavior).	A referral form that reflects the agreed-upon definition of Level 3 misbehavior has been developed. A notification form that reflects the agreed-upon definition of Level 2 misbehavior has been developed. (Alternatively, both Level 2 and Level 3 may be on one form.) Accurate data are kept and analyzed quarterly for all Level 2 and Level 3 misbehaviors and consequences.	Data are collected on the implementation of the 3-level system for responding to misbehavior and on staff and administrator satisfaction with the system. **Evidence:** All aspects of the policy are documented in the Foundations Archive and Staff Handbook.
D3 Staff Responsibilities for Responding to Misbehavior	Staff have generated and administrators have approved a menu of corrective consequences for use in common areas.	Staff have generated and administrators have approved a menu of corrective consequences for use in classrooms.	Staff have been trained in how to use Level 2 notifications as a process for moving toward collaborative planning for severe or chronic behavior problems.	Staff have been trained in writing objective and appropriate office referrals for Level 3 misbehavior. **Evidence:** Menus and procedures are documented in the Foundations Archive and Staff Handbook.
D4 Administrator Responsibilities for Responding to Misbehavior	Procedures have been developed for responding to Level 2 notifications to ensure that the reporting staff member receives timely feedback and that administrators and support staff take appropriate actions.	Office procedures for dealing with students sent to the office have been analyzed and streamlined. Students do not get too much attention from office staff or staff members who visit the office	Administrators are familiar with the game plan for dealing with Level 3 incidents. The game plan includes a menu of alternative consequences to out-of-school suspension.	If the school has an ISS program, that program has been analyzed and revised as needed to ensure that it is highly structured and includes an instructional component. **Evidence:** All procedures for Level 2 and Level 3 infractions are documented in the Foundations Archive.
D5 Preventing the Misbehavior That Leads to Referrals and Suspensions	Foundations Team has examined data on Level 2 and Level 3 infractions to determine what misbehaviors get students into trouble.	Foundations Team has reviewed the lessons in Module D (how to interact appropriately with adults) and discussed whether they might reduce misbehaviors that get students into trouble.	To avoid duplication, the Foundations Team has compared the Module D lessons with other social skills or social-emotional curricula currently in use. Staff have agreed on a plan for when and how to teach expected behaviors to all students.	Foundations Team has discussed whether re-teaching the Module D lessons (or similar) in ISS or detention settings would be beneficial; if so, the team has planned when and how to re-teach. **Evidence:** Lesson plans and teaching logistics and schedule are documented in the Foundations Archive.

If any items are rated as less than In Place or if it has been more than 3 years since you have done so, work through the Module D Implementation Checklist.

Foundations Implementation Rubric and Summary (p. 6 of 8)

School Name _____ Date _____

Module E

Presentation	Preparing (1)	Getting Started (2)	Moving Along (3)	In Place (4)
E1 Ensuring a Safe Environment for Students	☐ Team members are aware of their responsibilities for overseeing school safety efforts. The team coordinates with other teams or task forces that may be doing similar work and avoids duplicating other efforts.	☐ Foundations Team has viewed or read Module E and has compared that content with the school's current efforts toward safety, managing conflict, and bullying prevention. The team has developed a proposal for closing any gaps in the current efforts.	☐ Foundations Team has made staff aware of the importance of a comprehensive view of safety that includes preparing for outside attackers as well as the more common occurrences of playground injuries, student fights, bullying, and so on.	☐ Foundations Team has assessed problems with safety, conflict, and bullying within the last 3 years. If problems exist, a plan for using or adapting information from this module and integrating them with current curriculum or procedures has been completed. **Evidence:** Data analyses are documented in the Foundations Process Notebook, and final policies and procedures are documented in the Foundations Archive.
E2 Attributes of Safe and Unsafe Schools	☐ Team members and other staff directly involved with safety concerns have viewed or read Presentation 2 and have completed (individually) the form Understanding the Attributes of Safe and Unsafe Schools.	☐ Foundations Team has compiled individual responses to Understanding Attributes of Safe and Unsafe Schools and correlated those data with safety assessments completed in the last 3 years. Information about strengths and concerns has been shared with staff, and priorities have been set.	☐ Foundations Team and other staff involved with safety concerns have completed the form Assessing Emergency Preparedness, evaluated current plans for natural disasters and man-made emergencies, revised any weak procedures, including training on policies regarding seclusion and restraint.	☐ Foundations Team has completed the form Lessons to Increase Safety and Belonging, reviewed the Module E sample lessons, and evaluated whether current problems and policies address all features of the sample lessons. If there are gaps, a plan to teach some or all of the *Foundations* lessons is established. **Evidence:** Lesson plans and procedures are documented in the Foundations Archive.
E3 Teaching Conflict Resolution	☐ Foundations Team has assessed whether the school has a conflict resolution strategy that students and staff use when necessary. If so, document the effective procedures in the Foundations Archive (and skip the rest of this row).	☐ Foundations Team has reviewed the concepts and lessons in the Stop-Think-Plan (STP) approach and has prepared an implementation plan for staff.	☐ With staff input, lessons have been revised, an implementation plan has been established, and a process is in place for training all staff in how to encourage students to use the conflict-resolution strategy.	☐ Foundations Team has established a process for evaluating the effectiveness of STP by analyzing multiple data sources. The policy and lessons are revised and staff are retrained when necessary, and successes are celebrated. **Evidence:** Data analyses are documented in the Foundations Process Notebook, and lessons and teaching procedures are documented in the Foundations Archive.
E4 Analyzing Bullying Behavior, Policies, and School Needs	☐ Foundations Team is aware of the content of this presentation and can compare it with current policies and procedures related to bullying.	☐ Foundations Team has completed the form School-Based Analysis of Bullying Data and has identified whether new or revised procedures need to be implemented to enhance the current use of data related to bullying.	☐ Foundations Team has completed the form School-Based Analysis of Bullying Policies and has identified whether new or revised policies need to be implemented to enhance current policies related to bullying.	☐ Quarterly, the Foundations Team reviews data related to bullying. Annually, the team uses those data to answer each of the questions in the form STOIC Analysis for Universal Prevention of Bullying (or an equivalent process), and improvement priorities are established. **Evidence:** Data analyses are documented in the Foundations Process Notebook.
E5 Schoolwide Bullying Prevention and Intervention	☐ Foundations Team has completed the form Staff Training in Preventing and Responding to Bullying and has developed and implemented a plan to fill in any identified gaps in current practices.	☐ Foundations Team has completed the form Student Training in Preventing and Responding to Bullying. As part of a previously adopted bullying curriculum or through the *Foundations* lessons, students are taught about bullying prevention.	☐ Foundations Team has completed the form Family Training in Preventing and Responding to Bullying and has developed an implementation plan to fill in any identified gaps in current practices.	☐ Foundations Team has completed the form Active Engagement for the Prevention of Bullying and has developed an implementation plan to fill in any gaps in current practices. Bullying issues are a regular part of the team's work and are integrated into staff development efforts. **Evidence:** Ongoing discussions are documented in the Foundations Process Notebook. Established programs to enhance student engagement are documented in the Foundations Archive.

If any items are rated as less than In Place or if it has been more than 3 years since you have done so, work through the Module E Implementation Checklist.

School Name _____ Date _____

Foundations Implementation Rubric and Summary (p. 7 of 8) — Module F

Presentation	Preparing (1)	Getting Started (2)	Moving Along (3)	In Place (4)
F2 Supporting Classroom Behavior: The Three-Legged Stool	☐ A research-based model for classroom management has been adopted at the building or district level. All teachers have access to training, and teachers new to the building or district receive the same training.	☐ School and district personnel are identified as resources for teachers who would like observations, feedback, and coaching. An effort is made to actively market the benefits of coaching support.	☐ The administrator has communicated clear outcomes and goals of effective classroom management: • 90% engagement • 95% respectful interactions • 95% of behavior matches posted expectations	☐ The model creates a common language among teachers, support staff, coaches, and administrators for problem solving and intervention. Data are collected and analyzed to evaluate classroom management efforts. **Evidence:** Information on the model, administrative walk-through visits, and coaching supports is included in the Foundations Archive and Staff Handbook.
F3 Articulating Staff Beliefs and Solidifying Universal Procedures	☐ Foundations Team has reviewed sample staff beliefs about behavior management.	☐ In faculty and staff meetings, faculty and staff have examined and discussed sample staff beliefs about behavior management.	☐ All staff have developed and adopted a set of written staff beliefs regarding discipline and behavior, and ensured that it aligned with the school's mission statement.	☐ To solidify the culture of the school and to guide the ongoing development of school policies and procedures, staff beliefs are reviewed, discussed, and revised as needed at least annually. **Evidence:** Staff beliefs and the review process are documented in the Foundations Archive and Staff Handbook.
F4 Early-Stage Interventions for General Education Classrooms	☐ Foundations Team and support staff (counselor, school psychologist, and so on) understand the concept of early-stage intervention.	☐ Foundations Team, support staff, and principal (or district administrators) agree on the interventions that should be included in the early-stage protocol.	☐ All teachers and support staff have been trained on the interventions in the school or district early-stage protocol, including how and why to keep records of each intervention.	☐ Data Collection and Debriefing (or an equivalent) is adopted as a required intervention for most chronic behavioral problems. Data must be charted before assistance is requested from support staff or problem-solving teams. **Evidence:** Expectations about when and how to get assistance are included in the Foundations Archive and Staff Handbook.
F5 Matching the Intensity of Your Resources to the Intensity of Your Needs	☐ Foundations Team and support staff (counselor, psychologist, and so on) have identified a set of red-flag criteria and (if possible) have conducted universal screening to identify students who may need individual behavior support.	☐ Foundations Team, support staff, and principal (or district administrators) agree on who can serve as advocates for students who need additional support.	☐ The advocates meet regularly to discuss progress and case studies to ensure that each student's needs are being met. Patterns of need are communicated to the Foundations Team so prevention efforts can be implemented.	☐ All support staff and problem-solving teams have written brief job descriptions that outline the services they can provide. The documents are shared with staff to inform them about available resources. **Evidence:** Suggestions for accessing these services are in the Foundations Archive and Staff Handbook.
F6 Problem-Solving Processes and Intervention Design	☐ Foundations Team understands that it will not conduct staffings (team-based problem solving) on individual students, but the team should examine current processes for supporting students and staff.	☐ Foundations Team and support staff (counselor, school psychologist, and so on) have discussed the range of problem-solving support (individuals and teams) currently available to students and staff.	☐ Foundations Team and support staff have discussed the problem-solving processes suggested in *Foundations* (e.g., the 25-Minute Planning Process), and have determined whether the processes would strengthen current practices.	☐ A flowchart or description of how the school meets the needs of students and staff has been created. It clarifies how the intensity of student needs matches the intensity of both problem-solving processes and intervention design and implementation. **Evidence:** This information is documented in the Foundations Archive and summarized in the Staff Handbook.
F7 Sustainability and District Support	☐ Foundations Team archives data, in-process work, and all completed policies and procedures, and builds on this work each year.	☐ Foundations Team orients new staff and re-energizes returning staff about all policies and procedures, and emphasizes unity and consistency.	☐ Foundations Team uses the rubric annually and the Implementation Checklists as individual modules near completion and every 3 years thereafter. The team uses this information to guide staff in setting improvement priorities.	☐ In larger districts (more than four schools), a district-based team works on sustainability. The team reminds schools about important milestones (e.g., surveys, year-end tasks, etc.) and ongoing staff development opportunities on behavior support. **Evidence:** This information can be found in district communications (e.g., emails) to schools and agenda items for principals' meetings.

If any items are rated as less than In Place or if it has been more than 3 years since you have done so, work through the Module F Implementation Checklist.

Foundations: A Proactive and Positive Behavior Support System Date _____

Foundations Implementation Rubric and Summary (p. 8 of 8)

	Preparing (1)	Getting Started (2)	Moving Along (3)	In Place (4)
Module A Presentations				
A1. Foundations: A Multi-Tiered System of Behavior Support				
A2. Team Processes				
A3. The Improvement Cycle				
A4. Data-Driven Processes				
A5. Developing Staff Engagement and Unity				
Module B Presentations				
Hallways				
Restrooms				
Cafeteria				
Playground, Courtyard, or Commons				
Arrival				
Dismissal				
Dress Code				
Other:				
Other:				
Other:				
Other:				
Module C Presentations				
C2. Guidelines for Success				
C3. Ratios of Positive Interactions				
C4. Improving Attendance				
C5 & C6. School Connectedness and Programs and Strategies for Meeting Needs				
C7. Welcoming New Staff, Students, and Families				
Module D Presentations				
D1. Proactive Procedures, Corrective Procedures, and Individual Interventions				
D2. Developing Three Levels of Misbehavior				
D3. Staff Responsibilities for Responding to Misbehavior				
D4. Administrator Responsibilities for Responding to Misbehavior				
D5. Preventing the Misbehavior That Leads to Referrals and Suspensions				
Module E Presentations				
E1. Ensuring a Safe Environment for Students				
E2. Attributes of Safe and Unsafe Schools				
E3. Teaching Conflict Resolution				
E4. Analyzing Bullying Behaviors, Policies, and School Needs				
E5. Schoolwide Bullying Prevention and Intervention				
Module F Presentations				
F2. Supporting Classroom Behavior: The Three-Legged Stool				
F3. Articulating Staff Beliefs and Solidifying Universal Procedures				
F4. Early-Stage Interventions for General Education Classrooms				
F5. Matching the Intensity of Your Resources to the Intensity of Your Needs				
F6. Problem-Solving Processes and Intervention Design				
F7. Sustainability and District Support				

APPENDIX B
Module E Implementation Checklist

The Implementation Checklist is a detailed checklist of the processes and objectives in each *Foundations* module. The Module E checklist (Form E-02) appears in this appendix and can be printed (see Appendix C for directions).

As you near completion on the module, use the Implementation Checklist to ensure that you have fully implemented all recommendations. If you've decided not to follow some recommendations—you've adapted the procedures for your school—indicate the reason on the checklist. If data show problems later, this record of what you implemented and what you chose not to implement could be helpful in deciding what to do to address the problem.

In addition to using the checklists as needed, plan to work through all *Foundations* checklists every 3 years or so. See the sample schedule below. Additional information about Implementation Checklists appears in Module F, Presentation 7, Task 1.

Sample Long-Term Schedule: Improvement Priorities, Data Review & Monitoring

Year 1	Work on:
	• Modules A and B (continuous improvement process, common areas and schoolwide policies)
	• Cafeteria
	• Guidelines for Success
	In late spring, work through the Foundations Implementation Rubric for Modules A, B (cafeteria), and C2 (Guidelines for Success).
	Use the Modules A and B Implementation Checklists to assess status as you near completion of those modules.
Year 2	Work on:
	• Module C (inviting climate)
	• Hallways
	In the fall, evaluate cafeteria data.
	In late spring, work through the Foundations Implementation Rubric for Modules A, B (cafeteria and hallways), and C.
	Use the Module C Implementation Checklist to assess status as you near completion of Module C.

Year 3	Work on: • Module D (responding to misbehavior) • Playground In the fall, evaluate hallway data. In late spring, work through the Foundations Implementation Rubric for Modules A, B (cafeteria, hallways, and playground), C, and D. Use the Module D Implementation Checklist to assess status as you near completion of Module D.
Year 4	Work on: • Module E (safety, conflict, bullying prevention) • Arrival and dismissal In the fall, evaluate playground data. In late spring, work through the Foundations Implementation Rubric for Modules A, B (cafeteria, hallways, arrival and dismissal), C, D, and E. Use the Module E Implementation Checklist to assess status as you near completion of Module E. Monitor Year 1 priorities: • Module A Implementation Checklist • Module B Implementation Checklist for cafeteria • Module C Implementation Checklist for Guidelines for Success (C2 only)
Year 5	Work on: • Module F (classroom management and sustaining *Foundations*) • Assemblies • Guest teachers In the fall, evaluate arrival and dismissal data. In late spring, work through the Foundations Implementation Rubric for Modules A, B (playground, arrival and dismissal, assemblies, guest teachers), C, D, E, and F. Use the Module F Implementation Checklist to assess status as you near completion of Module F. Monitor Year 2 priorities: • Module B Implementation Checklist for hallways • Module C Implementation Checklist

Year 6	In the fall, evaluate assemblies and guest teacher data.

Work through the Foundations Implementation Rubric for all modules.

Monitor Year 3 priorities:
- Module B Implementation Checklist for playground
- Module D Implementation Checklist |
| Year 7 | In the fall, work through the Foundations Implementation Rubric for all modules and all common areas and schoolwide policies.

Monitor Year 4 priorities:
- Module A Implementation Checklist
- Module B Implementation Checklist for arrival, dismissal, and cafeteria
- Module C Implementation Checklist for Guidelines for Success (C2 only)
- Module E Implementation Checklist |
| Year 8 | In the fall, work through the Foundations Implementation Rubric for all modules and all common areas and schoolwide policies.

Monitor Year 5 priorities:
- Module B Implementation Checklist for assemblies, guest teachers, and hallways
- Module B Implementation Checklist for hallways
- Module C Implementation Checklist
- Module F Implementation Checklist |
| Year 9 | In the fall, work through the Foundations Implementation Rubric for all modules and all common areas and schoolwide policies.

Monitor Year 6 priorities:
- Module B Implementation Checklist for playground
- Module D Implementation Checklist |

Module E Implementation Checklist (p. 1 of 5)

Implementation Actions	Completed Y/N	Evidence of Implementation	Evidence Y/N
Presentation 1: Keeping Students Safe From Physical and Emotional Harm	✓		✓
1. The Foundations Team (or a subset of the team) has viewed or read Presentation 2 on safety, completed the Presentation 2 portion of this Implementation Checklist, and, if needed, established a plan of action.	☐	Foundations Process: Safety	☐
2. The team (or a subset of the team) has viewed or read Presentation 3 on conflict resolution, completed the Presentation 3 portion of this Implementation Checklist, and, if needed, established a plan of action.	☐	Foundations Process: Safety	☐
3. The team (or a subset of the team) has viewed or read Presentations 4 and 5 on reducing bullying, completed the Presentations 4 and 5 portions of this Implementation Checklist, and, if needed, established a plan of action.	☐	Foundations Process: Safety	☐
Presentation 2: Attributes of Safe and Unsafe Schools			
1. The Foundations Team or safety task force has completed the Attributes of Safe and Unsafe Schools form (Form E-03), then as a group discussed and reached a consensus score for each item. Consensus scores have been recorded and used to establish priorities for improving safety in the school.	☐	Foundations Process: Safety	☐
2. The team or task force has identified any other staff members or groups working on school safety and has coordinated with those people or groups to ensure that efforts are not duplicated. The team or task force has also determined whether any school safety assessments were conducted in the last 3 years.	☐	Foundations Process: Safety	☐
3. The team or task force has completed Assessing Emergency Preparedness (Form E-04) and, if needed, established priorities for improvement.	☐	Foundations Process: Safety	☐
4. All possible emergency situations (natural disaster, man-made, medical, and student behavior) that need written response plans have been identified, and all plans are complete and current.	☐	Foundations Archive: Safety Policies	☐

(continued)

Module E Implementation Checklist (p. 2 of 5)

Implementation Actions	Completed Y/N	Evidence of Implementation	Evidence Y/N
Presentation 2 (*continued*)	✓		✓
5. A system is in place to ensure that all emergency plans are reviewed and updated annually.	☐	Foundations Process: Planning Calendar	☐
6. The team or task force has completed the Evaluation Form: Lessons to Increase Connectedness and Safety (E-05) and used that information to establish priorities for improving safety in the school.	☐	Foundations Process: Safety	☐
7. The team or task force has developed and implemented a plan for informing students and parents annually about all important safety considerations, including but not limited to student lessons.	☐	Foundations Archive: Safety Policies Student and Parent Handbk: Policies and Procedures	☐
8. The team or task force has reviewed the sample lessons in Presentation 2 and developed a plan to use those lessons (with modifications as needed), implement other published curricula, or create new lessons. A plan for initial delivery and subsequent review has been developed and implemented.	☐	Foundations Archive: Lesson Plans for Teaching Safety Expectations Foundations Process: Planning Calendar	☐
Presentation 3: Teaching Conflict Resolution			
1. The Foundations Team (with the administrator) has reviewed the tasks and sample conflict resolution lessons and has determined (or guided the staff through determining) whether to implement STP. If not, the team has clarified the reason why (e.g., the school already has a conflict resolution strategy that students and staff actively use, or conflict resolution is not currently a priority).	☐	Foundations Process: Safety	☐
2. If the school will adopt STP, the team has completed the following implementation steps: • Ensure that staff, especially teachers, are aware of STP's major steps. • Design schoolwide lessons and implement them. • Determine how supervisors will be trained and implement that plan. • Work through possible areas of staff resistance to implementing STP. • Decide on schoolwide procedures for teaching students about dispersing from a conflict. (*continued*)	☐	Foundations Process: Safety, Presentations/ Communications With Staff Foundations Archive: Lesson Plans for Teaching Safety Expectations, Safety Policies Staff Handbook: Policies and Procedures Student and Parent Handbook: Policies and Procedures	☐

Module E Implementation Checklist (p. 3 of 5)

Implementation Actions	Completed Y/N	Evidence of Implementation	Evidence Y/N
Presentation 3 (*continued*) • Inform staff of the content of any extension lessons. • Establish feedback loops so that information about actual conflicts goes to the people who teach the lessons. • Decide how to involve parents. • Develop a plan to get students to generalize the STP strategy. • Evaluate the effectiveness of the STP implementation and make adjustments as needed. • Develop emergency procedures so that if STP fails, all staff know what to do. • Develop long-range procedures for dealing with students who chronically fight or exhibit aggressive behavior, including re-teaching of STP processes	✓		✓
3. The team has developed and implemented a plan for sharing conflict resolution information and strategies with parents, including presentations at a PTA meeting or Back to School Night, website content, newsletters, email blasts, and video examples posted online.	☐	Foundations Process: Planning Calendar, Communications W/ Parents Foundations Archive: Lesson Plans for Teaching Safety Expectations	☐
Presentation 4: Analyzing Bullying Behavior, Policies, and School Needs			
1. The Foundations Team (with the administrator) has viewed or read the tasks in Presentations 4 and 5 and determined (or guided the staff through determining) whether the tasks and suggested actions will be implemented. If not, the team has clarified the reason why (e.g., the school already has an approach to bullying prevention and intervention that accomplishes the suggested actions).	☐	Foundations Process: Meeting Minutes, Presentations/ Communications With Staff	☐
2. The team or bullying prevention task force has completed School-Based Analysis of Bullying Data (Form E-06). Based on that information, any gaps or weaknesses in current data collection policies and procedures have been identified and addressed.	☐	Foundations Process: Meeting Minutes Foundations Archive: Bullying Prevention	☐

Module E Implementation Checklist (p. 4 of 5)

Implementation Actions	Completed Y/N	Evidence of Implementation	Evidence Y/N
Presentation 4 (*continued*)	✓		✓
3. The team or task force has completed School-Based Analysis of Bullying Policies (Form E-09). Based on that information, any gaps or weaknesses in current policies and procedures have been identified and addressed. The completed policies ensure that all staff, students, and families have the information they need to prevent bullying and respond effectively when it occurs.	☐	Foundations Process: Meeting Minutes, Presentations/ Communications With Staff, Communications With Parents Final policies will be placed in the Foundations Archive: Schoolwide Policies, Bullying Prevention	☐
4. The team (or task force) analyzes all data related to bullying at least annually and answers the questions on STOIC Analysis for Universal Prevention of Bullying (Form E-10). If needed, additional data are collected (e.g., to determine why a particular location is a hot spot for bullying), and a plan is developed and implemented to address concerns.	☐	Foundations Process: Data Summaries, Current Priorities	☐
Presentation 5: Schoolwide Bullying Prevention and Intervention			
1. The Foundations Team or bullying prevention task force has completed Staff Training in Preventing and Responding to Bullying (Form E-11). Based on that information, any gaps or weaknesses in current staff training have been identified and addressed.	☐	Foundations Process: Presentations/ Communications to Stafff	☐
2. The team or task force has completed Student Training in Preventing and Responding to Bullying (Form E-12). Based on that information, any gaps or weaknesses in current student training have been identified and addressed.	☐	Foundations Archive: Lesson Plans for Bullying Prevention	☐
3. The team or task force has completed Family Training in Preventing and Responding to Bullying (Form E-13). Based on that information, any gaps or weaknesses in communicating with and training families have been identified and addressed. Scripts for staff that facilitate conversations with families of students who were involved in bullying incidents have been developed. (*continued*)	☐	Foundations Process: Communications With Parents Foundations Archive: Bullying Prevention	☐

Module E Implementation Checklist (p. 5 of 5)

Implementation Actions	Completed Y/N	Evidence of Implementation	Evidence Y/N
Presentation 5 (*continued*)	✓		✓
4. The team or task force has completed Active Engagement for the Prevention of Bullying (Form E-14). Based on that information, any gaps or weaknesses in current engagement practices have been identified and addressed, especially related to students who are victimized by and students who engage in bullying behavior.	☐	Foundations Archive: Students' Basic Needs, Bullying Prevention	☐

APPENDIX C
Guide to Module E Reproducible Forms and Samples

Additional resources are available to help you implement *Foundations*. A thumbnail of the first page of each form, figure, or sample appears in this appendix. Unless noted, all files are in PDF format. See the Using the Files document for more information about using fillable PDF forms.

Access to these print resources depends on the video option purchased.

Foundations DVD option. The CD in the DVD case contains the print resources.

Foundations streaming video option. Find your School Code on the title page of this book. Go to the website streaming.ancorapublishing.online and enter your School Code and your school email address. You will enter this email address each time you log in. Select the desired module, then click on Download Print Resources to the left of the menu of tasks. A menu will open in a new browser window. Click on a link to view or download the file. You must download files to your computer to modify them or use the fillable PDF features described in Using the Files.

Note: The only web browsers supported are Chrome, Internet Explorer, and Edge. Use of other browsers may cause problems with viewing the videos.

Folders on the CD are:

- Forms (E-01 through E-14)
  - Excel Spreadsheet
  - Fillable Forms
  - Print Forms
  - Word Form
- Other Resources (E-15 through E-17)
- Samples (E-18 through E-27)
- Lessons
  - E2 Increasing Connectedness and Safety
  - E3 Conflict Resolution (STP)
  - E5 Bullying Prevention
- PowerPoint Presentations (E1 through E5)
  - E1 Keeping Students Safe.pptx
  - E2 Safe and Unsafe Schools.pptx
  - E3 Conflict Resolution.pptx
  - E4 Analyzing Bullying Behavior.pptx
  - E5 Bullying Prevention.pptx

Folders on the streaming video site are:

- Forms (Fillable)
- Forms (Excel Spreadsheet)
- Forms (Print)
- Forms (Word)
- Lessons E2
- Lessons E3
- Lessons E5
- Other Resources
- PowerPoint Presentations
- Samples

Forms
(E-01 to E-14)

For Single-School Use Only

Permission to copy and use the reproducibles is granted only to staff members who work in schools that have purchased the *Foundations* module.

E-01 Foundations Implementation Rubric and Summary (8 pages)

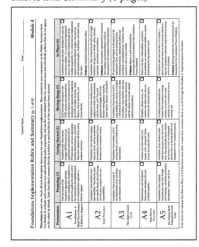

E-02 Module E Implementation Checklist (5 pages)

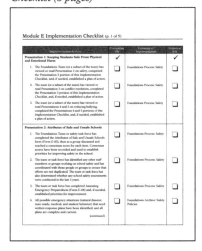

Form E-03 Understanding the Attributes of Safe and Unsafe Schools

Form E-04 Assessing Emergency Preparedness

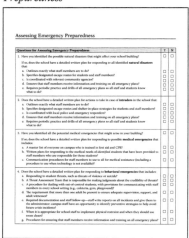

E-05 Evaluation Form: Lessons to Increase Connectedness and Safety

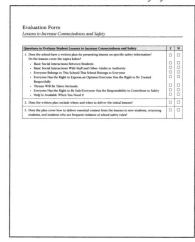

E-06 School-Based Analysis of Bullying Data (2 pages)

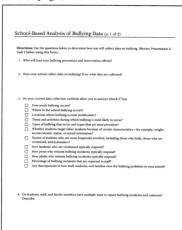

E-07 Bullying Incident Report (Word format, 3 pages)

E-08 Schoolwide Bullying Incident Log (Excel format)

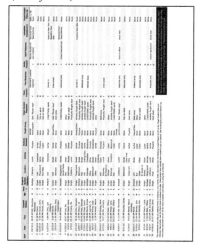

E-09 School-Based Analysis of Bullying Policies (2 pages)

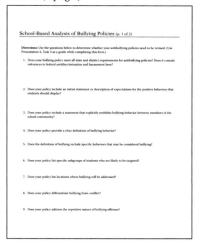

E-10 STOIC Analysis of Universal Prevention of Bullying

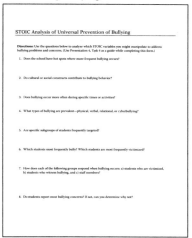

E-11 Staff Training in Preventing and Responding to Bullying

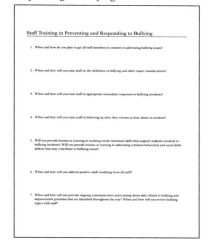

E-12 Student Training in Preventing and Responding to Bullying

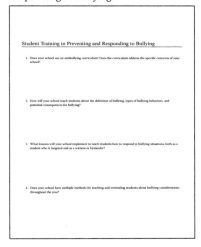

E-13 Family Training in Preventing and Responding to Bullying

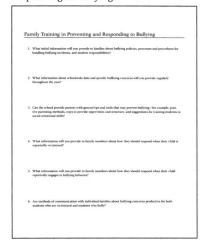

E-14 Active Engagement for the Prevention of Bullying

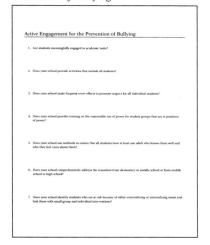

Other Resources
(E-15 to E-17)

E-15 Attributes of Safe and Unsafe Schools and Associated Protective and Risk Factors

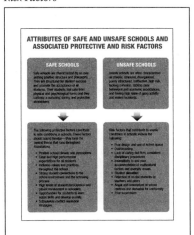

E-16 Red Card

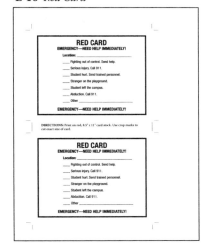

Appendix C: Guide to Module E Reproducible Forms and Samples

E-17 Summary of the Joint Statement on the Impact of Entertainment Violence

Samples
(E-18 to E-27)

E-18 Stop–Think–Plan negative and positive strategies poster

E-19 Parent handout on STP (3 pages)

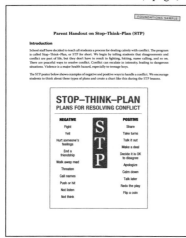

E-20 Range of consequences and interventions for bullying

E-21 Statement Regarding a Balanced Approach to Consequences and Supports for Bullying Intervention

E-22 Staff training activity (2 pages)

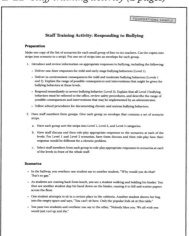

E-23 Thought Exercise

E-24 Monthly Antibullying Themes and Activities (3 pages)

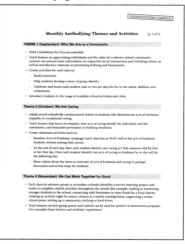

252   Module E: Improving Safety, Managing Conflict & Reducing Bullying

E-25 *Dealing With Technology: Tips and Strategies for Parents (3 pages)*

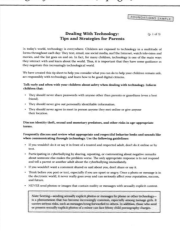

E-26 *Script for Talking With Families About a Student Who Was Victimized*

E-27 *Script for Talking With Families About a Student Who Bullied*

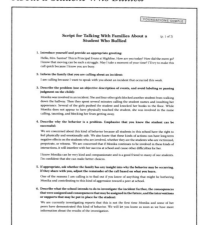

Lessons
E2 Increasing Connectedness and Safety

Lesson 1 Outline *Basic Social Interactions Between Students*

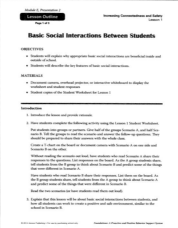

Lesson 2 Outline *Basic Social Interactions With Staff and Other Adults in Authority*

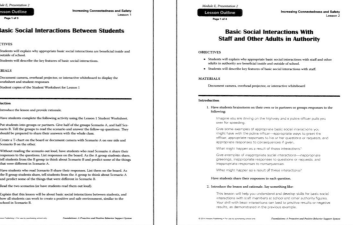

Lesson 3 Outline *Everyone Belongs in This School/This School Belongs to Everyone*

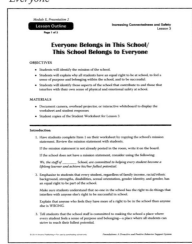

Lesson 4 Outline *Everyone Has the Right to Express an Opinion/Everyone Has the Right to Be Treated Respectfully*

Lesson 5 Outline *Threats Will Be Taken Seriously*

Appendix C: Guide to Module E Reproducible Forms and Samples

Lesson 6 Outline *Everyone Has a Right to Be Safe/Everyone Has the Responsibility to Contribute to Safety*

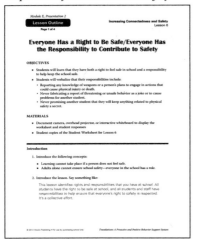

Lesson 7 Outline *Help Is Available When You Need It*

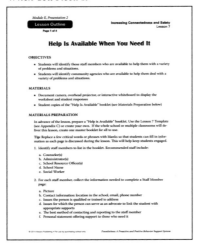

Lessons
E3 Conflict Resolution (STP)

Lesson 1 Outline *What Is a Disagreement? What Is a Conflict?*

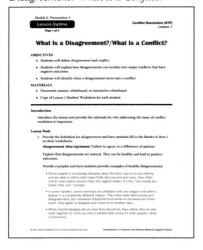

Lesson 2 Outline *Reading Social Cues to Avoid Conflict*

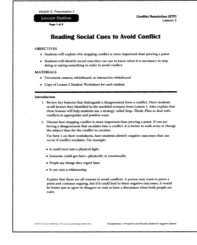

Lesson 3 Outline *Conflict and Electronic Communication/Social Media*

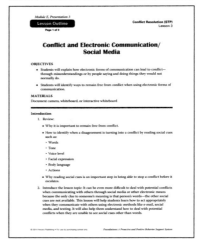

Lesson 4 Outline *Stop–Think–Plan: A Strategy to Resolve Conflict (Stop)*

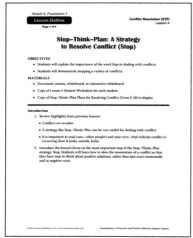

Lesson 5 Outline *Stop–Think–Plan: A Strategy to Resolve Conflict (Think)*

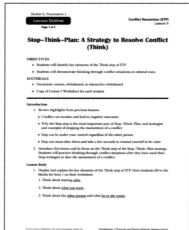

Lesson 6 Outline *Stop–Think–Plan: A Strategy to Resolve Conflict (Plan)*

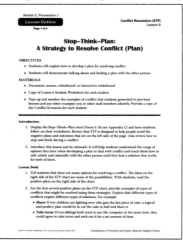

Lesson 7 Outline Determine Whether You Need Help

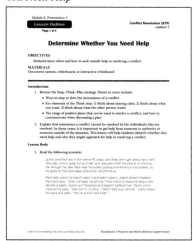

Lessons
E5 Bullying Prevention

Lesson 1 Outline What Is Bullying?

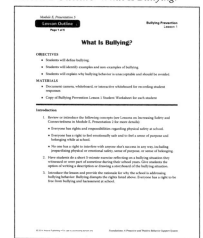

Lesson 2 Outline What Is Harassment?

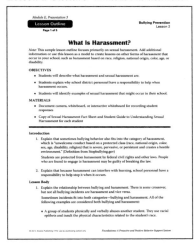

Lesson 3 Outline Personal Power and Control, Part 1

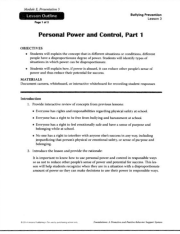

Lesson 4 Outline Personal Power and Control, Part 2

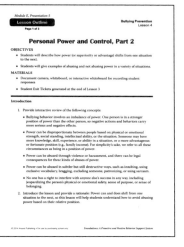

Lesson 5 Outline Group Power and Control: Everyone Shares Responsibility

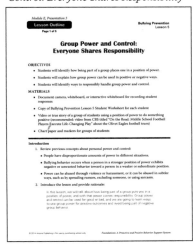

Lesson 6 Outline Teasing and Destructive Humor Can Be an Abuse of Power

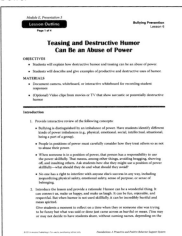

Lesson 7 Outline When You Are on the Receiving Side of an Abuse of Power

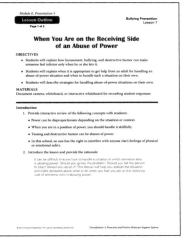

Appendix C: Guide to Module E Reproducible Forms and Samples

Lesson 8 Outline *Giving and Getting Feedback*

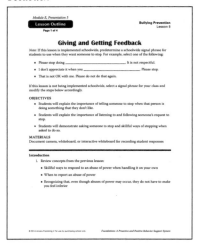

Lesson 9 Outline *How to Respond if You Are Targeted, Parts 1–4*

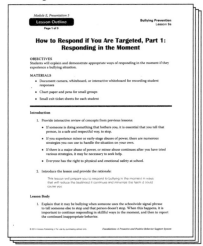

Lesson 10 Outline *How to Respond if You Are a Bystander*

Lesson 11 Outline *Potential Long-Term Ramifications—What You Need to Know*

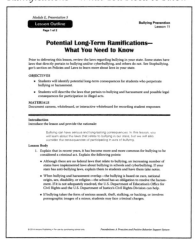

PowerPoint Presentations
(E1 to E5)

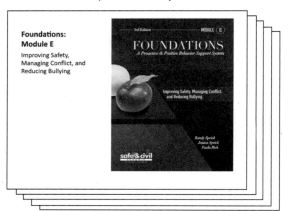